Poetry

BLOOMSBURY WRITER'S GUIDES AND ANTHOLOGIES

Bloomsbury Writer's Guides and Anthologies offer established and aspiring creative writers an introduction to the art and craft of writing in a variety of forms, from poetry to environmental and nature writing. Each book is part craft-guide with writing prompts and exercises, and part anthology, with relevant works by major authors.

Series Editors:

Sean Prentiss, Vermont College of Fine Arts, USA
Joe Wilkins, Linfield College, USA

Titles in the Series:

Environmental and Nature Writing, Sean Prentiss and Joe Wilkins
Short-Form Creative Writing, H. K. Hummel and Stephanie Lennox
Creating Comics, Chris Gavaler and Leigh Ann Beavers
Advanced Creative Nonfiction, Sean Prentiss and Jessica Hendry Nelson
The Art and Craft of Asian Stories, Xu Xi and Robin Hemley
Advanced Fiction, Amy E. Weldon

Forthcoming Titles:

Experimental Writing, William Cordeiro and Lawrence Lenhart
Fantasy Fiction, Jennifer Pullen
Environmental and Nature Writing 2ⁿᵈ ed, Sean Prentiss and Joe Wilkins
Speculative Fiction, Benjamin Warner and Ron Tanner

Poetry

A Writer's Guide and Anthology

2nd edition

Amorak Huey and
W. Todd Kaneko

BLOOMSBURY ACADEMIC
LONDON • NEW YORK • OXFORD • NEW DELHI • SYDNEY

BLOOMSBURY ACADEMIC
Bloomsbury Publishing Plc
50 Bedford Square, London, WC1B 3DP, UK
1385 Broadway, New York, NY 10018, USA
29 Earlsfort Terrace, Dublin 2, Ireland

BLOOMSBURY, BLOOMSBURY ACADEMIC and the Diana logo are trademarks of Bloomsbury
Publishing Plc

First published in Great Britain 2024

Amorak Huey and W. Todd Kaneko have asserted their right under the Copyright, Designs and
Patents Act, 1988, to be identified as the authors of this work.

For legal purposes the Acknowledgments on p. 276 constitute an extension
of this copyright page.

Cover design: Rebecca Heselton
Cover illustration © djvstock/Adobe Stock

Bloomsbury Publishing Plc does not have any control over, or responsibility for, any third-party
websites referred to or in this book. All internet addresses given in this book were correct at the
time of going to press. The author and publisher regret any inconvenience caused if addresses
have changed or sites have ceased to exist, but can accept no responsibility for any such
changes.

The authors and publisher gratefully acknowledge the permission granted to reproduce
copyrighted material in this book. The Third Party copyrighted material displayed in the pages of
this book is done so on the basis of fair use for the purposes of teaching, criticism, scholarship
or research only in accordance with international copyright laws, and is not intended to infringe
upon the ownership rights of the original owners.

A catalogue record for this book is available from the British Library.

Library of Congress Cataloging-in-Publication Data
Names: Huey, Amorak, author. | Kaneko, W. Todd, author.
Title: Poetry: a writer's guide and anthology / Amorak Huey and Todd Kaneko.
Description: 2nd edition. | London ; New York : Bloomsbury Academic, 2024. | Series: Bloomsbury
writer's guides and anthologies | Includes bibliographical references and index.
Identifiers: LCCN 2023025523 (print) | LCCN 2023025524 (ebook) | ISBN 9781350325890
(paperback) | ISBN 9781350325883 (hardback) | ISBN 9781350325906 (pdf) |
ISBN 9781350325913 (epub)
Subjects: LCSH: Poetry–Authorship. | Poetry. | Poetry–Collections.
Classification: LCC PN1059.A9 H84 2024 (print) | LCC PN1059.A9 (ebook) |
DDC 808.1–dc23/eng/20230726
LC record available at https://lccn.loc.gov/2023025523
LC ebook record available at https://lccn.loc.gov/2023025524

ISBN: HB: 978-1-3503-2588-3
PB: 978-1-3503-2589-0
ePDF: 978-1-3503-2590-6
eBook: 978-1-3503-2591-3

Series: Bloomsbury Writer's Guides and Anthologies

Typeset by Deanta Global Publishing Services, Chennai, India
Printed and bound in Great Britain

To find out more about our authors and books visit www.bloomsbury.com and
sign up for our newsletters.

CONTENTS

PREFACE

A Word of Welcome for Teachers and Students

You do not need this textbook to become a poet.

Nor do you need a resume stuffed with published books before you can claim the title of poet. You don't need to complete an advanced degree or take even a single class. That's because "poet" is not some lofty title which only a select few deserve to claim. Whether you are a poet is determined by two questions:

Do you read poems? Do you write them?

If so, then, yes, you are a poet.

You learn to write poetry—and then you learn to write it better—by doing two things: reading poetry and writing your own. It's truly that simple. Read lots of poems and write every day, or nearly every day, or as often as your life will allow, and your poetry will grow and evolve and improve.

This textbook and a well-taught poetry class can, however, provide shortcuts to that growth.

A class provides you with a dedicated audience of your peers and your teacher: readers willing to engage with and respond to your poems. Your teacher can serve as a mentor and guide through the challenging early stages of reading and writing poetry. You'll have questions as you read and write; your teacher can help you try to answer them. An encouraging teacher can also allay some of the natural fears that you're not good enough or that you somehow don't deserve to be writing—while simultaneously raising the bar for your work, pushing you to accomplish more than you imagined possible.

Imagine poetry is a muscle. If you wanted to make your body stronger, you'd head for a weight room. But when you first walk in, the dazzling array of machines and free weights can be intimidating and confusing. How much should you be lifting? How many repetitions is enough? When do you risk hurting yourself? Which machines develop which muscle groups? The bulked-up veterans in the room are equally intimidating; they all seem to know what they're doing and they seem to be stronger than you could ever make yourself. If this sounds like how you feel about poetry, know that you're not alone. It's called Imposter Syndrome, and it's a near-universal sensation. We all feel it. The good news is that your teacher can serve as a personal trainer, walking you through the process until you've gained the confidence you need to forge ahead on your own, stronger than before.

This book, too, can play a role in your development as a poet. It is based on three core beliefs about writing in general and writing poetry in particular:

1. **Writing is a muscle.** We strengthen that muscle through exercise and repetition, through a regular routine of reading and writing.
2. **Writing poetry is a rhetorical practice.** We shape our poems by making intentional choices about the language we use and by being aware of the effects those choices have on our readers.
3. **Reading is essential.** We become better writers by reading.

This approach is not intended to discount the mystery and magic of creating art. There's certainly something about the creative process that defies easy definition and exists outside the realm of textbooks and guidelines. To be a good writer requires you to approach the world with sensitivity and perception. You must be willing to interrogate your own motives and mindsets. You should be eager to dig past the surface of your daily life, to look for moments of particular beauty and truth.

Then, after all that, you have to *want* to write. No one *has* to be a poet. If you'd rather play soccer or knit sweaters, master the bassoon or play Dungeons and Dragons, that's terrific. When people ask skeptically, "Can creative writing even be taught?" and you can tell by their tone that they think the answer is no, this part of it is probably what they have in mind. It's probably true that no one can teach you the desire to write. That has to come from inside you. But if you have that urge? What we can do— what we hope this book does—is help you harness that desire, focus it, and make the most of it, so that the poems you produce are the best versions of themselves.

How This Book Is Built

An Introduction to Poetry

The opening section of the book sets up our approach to writing and teaching poetry. We believe the most effective way to teach poetry writing is by focusing on how contemporary poems are built rather than by searching for meanings or symbols. We focus on practice rather than interpretation. We encourage teachers and writers to move away from the search for meaning as the primary way of interacting with a poem. Instead, we urge readers to focus on the experience a poem creates—and how, specifically, the poet uses language to create that experience. Also in this section, we challenge some myths about talent, we explore where poems come from and what it means to be a poet, and we dig into the connections between reading poems and making poems.

The Elements of Poetry

This section is the heart of this book. First, we explain what it means to think of poems as being rhetorically constructed, built to appeal to an audience through logic, emotion, and character. Then we present thirty-eight elements of poetry as we've conceived them, in alphabetical order from ambiguity to weight. These are the rhetorical components of a poem: the building materials and tools every poet relies on when making a poem. Just as a contractor building a new home needs drywall and nails, lumber and paint and a measuring tape, each serving a different but essential purpose in the process, so too does a poet rely on these elements in the writing process. By studying the elements and learning how they work in a poem, you'll be equipped to employ them to best effect in your own writing. Our goal with these elements is to make you a more intentional writer, more keenly aware of how language works and how to manipulate it.

Beyond the Elements

Here you'll find useful guidance about how to make best use of your workshop experience. Giving meaningful feedback to your classmates—and learning what to do with the feedback you receive—is a challenge, and we'll guide you through that process. There's also an important chapter on revising poems. Too often, we think of poems as set in stone upon their first draft, finding ourselves at a loss when a teacher requires revision. This chapter will offer practical strategies for moving past that first draft and making your poems better through the revision process. There's a chapter on poems to avoid: poems we've all read before (if we're being honest, poems we've all written before) but that are generally best left in the past. We address how and why to use published poems as models for your own in a chapter on imitation as a learning device. There's a chapter on fixed forms, both traditional and contemporary. Finally in this section, there's a chapter on prosody for those interested in exploring how metrical rhythm works in poems.

An Anthology of Contemporary Poems and Poetic Modes

Here, you'll find successful poems by contemporary poets. We offer this selection of poems both as models for your own work and as examples of the range and quality of poetry being produced in the twenty-first century.

This anthology is just a starting point for that—contemporary poetry is vast and diverse, and it's impossible to generalize about the artform as a whole. We offer these poems as an introductory sampling.

There's tremendous value in studying classic literature, and we encourage all poets to read widely in poems of all eras. However, we believe that studying poems written now or close to now is the best first step on the path toward learning how to write your own contemporary poems. We reject the notion that poetry is best studied as historical artifact; as one colleague put it, that would be akin to having to prove you understand Mozart before you're allowed to listen to current pop music. We have arranged this anthology by poetic mode; again, the organization is alphabetical, from apostrophe to protest. These modes are, in essence, rhetorical stances chosen by the poet, each different mode offering a different lens through which to explore the beauty and chaos of the human experience.

A Note about Difficult Content

One of the things poems do is challenge us. Poems are often confounding syntactically or formally; they ask more of their readers than do most works in prose. Some poems are also challenging in their subject matter. Layli Long Soldier's "38," for example, presents a narrative about the execution of thirty-eight men executed by the state for doing little more than trying not to starve. Patricia Lockwood's "Rape Joke" deals with a sexual assault. Reading about such things can be emotionally difficult. These poems and others like them are included here not to titillate or traumatize, but to illustrate how poets can take on such tough topics and make art from them—not in a way that minimizes or covers up the trauma and emotion connected to the events depicted, but in a way that explores it and reveals it. These poems explore how language and art help us make sense of experiences and events that are fundamentally impossible to understand.

Our best advice to teachers is to prepare your students for reading these poems by discussing what they teach us about poetry. Focus on what it means for a poet to be unafraid to write about extremely vulnerable or risky experiences, and to do so not in an attempt to be shocking. Help them to understand the difference between reading a poem for its content and reading a poem to figure out how it's built. Moreover, given the wide range of human experience, it's impossible to predict what material a reader will find emotionally difficult, so be sympathetic to students who might be uncomfortable with a poem's content. Given the way poems create emotional responses in a reader, try to be understanding when students encounter material they struggle to interact with. A student who is prepared for a poem's traumatic subject matter will be better able to deal with a craft conversation about that poem than a student encountering the subject cold and having to process it in real time, for the first time.

For students, approach these poems as you would those with less challenging content: ask what you can learn from them that you can apply to your own writing. Consider what it means to explore cruelty or trauma in a poem and how a writer uses poetry to transform traumatic experiences into art. These poems teach us something about what it means to tell the truth about the world, even when that truth is ugly.

How to Use This Book

This book is designed to offer practicality and flexibility for teachers and students using it in a class as well as for poets who've picked it up outside of a formal course of study. In essence, it can be read in any order. You could start by reading the poems in the anthology and then move on to the elements, first considering your own emotional and intellectual reactions to the poems before exploring in more depth the rhetorical components that make them work. A teacher might begin by having the class read the "Proceed with Caution" chapter to get those poems out of everyone's system before they start writing. You can explore the elements and modes in any order or any combination; it's easy to imagine a course starting, for instance, with lines and music on the element side, and meditative and lyric poems on the mode side.

No element in this book stands entirely alone; you'll find cross-references throughout, and you could read that way, moving from ambiguity to precision to syntax to diction to language to voice, or along some similar path. The same applies to the modes. There is overlap among them, and poems can be categorized in more than one way. Mary Jo Bang's "The Role of Elegy" is both elegy and ars poetica. Jennifer Joshua Espinoza's "A Family History is Sacred" is both documentary and narrative. Kiki Petrosino's "Nocturne" is both nocturne and lyric poem (and you'll see it's also a documentary poem if you read it in the context of the book *Hymn for the Black Terrific*, where it was published). And so on. Both the modes and elements we present here should be seen as expansive and inclusive, rather than as restrictive, as places to start rather than places to finish.

Many poetry textbooks start by teaching formal verse: the sonnet, the villanelle, the sestina, the haiku, etc. Many teachers begin with prosody, learning to scan a poem for its rhythmic structures. There's a certain comfort in these strategies; they are rooted in poetic tradition and history, and they offer a sense of stability, uniformity. You can tell a sonnet is a sonnet by counting lines and syllables; you recognize a sestina by looking for the pattern in the last word of every line. We have not centered this way of teaching poetry, but in our chapters about fixed forms and prosody, we explore how such traditional and historical approaches remain valuable to contemporary poets. To learn more about formal and metrical verse, you can also explore materials beyond this book that we highlight in Appendix B: Additional Reading.

As for the poems in this anthology, we think these are amazing poems—and they are merely the tip of a massive iceberg. If this is your introduction to contemporary poetry, make sure it's just that: an introduction. When you find poems that particularly engage you in this collection, seek out more work by those poets. All of the poets in this book have poems published online that you can find with a quick search, and they also have books you can buy or check out from the library (if your library's poetry collection is limited, as many are, use interlibrary loan, or offer a gentle suggestion that they buy more poetry).

You should make a habit of discovering new poems and poets; the internet is a great resource for that as well. The websites Verse Daily (www.versedaily.org) and Poetry Daily (www.poems.com) and the Poem-A-Day feature from the Academy of American Poets (www.poets.org) feature new contemporary poems every day, as well as substantial archives. We suggest starting there. For teachers, we encourage you to supplement the poems in this collection with your own favorites, with poems you love to read and teach, as well as other examples of poems in these modes.

As you look for starting places for your writing, we have offered 100 poetry prompts in Appendix A. Each of these suggestions can be used as a spark for your own poems. In addition, the modes themselves can be used as writing assignments: write a documentary poem. Write a portrait. Write an elegy, a love poem, a list poem. You can also use the elements as prompts: write a poem in which you experiment with punctuation and syntax. Write a poem in which you focus on both concision and precision. The exercises are nearly endless through this kind of mixing and matching.

In the end, we want you to use this book in the way that makes the most sense for you or your class. Everyone learns differently, every teacher teaches differently, and every class has its own set of objectives and desired outcomes. We hope this book makes clear that there is no single path to a life in poetry and that there are no universal truths about poetry, no absolute rules every poem or poet must follow. We hope this book reminds you to be generous with yourself as you develop your voice. This book is intended to be practical and adaptable, useful in a variety of contexts and approaches. We hope you enjoy it, and we hope it makes you a stronger, more confident poet.

Amorak Huey & W. Todd Kaneko

P.S. If you find this book helpful as you begin your poetry-writing journey, we'd love to hear from you. Find us on the usual social media channels to reach out and tell us how your poetry life is going.

SECTION I

An Introduction to Poetry

1

Why Do We Write Poems?

A baby cries in the dark and is held.

Cries again and is fed.

In this way, we learn that expression leads to communication. We learn the bonds between language and love.

The answer to why we write poems is as simple as this. We are lonely or afraid or cold or hungry. Our need for utterance is primal, innate.

We speak in order to find out whether anyone is listening.

Our ability to acquire and use language is encoded in our DNA; language is fundamental to what it means to be human and alive. Since we were huddled around campfires in caves, we have shared stories and songs and poems. We tell stories in order to remember our histories, our families, our experiences; we make them into art to help us understand ourselves. We aim to entertain and connect with each other. We pass down our stories to preserve what matters to us. Anthropologists have observed that tribal cultures with little or no other forms of art still have a strong tradition of poetry. It's ingrained in us. We are all poets and always have been.

But why poems specifically? And why poems in the twenty-first century, so many thousands of years removed from the cave and campfire? Wouldn't it be easier to post a status, send a text, caption a photo you took on your phone? Wouldn't a memo, a letter, an essay, even a novel be a more straightforward way of making your point, telling your story?

Yes, of course.

That's precisely why we write poems: because they are not always easy. They are not always intuitive. They can be difficult, challenging, weird.

If someone asked you where you wanted to have lunch and you wrote a poem in response instead of sending a quick text message or replying to their Facebook thread or Snapchat, that would be awkward. If you needed to summarize what happened at a meeting and you wrote a poem instead of a memo or a news article, that would be inefficient. Clearly, a poem is not the best mechanism for the straightforward delivery of information. This is good to know, because it frees us poets from that burden. If we're not obligated to present information in the most clear and concise manner possible, we must be doing something else when we write poems.

So what are we doing? We are creating an experience for our readers. We are exploring the world as we see it. We are building a work of art using language as our medium. Language is to a poet as paint to a painter, as marble or bronze or wood to a sculptor, as brick and mortar and steel to an architect, as the body to a dancer, the voice to a singer. Language is limited, naturally. Magritte's famous painting of a pipe is not itself a pipe, nor is the word "pipe" a pipe. But that word is what we have; it's the medium we have chosen. So poets are always pushing against the limits of language, trying to expand the possibilities of what words can do on the page, seeking a new way to say what they mean, even—especially—when what we're trying to say is complicated or difficult.

Looking at a painting of a sunset is not quite the same thing as looking at a sunset, but that doesn't mean it is a lesser experience—merely a different one. The painting presents a version of the sunset that has been filtered through human eyes and human hands and the limits of paint as a medium, so the pleasure of looking at the painting is twofold: first, the experience of a sunset; and second, the experience of seeing how another person views that sunset and tries to reproduce it. What colors, shapes, images appear to matter most to the artist? It's the same with a poem. Reading a love poem is not exactly like being in love, but it can activate many of the same parts of the brain—and in addition to that, it yields the experience of understanding someone else's conception of love, both where it matches your own perceptions and where it challenges or expands them. The best poems, our favorite poems, those that speak to us most deeply, alter our own perceptions and become part of us.

Poems are embedded in who we are, an essential part of the human experience, but they are decidedly not our most natural mode of written communication. Prose is easier on the eye; we are more used to reading words and sentences that fill the margins of the page or screen. Poetry, with its line breaks and associative leaps, its seeming lack of chronology or argument, its focus on image or music, is inherently disruptive. Poems slow us down, call our attention to unusual moments or unfamiliar images, delight in daring us to understand. Poems resist easy paraphrase. They ask us to embrace ambiguity, to accept uncertainty. That's a feature, not a bug; it's inherent in the artform.

Why do we write poems? We write poems because we have something to say. We write poems because the world can be hard and we want to make sense of our place in it. We write poems because we are moved by our experiences and want to share them. We write poems because writing something down helps us understand it differently. We write poems to help us accept loss or celebrate love or both at once. But we also write poems to reach an audience. We write poems to connect with readers, with other human beings who have also loved and lost and felt and wondered at the world's chaos. We write poems in hopes that our words will touch others as pieces we have read have touched us. We write poems to join in an unending conversation about what it means to be human, to be alive, to suffer and thrive and grow and love and lose, to despair and to triumph.

The sound that baby makes as she cries out in the dark cry begins as expression and ends as communication. So, too, does poetry.

2

Who Gets to Be a Poet?

Who gets to be a poet?

Anyone.

Everyone.

You.

You get to be a poet. You are a poet.

To be a poet asks two things of you: that you read and write poems. Presumably if you are holding this book, you are on your way to doing both things. Hence: *you are a poet.*

To be sure, there is some perceived cultural baggage with calling yourself a poet, a sense from some corners that the label is more title than job description, that to use it is to lay claim to some particular talent.

So let's talk about talent. Specifically, why the notion of talent can actually be a harmful one for young writers. When a teacher tells a student they have a talent for writing, the message is that this one student has an inherent gift that makes them better at writing than other people. Perhaps, then, the message is also that because this writer is special, they will not have to work as hard as others. When this talk of talent is had in front of other writers who have not been blessed with the same adjective, the message is that the rest of you clowns can never measure up to the chosen one. Presented as some magical kind of innate ability, the concept of talent does more harm than good. So let's recast the word. Let's set aside talk of inherent skill and think instead about the attributes and habits of mind that lead to success for any poet.

Discipline

There is a German word all writers should know: *Sitzfleisch*. Loosely translated, the word means *the ability to sit on one's buttocks and persevere in a tedious activity*—obviously a great trait for a writer to have.

Writing is hard; there is no arguing with that. It's lonely work during those dark hours of the night when it's just you pecking away at the keyboard until you fall asleep or run out of coffee. There's no one else with you on the page except the people you have made up and the phrases you have concocted to represent them. A poem will go well for a while, but everything will upend itself without warning and then your friends start texting you—you know, the people who wanted you to go out with them this night, but you told them you had to work, and they smiled as though they understood but really they rolled their eyes and went on their way to revel at a party or a tavern somewhere while you sat in front of your computer eating stale snacks and wishing that you could be doing anything else but writing. Watching TV. Petting your dog. Going for a walk before winter sets in. Anything at all.

Writing is an activity usually done solo, whether it's in the middle of the day or in the tiny hours of the morning. You might try to go to a coffee shop, but even there you are by yourself while you write. Your friends call and invite you to a party or a dance club or brunch, and you'll decline because you have this poem you are working on and you're afraid that if you look away from it for too long, it will wriggle free and escape before you have a chance to finish it. Your friends won't understand unless they are writers. Screenwriter Lawrence Kasdan famously said that being a writer is rather like having homework every night for the rest of your life. Alas, it's true.

Sounds awful, right? Why would anyone pursue a life like this?

Writing is supposed to be fun, and often it is—a writer is always involved in a kind of serious play with the elements of poetry. Sadly, the process can also feel tedious—yeah, maybe you will receive a gift once in a while, a poem that comes to you fully formed and ready to go. However, such gifts are rare, and sometimes when you look at those poems again the next morning, you'll realize that what seemed like a precious statuette is missing an ear or has a big crack running down the side. Mostly, writing is lots of time spent between the writer and the page, time that can be as frustrating as it is exhilarating.

A writer has to have *Sitzfleisch*. They sit in the chair and write because that's what writers do.

Courage

It takes a brave person to write poems. It takes courage to walk into Thanksgiving dinner with the family, and when your grandfather asks you what you're doing with your life, you reply, "I want to write poetry."

More than that, though, poetry demands that a writer be vulnerable to the world and allow that vulnerability to appear on the page. Sometimes, in the midst of writing a poem, a writer might discover a difficult truth about themselves, about someone they care for, or about the world. When this happens, it's tempting to look away toward something easier to write about, but writers have nerves of steel, or at least they act as if they do. It's a brave thing for a writer to write about difficult material—and not just brave but generous to share that material with a reader. Without that bravery and generosity, a poem can lack density or gravity or a sense that it is significant.

Additionally, it takes courage to share unfinished poems with other people, as we do in a creative writing workshop. Even a poem about the most innocuous of topics is still a representation of you as a writer. It is scary to share this thing you made with readers and to listen to them dissect it, but poems are made to be read. Letting a poem go can be difficult, but that's what poets do every time they hand a poem to a reader or submit it for publication.

Courage might mean walking into a poem with nothing but a title or a beginning and trusting the writing process to get you through to the other side with something that resembles a poem. This requires a poet to learn to trust in themselves and in the writing process. This trust is not easy to acquire, nor easy to hold onto once acquired, but it's what poets must have.

Doubt

It might seem that doubt is the opposite of courage, and maybe it is, but poetry makes room for contradictory things to exist simultaneously. There are times when a writer questions their ability to be a writer, times when they wonder if there is something better they should be doing with their time, if they have the discipline to work hard enough to create a great piece of art, if perhaps they are not capable of creating the poem they imagine.

This feeling is normal.

Writers are supposed to struggle with the words on the page—if it were easy, it might not be worth doing. Writers are supposed to feel uneasy when they share their work because of all the discipline and courage they have devoted to the writing process. Writers are supposed to feel doubt when there is suddenly an audience where there was once just the sound of a keyboard and an empty room. Writers are supposed to feel uneasy because they have this idea of what the poem is supposed to look like in their head and it never exactly matches the poem that ends up on the page.

Get used to the feeling of doubt in your gut and embrace it as part of being a writer. Use your doubt to help you reflect on how your poems might work more efficiently or how they might better have the desired effect on the reader.

Sure, there are writers who claim they don't experience doubt, writers who say they know it all and that if someone doesn't like their work, then that someone doesn't recognize greatness. This kind of writer has shut down and is no longer open to growing as a writer. It's not that they don't doubt, but they have suppressed that feeling to the point that they can't use it to see their writing more clearly.

When you feel doubt, that's just a reminder that you care deeply about your writing. You care. That's okay. It's a good thing. It's essential, even.

Inspiration

We often think of inspiration as an external force, something from outside the poet—and thus beyond our control. A thing to wait for. In the old days, people chalked talent up to supernatural forces, the most well known of which are the Greek Muses: the nine daughters of Zeus who presided over inspiration in the arts, sciences, and literature. This trickled down to a romantic notion that an artist waits to be inspired to create because great art comes from divine inspiration.

Nowadays, we pretty much agree that the Muses are creatures of myth, yet many people complain that they cannot write a poem because they are waiting for inspiration. This may be an excuse to avoid sitting down to do the hard work of writing a poem. To rely on inspiration for a poem is to wait around until writing the poem seems easier, and it isn't likely to get any easier without sitting down to write.

Rather than wait for inspiration, a writer should be out looking for inspiration, actively seeking out the things they want to write about, the things they simply must write about. These can be big worldly things like injustice perpetrated against marginalized groups or the effects of violence on citizens of war-torn countries, but they can just as easily be more personal topics such as a favorite television show or a neighbor's dog—the important thing is that the world is out there just waiting to offer up inspiration. All a writer needs is the willingness to seek it out.

Perception

Part of becoming a poet is learning to think like a writer. We just told you that the world is out there offering up inspiration at every turn; it's up to you as a writer to learn to look for it. Work at being perceptive and look for beauty wherever you can find it, even (especially?) when that beauty is hideous.

Writers travel through the world with their eyes open not just looking for material to write about, but for material they can attempt to understand through their writing. This could be something about nature or politics or human relationships, but it could also be something like the patch of rust on your father's old car or the way your sister sits in the living room by herself after a long day of work at the auto plant.

In particular, poets pass through their days looking for language—words and phrases and descriptions they can use. To be a poet, in other words, means you read the world. You read voraciously, widely, deeply. You read poetry, fiction, nonfiction. You read news stories and soup-can labels, cereal boxes and years-old Tumblr threads. You read writing that soothes you and writing that makes you uncomfortable. Writing that speaks to your beliefs about the world and writing that expands your beliefs about the world. You read to make yourself a better writer, but also to make yourself a better person. You read with an open mind and an open heart.

Many poets carry a notebook to record those fragments as they encounter them in their daily routines. Later, then, each note, each fragment becomes a starting place: a title, a line, an image that may unlock a poem.

Tradition and Community

Writing might happen in solitude, but to be a writer is to be part of a community, whether you know it or not.

People who think like writers have a common experience with the world and can come together and connect through writing. You can find a writing community in creative writing workshops, in book groups, in classes at school. Or you can open up the pages of a literary journal to see who has their poems published inside. Or look at the books on the shelves of your local bookstore, books full of poems that were once written on scraps of paper in someone's wallet or in a spiral notebook at the bottom of someone's backpack—poems like yours, written by people like you. True education, the kind that helps you become a stronger poet, does not happen only alone, you in a room interacting with some learning-management software; no, this education happens when you find other people who care about poetry and build a community with them.

To write poems is to be part of a tradition. Shakespeare wrote poems. So did Sappho, Lord Byron, Emily Dickinson, and Edgar Allen Poe. Today, people still write poems: Oliver de la Paz, Kazim Ali, Omar Sakr, Layli Long Soldier, Natasha Trethewey—all people in the anthology portion of this book. When you write poems, you are entering into the tradition of poetry and the conversations about the world that poetry has created and perpetuated since the world's first line break. The conversations that are still ongoing today. Contemporary poems are different from the poems of yesteryear, in terms of both form and content, but the poems you write today are your conduit to the writers of the past and the writers of the future.

Empathy

The best poetry is generous. You should approach the world with empathy and be sensitive to the emotions and experiences of people whose lives are different from your own. It can be difficult to figure out how to walk in another person's shoes and try to understand their lives and how they think about the world, but you can try to do so in your poems. Despite differences, you are drawn to finding commonality with others through our shared participation in the act of being human.

As a poet, you live in the world—in a city, a region, a state, a nation. If you pay attention to what that means, you will see all sorts of things happening that you cannot ignore: war, oppression, tyranny—you are witness to these things and your poems strive to bring readers' eyes to them as well. You cannot cure the world's pain, but your poems can demand that people pay attention. Your poems bear witness. Your poems make you an activist. Metaphor is your sword, the line break is your bow and arrow, and there are dragons out in the world for you to fight. Poems are about the human experience, and where the human experience is threatened, it is the poet's duty to step in with words, and in doing so, rally others to your cause.

Mystery

We may be dismissing innate talent as a prerequisite for being a poet, but that doesn't mean there's nothing mysterious about the art, or that you are not driven by a desire to create that you can't quite name.

You wouldn't ask lightning why it sparks a fire in dry tinder. No one asks water why it flows to the lowest point in the road. To be a poet means that you have an uncontrollable urge to make things with words, poems that say things we want to say, poems that tickle the brains and hearts and bellies of people we want to reach. Being a poet sometimes means you have these things that you can do with words and you can't stop doing those things without ending up in jail or in rehab or at a dead-end job where your soul is slowly crushed. You've never asked what it means to be a poet because you can't imagine being anything else.

Poetry is how you express yourself as an individual in the world, your worldview, your emotions, and your thoughts all on the page to let everyone know that you are you. The world is an immense and busy place where you are just one of millions of people. The universe is even more immense and busier with little time for inconsequential things. But here, in the poem, you are you.

Or you are someone else. Poetry can be like putting on a mask. In your poems, you can be Batman, Benjamin Franklin, or Beyoncé. You can be a soldier fighting overseas or a college student or a stay-at-home-dad or any combination of these things. Adopting a persona can mean you aren't you, so you are free to do all sorts of things in the poem you wouldn't otherwise feel comfortable doing.

So who gets to be a poet? You do. Your discipline, fearlessness, desire, and knowledge make you a poet. You are a poet because you've decided to be a poet.

And what does it mean to be a poet? Simple: it means you read poems and you write poems. So go.

3

Where Do Poems Come From?

So just go write poems. That's it, right? But maybe that's easier said than done.

Where to start? How to start?

These are perhaps the most vexing questions for young poets, indeed for all poets. That unforgiving blankness of the blank page or computer screen taunts us as we stare into its void, wishing a poem would somehow appear there. Wishing won't get much written, alas. What we need is some kind of spark.

The good news is there are plenty of ways to seek out that spark other than waiting for that divine inspiration we just debunked in the previous chapter. There are exercises you can give yourself, habits you can develop, practical approaches to writing a poem that will work a good deal better than waiting for a poem to arrive gift-wrapped by the muses.

Here's a useful metaphor: Writing is a muscle that you strengthen through repetition. It never gets easy, but it absolutely gets easier. Here are some principles and practices to help you find your poems.

Writer's Block Is a Myth

One way of thinking about writer's block is that it's a myth. It's an excuse we give ourselves for those periods of time when we're not writing, or not writing well, or not writing as much as we'd like to. Look, writing is hard. We all go through stretches where we're not being productive. But writer's block is a label we sometimes use to let ourselves off the hook for not writing when in fact there is no concrete, tangible block in our path. Often what is in the way are only the usual fears about not being good enough, about not being able to write the poem we want to write.

The first step to overcoming these fears is to focus initially on the process of writing, not the product of writing. When you're already thinking about the final version of a poem, it can be all but impossible to write the first words. So, at first, do not worry about what the poem will be when it's finished. Focus, rather, on the process. On good writing habits. On the best practices of successful writers.

The more frequently you write poems—particularly when it's a daily or near-daily practice—the more you find yourself open to poems. If you know all day that you're going to write a poem in the evening, you find yourself spending the day looking for subject matter, for images or phrases or details that you can repurpose later in your writing. You become a better observer of the world, in other words, and that's one of the most important things a writer can be.

Many poets carry a notebook for jotting down stray lines that cross their mind during the day, for recording overheard scraps of conversation, for making lists of sights seen, sounds heard, smells and sensations encountered. These are the small details that fill our hours and make up our lives, and for many people, they pass away without much thought being paid to their passing. But when you're an active poet, ever alert for material, you must seize these details, make note of them, remember them, use them, dress them up and send them back out into the world in your poems.

It's a simple matter of paying attention. The more you pay attention to the world around you, the more you'll have to write about. When you are taking notes and thinking about poems, that's part of the writing process.

Writer's Block Is Not a Myth

Just as it's important to understand the myth behind writer's block, it's just as important to acknowledge that sometimes in your life, writing is difficult, or even impossible. Sometimes the problems of daily life get in the way of the creative process and nothing we do can translate our inner turmoil, our daily grind, our inescapable responsibilities, and so on into poems.

As a writer, you have to know when to let yourself off the hook and tend to what's immediately important and not let not the guilt of not writing get in the way of being a human who writes. Do this for the sake of your mental and physical health, your well-being, and ultimately for the sake of your relationship with your writing.

There are some who suggest that in order to be a writer you have to write every day. They say that a good writer knows how to overcome those things that block the writing process, and to do otherwise is to give up on being a writer. To those people, we would say that a daily commitment to writing is a privilege enjoyed by those who have the resources to afford it. A daily practice can be valuable, but it's not for everyone, and it's not always possible. There is no one prescribed way of going about being a writer, no one way of living with poetry.

Yes, it's important to commit to your writing, and to actually write—that's something that all writers do to some extent. But it's just as important to recognize that sometimes a field has to lay fallow for a spell before new crops can arise. And sometimes when a writer isn't writing, they are readying themselves—or even saving themselves—to write.

Chase Your Obsessions and Interests

You already have most of what you need to write about in your heart and brain. Young poets may think they need to write about pre-approved "poetic" topics, which usually means lofty and abstract concepts like love and grief, or important-seeming subjects such as Greek mythology or classical music or daffodils.

We do sometimes write about these things, to be sure, but there is by no means a list of topics that belong in poetry and another list of topics that do not. It is the twenty-first century, and we should write about the world we live in. That means Wonder Woman, Mountain Dew commercials, Wikipedia, and real estate pitches belong in our poems just as much as the activities of the royal English court belonged in the poems of Alexander Pope or John Dryden. The world around us provides us with the language we hear and speak and breathe in on a daily basis; this language then is the foundation of our poems.

Besides, you should write about the things that interest you. Indulge your obsessions. If you love the spectacle and drama of professional wrestling, you should write poems centered on professional wrestling. If you grew up listening to heavy metal music and Slash's guitar solos make you weak with nostalgia, then by all means, your poems should explore those topics, those memories, those emotions. Whether your passion is for rugby, scrapbooking, autograph collecting, photography, romantic comedies, Doctor Who, or whatever else, there is a place for that in your poems. Poems exist to make sense of the things that matter most to us, right? Don't be self-conscious about what you love; embrace it. Write it.

Poems Come from the World around You, So Pay Attention

Poems can come from anywhere. They come from developing that sense of perception we talked about in the previous chapter. They come from moving through your life looking for poems in the words and world you encounter. They come from experiences and observations that inspire you; they come from prompts or experiments like the ones in the appendix at the end of this book.

Poems Come from Playfulness

One thing that can derail young poets before they ever get started is feeling pressure to decide what they want to write about—and what, exactly, they want to say about that subject. And sometimes, poems come from having such a blueprint to follow from the start. But just as often, a good poem can come as a total surprise—so long as you give yourself permission to start writing without a plan, to explore without a map. Consider the act of getting a draft down on paper as a sort of freeform play. You're moving letters and words around on the page to see what happens. Like assembling Legos without any particular set of instructions, you're just messing around. Experimenting. Seeing what happens. Give yourself permission to write aimlessly.

There is no one single correct process. What works for one poet might not work for the poet sitting next to them—and what works for you in one poem might lead to a false start in the next. Sometimes you need to write a lot. Sometimes you need to give yourself a break. Sometimes a poem comes out nearly done; other times a piece requires months or even years of revision before you feel as though you have the words right.

The keys are being generous with yourself and being disciplined when you are able. Give yourself permission to explore, to play, to try new approaches, to expand your comfort zone. The poems will come.

4

Reading, Writing, and Making Meaning

So far, we've talked a lot about the process and purpose of writing poems—sort of a big-picture look at what poets do and how they (try to) do it. Now let's talk a bit about poems themselves. Curious things, poems. Difficult little buggers sometimes. As we've said, they don't always convey information or narrative or message in the most straightforward manner. If you sometimes struggle with understanding what poems mean, you are not alone.

When we read prose, we are used to the text conveying information for us to use, whether it's to assemble a pressboard bookcase, to comprehend how atoms bond together to create new molecules, or to follow our hero as she leads her armies through steamy swamps to fight the goblin armies of the Doom King.

We are used to following a text toward meaning, toward some kind of understanding about the subject. What happened? How does that work? Why is this thing important? What's going to happen next? The language on the page raises questions for us as readers—and then, in prose, it typically provides the answers to those questions.

But poems often resist providing meaning in the traditional sense. Instead of providing answers, they just raise new questions. We may get to the end of a poem and feel less certain than when we began. We may feel lost from the start.

We're here to assure you: that's all okay. Poems are sometimes difficult. They do sometimes ask more of us than prose does. We probably have to sit with a poem longer than we would with, say, a greeting card whose message is immediately clear. Poems can and should reward more careful reading and re-reading; they ask the reader to devote a more focused, patient kind of attention.

We Have Been Taught That
Poems Have Meanings

So many of us sat through middle or high school English classes tormented by the question of what a poem means. Perhaps the teacher stood at the front of the room, spectacles down at the tip of his nose, his bushy mustache twitching as he read lines from a poem by Frost or Whitman or Dickinson and then demanded to know what they meant. When we raised our hands to take a crack at answering, more than likely we were told that we were wrong.

No one likes to be told they are wrong.

Being told you are wrong all the time turns a potentially interesting conversation about a poem into an excruciating hour in which there are two kinds of answers: the answers that the teacher knows and the stuff everyone else in the room says. The teacher is drawing from time spent studying the poem and the historical context in which it was written. Students have no access to this context and information, so their best guesses at interpretation are based on the text in front of them.

This is how many students learn to dislike poetry. They have been taught that reacting to a poem requires outside information and that poems themselves are arcane historical documents (as opposed to, you know, works of art). They have been taught not to trust their own experience with the words on the page. Imagine a student reading a classic poem such as William Blake's "The Tyger," and being initially excited by the energy and fire of the poem and the dangerous power of the tiger and the cool rhymes, only to come to class to be told that to understand the poem, they'll first need to understand what Romantic poets thought about theology.

This focus on meaning—especially meaning supplemented by or reliant on biographical details about the poet or historical information about the period in which a poem was written—puts an awkward distance between the poem and the reader. It enforces the notion that a poem has one singular meaning that can be somehow objectively determined, like an algebra problem or a riddle. It doesn't inspire most students to craft their own complex, obscure historical document. This is not to suggest that knowing something about the historical context of a poem or about an author's life story cannot enrich the reading experience for some poems; clearly, it can. However, it's important to move past thinking that knowledge is necessary for having any sort of experience with any poem at all. In order to write poetry yourself, you may need to move past the way many of us were taught about poetry and start to think differently about meaning.

So, yes, poems totally have meanings. Otherwise, they would be nonsense (not necessarily a bad thing, but nonsense isn't what we're talking about here). When you write something down and give it to someone to read, you're after communication and connection with an audience. As we've said (more than once), poetry isn't the genre best suited for the direct delivery of a singular message, but we do want our poems to mean *something* to our readers. But remember that meaning may be complicated, challenging, even contradictory.

Poems Are Always about Two Things

Maybe it's more accurate to say that poems are always about *at least* two things. The literary critic Cleanth Brooks observes in an essay titled "The Heresy of Paraphrase" that it's impossible to summarize a poem and capture all of its meaning. You can summarize a book report or a financial statement, for instance, and relay the important main points the original text is intended to communicate. Any paraphrase of a poem, however, loses the nuance of sound and mood and metaphor—in other words, the very elements that make a poem a poem. This also has to do with the nature of metaphor: as poems work with literal and figurative meanings to create metaphor, they acquire layers of meaning, sometimes even contradictory layers.

This complexity, this layering of ideas and associations, is exactly the work a poem does. You want your poems to fight against the notion that truth can be represented by a single, monolithic idea. You want your words and lines to evoke multiple, simultaneous reactions from your readers. This sometimes makes poems a bad fit for modern education, where standardized testing demands that everyone agree on a single "correct" answer, but we think poems are pretty much the opposite of a standardized test—and we think that's a good thing.

You see the multiple meanings at play in the poems included in this anthology. The poem "Ars Poetica" by Traci Brimhall explores the poet's approach to poetry, certainly, but it is also very much about the aftermath of a car accident. "Wonder Woman Dreams of the Amazon" by Jeannine Hall Gailey is a fun piece about the origin of a superhero; the poem is also about being a woman in the modern world. These meanings are at once overlapping and contradictory—and that is what makes the piece a poem.

Poems Are Not Completely Up to Reader Interpretation

Even though poems have multiple meanings, it's a mistake to say they can mean whatever a reader wants them to. From the poet's point of view, you want your language to direct readers toward specific experiences and understandings. If you write a poem about the death of your great-grandmother and a reader says, "I was so touched by this poem about your new kittens," the poem is probably too vague to be understood. A poem that can mean anything is a poem that says nothing.

Think of it this way: Yes, a poem is open to interpretation, but mostly in terms of the associations a reader brings to the poem. If you write a poem with a dilapidated old barn as its central image, that barn is going to mean different things to different readers: the reader who grew up in the country, the reader who has never been outside the city where they were born, the reader who spent summers at their grandparents' farm—all of them are going to bring different visual images and different emotional connections to that barn in your poem. That's okay. In fact, it's kind of amazing, and it's part of how the poem means at least two things. But you probably do want them all thinking about a barn. If your barn is so inadequately rendered on the page that it doesn't bring up those varied associations for your readers, that's when you've not fully done your job.

As you read the poems in this anthology, you might not always be certain exactly what the poet means, but you will rarely be mystified over what a poem is about. "Aubade with Bread for the Sparrows" by Oliver de la Paz is about feeding the birds on a winter morning, It leaves a reader pondering any number of things: the starkness of morning, the cruelty of the world, the immense loneliness in the dead of winter, or the complexity of religious faith and doubt—or maybe it reminds you of the way your uncle used to sit in the park every afternoon to throw bread crumbs to the pigeons. All of these different reactions to the poem are legitimate interpretations, but the poem itself is still *about* feeding the birds on a winter morning. The fact that the poem has a clearly rendered subject matter is what allows readers to have their individual reactions and experiences with the language of the poem.

Sometimes, Meaning Is Secondary

Instead of delivering a logical conclusion or a clear narrative climax, poems offer up an experience to the reader. Perhaps the point isn't about arriving at a specific destination at the end of a poem. Perhaps the point of the poem is the journey the reader takes between the beginning and the end. Perhaps the poem's aim is the music, not the interpretation of the music. Perhaps the poem aims to evoke a mood or explore an image without being beholden to a narrative arc or an internal coherence.

As Kim Addonizio's "You Don't Know What Love Is" unfurls on the page and offers up its images and language and metaphor, the reader experiences the complexity of love, the rebirth of a corpse pulled from a river, the rise and downfall of this figure, the physical intimacy between the speaker and a "you," before the return to the images of death and a funeral again at the

end. There are hints of a narrative here, but it's likely readers will come
to different conclusions about the story in that narrative and different
conclusions as to precisely what the poem is saying about love. This isn't to
say that the poem's meaning isn't important. Clearly, it is, but sometimes as
a reader, it's more important to engage in the experience of reading the poem
than it is to isolate and analyze all the possible symbols to arrive at some
kind of universally agreed-upon truth.

As a Writer, You Don't Have to Think about Meaning

That's a half-truth, because at some point you will want to think about
what the poem means. But meaning isn't something that you have to know
ahead of time. It's not something a writer needs to have planned out before
sitting down to write a poem. You don't have to go in thinking about the
different symbols you will use or how the poem is going to use a series of
references to Langston Hughes, or how the last stanza will be an homage
to Homer's *Iliad*. In fact, a poet shouldn't be thinking about symbols at all.
Declaring something in a poem to be a symbol is an act of interpretation,
not creating. As a poet, you should focus on using compelling images and
concrete, specific details. Let the scholars who study your work later decide
which ones are symbols, and for what.

When you start to write, it's often with the intention of exploring a
certain experience or an emotion, and you probably have some idea what
you want to say about that topic, but you must approach the process with
an open mind, willing to reverse course or follow some new path that
your language opens up. The best poems become their own thing during
the writing process. A poem that marches relentlessly toward a particular
conclusion is not exploring, it's explaining. It's also sure to lack the surprise
successful poems need.

The trick is to be flexible with your understanding of what the poem
is going to be about. Follow the language. Trust in your mind's strange
associative powers. When your images and metaphors open a doorway to
a new subject, go through it. At that point, the poem might have started to
find its own meaning, and that's a good thing indeed.

A note here about writerly intent: As a writer, you'll have specific aims
for your poems, experiences you'll want to capture, feelings you'll want to
evoke, perhaps even some message you'd like to convey. But once we share
our poems with the world, we don't get to walk around with them and say,
"Now, what I meant in this line is . . ." You have to trust that line says what
it needs to say all on its own. You need to have spent enough time and effort
on each word in that line so that you know it's ready to leave the safety of
your hands and venture into the world where readers will interpret as they

will. The flip side of this is that you hear beginning readers of poetry asking, "Why did the poet space these lines like that? What did they mean by this image?" These are the wrong questions. Readers don't have access to the writer's mind (in most cases), and even if they do, writers aren't always the best judges of their own work. What readers have access to is the poem on the page. The right questions to be asking are, "How does it affect my reading experience when the lines are spaced like that? What associations does this image conjure in my mind?" The answers here are slipperier, more ambiguous, and personal—but ultimately more meaningful than playing a guessing game about what the writer had in mind.

Your Three Brains

It's important for poets to have some understanding of how readers might process information and create meaning as they engage with a text. So let's examine your three brains: lizard, animal, and human.

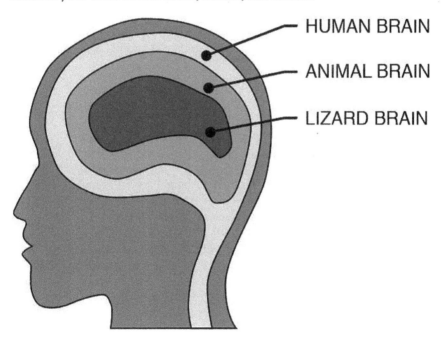

The Lizard Brain

The limbic cortex is the part of the brain where emotion and mood happens, the system in charge of primal feelings fear and hunger and lust. Some people call this "The Lizard Brain" because the limbic cortex is just about all a lizard has in terms of brain function, When you see a scary movie and the hairs rise up on the back of your neck, that's the lizard brain saying, "Um, maybe we should get out of here before the dude with the chainsaw comes back." When you are playing a sport and you feel the blood pounding in your temples and your muscles all twitch, that's the lizard brain saying, "It's game time, suckers!" When you are at a party and you lock eyes with an attractive someone across the room and you get that swirly feeling in your stomach, that's the lizard brain saying—well, you get the picture.

The Animal Brain

Wrapped around the lizard brain is the animal brain (not really; this is a metaphor), the part of the brain that tells us what to do when we feel the emotional surges in our lizard brain. When you are scared, you make decisions about how to proceed: do you flee in terror or do you rise up with both fists to take on that chainsaw killer? When you are at bat and the pitcher winds up, you watch the ball and decide whether you will swing, how hard you will swing, or whether you will lean into the pitch and try to get on base the easy (and painful) way. The animal brain reacts to stimuli from the lizard brain and starts to make decisions and plans in response to base desires and emotions.

The Human Brain

The outermost layer of the brain is the human brain, the part that is all about creating order and finding logical connections in the world. It's where you collect the data the world gives you for interpretation and use it to figure out how to take action. What is to be gained by fighting vs. fleeing Leatherface? What tools do you need for such a fight? Is he chasing you or running away? Maybe he just needs a hug?

Or in the case of reading a poem, what does it mean?

Sometimes a poem can be too straightforward, perhaps so simple that it has only one meaning, in which case we might say that the poem is too human-brained, stuck in a mindset of telling a logical story or creating associations that become too obvious by the poem's end. If a poem is too lizard-brained, it might need some way to ground the poem so that the reader understands what to do with the sensory information or imagery. Some poems are deliberately more lizard-brained than others, while others use the human brain to do most of their work—these things are not absolutes, nor are they mutually exclusive in any particular poem. But they can be helpful in thinking about what kind of meaning a reader is getting from a poem. Human brain and lizard brain—generally speaking, a poem needs both.

When something in a poem moves a reader emotionally, that's the lizard brain at work, responding viscerally to an image or phrase. Part of a poem's goal is to reach the lizard brain, but that's not always easy to do. The animal brain is between the human and lizard brains and it keeps them apart so they don't always know what the other is doing or feeling. If the human and lizard brains were in contact, finding meaning in poems would be so easy to do. We would more easily see the connections between things and the emotional value they have in poems.

All of this doesn't mean that we are back to square one where poems are undecipherable things that refuse to give us information. No, on the contrary—if we are armed with a way of articulating how meaning operates in a poem, both in terms of how a writer creates it and how a reader interprets it, we can start to get a handle on creating a poem without having to know what everything in a poem means.

Just as writing poems is like a muscle that develops with practice, so too is reading poems. The more poems you read, the more you spend time with words on the page, the more comfortable you become with the particular kinds of music, ambiguity, contradiction, and mystery you'll find in those words. This in turn will make you more confident when you make your own poems.

The Elements of Poetry

5

Rhetorical Construction

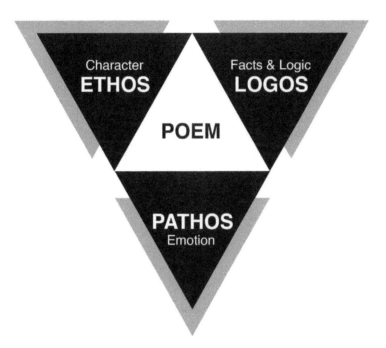

Simply put, rhetoric is the art of persuasion. A writer uses language deliberately in order to inform, instruct, or persuade an audience to a particular way of thinking or to spur them into action. The study of rhetoric goes back at least to Aristotle, who more than 2,000 years ago was thinking about the effects of language on its audience. Language is deployed rhetorically everywhere around you: television commercials, magazine advertisements, political speeches, piano lessons—it's all over the place. Thinking about language rhetorically is an important aspect of understanding how poems work on the page.

It is helpful to see poems as rhetorical constructions because it pushes the poet to consider the work poems do and because it provides helpful vocabulary for describing *how* poems do that work. As you become comfortable articulating how poems work, you will discover a greater variety of choices available to you. A poet isn't just putting words on the page haphazardly in order to express emotions. Rather, the poet carefully constructs a text built to appeal to the audience's sense of logic, emotion, and values. This is the rhetorical triangle, the points of which are logos, pathos, and ethos.

Logos

A common complaint about poetry is that people sometimes find poems difficult to understand, so perhaps a good place to start in response is to say yes, poems can be difficult to understand. People are more used to reading prose, which is typically bound by logic and framed in rhetorical structures aimed at explanation and providing systems of evidence-based claims and proof. Because the majority of textual communications happen in prose, this has become the default expectation for how readers set about finding meaning in a text.

A discussion of logos generally addresses how facts and logical structures are used in a text. Writers create authority for themselves and about their subjects through data, logical statements, and claims supported by evidence to make their argument clear to their audience. When readers look for meaning in a text, they are most often focused on how the writer has used logos to deliver information in a way that creates a convincing message.

This connects to why many people find poetry difficult: readers are used to looking for facts and logic to drive a text, but poems often create their own logic, which may be counter to what readers have learned to expect from prose. Often poems make a statement and then make a leap to some other seemingly unrelated subject. Some poems will forsake logic in favor of repetition, rhythm, voice, and language, prioritizing these elements over the need to provide any sort of causal system of creating meaning. Sometimes poems use faulty causality or a slippery slope argument, and sometimes they outright contradict themselves, making a statement and then reversing that statement a few lines later. Poems may omit the words that make clear the logical connections between ideas: "In conclusion," "as a result," "which leads us to"—these phrases are at home in prose but quite out of place in most poems.

When you write a poem, there's no need to adhere to the logical thinking as we understand it from our reading of prose. Logic is the realm of the human brain but sometimes the goal of the poet is to expand a poem's possibilities beyond the potential logical structures—or illogical structures, as the case may be—that take the poem into interesting and unknown territories.

Rhetorical Devices

A poem's logos is, in great part, a system of rhetorical devices aimed at engaging the reader. Here is a rundown of common terms—literary devices, they're called—that describe the moves poems make.

Allusion: A reference to something outside the poem, usually of cultural, historical, or literary significance.

Archaism: The use of old or outdated conventions or diction in a poem. This could take the form of simple rhymes and rhyme schemes, sentences that are written to sound "poetic," or just a lot of forsooths and hences.

Anthropomorphism: The attribution of human traits or qualities to animals or inanimate objects.

Colloquialism: An expression or phrase that is informal or conversational, belonging more to the realm of spoken language than written language. This also includes slang and regional dialects.

Didacticism: The idea that a poem should contain information and instructions for the reader, especially moral instruction. Sometimes considered a negative trait, as people don't want poems to preach at them.

Framing: The encapsulation of one thing inside another. Like a story within a story, except we're talking about poetry here.

Hyperbole: Exaggeration! Overstatement! (With a rhetorical purpose!)

Idiom: A phrase commonly used for its figurative meaning, though its literal meaning might not be obvious without context. *It's raining cats and dogs, best thing since sliced bread*, etc.

Irony, Dramatic: A scenario where the reader knows more about a given situation than do the characters involved in a narrative.

Irony, Situational: A scenario where what happens is the opposite of what is expected.

Irony, Verbal: An expression that means something different (usually the opposite) of what is said.

Juxtaposition: Placing one thing next to another for comparison and/or contrast. The close proximity forces readers to create associative meanings. One thing takes on the value of the other thing next to it. You can place an eagle next to a soldier and they can exchange values. The eagle becomes an insignia of war, while the soldier receives the majesty and sovereignty of the eagle.

Kenning: A two-part figure of speech that appears often as a hyphenated word offered in place of a thing's literal name. The sun is a *sky-candle*, the moon is a *night-eye*, and snowfall is *winter's curtains*.

Metonymy: Representation of a thing by that with which it is closely associated. The eagle represents the United States. The bear represents Russia—or California, depending on where you live. The White House represents the executive branch of the US government.

Mimesis: The imitation and interpretation of reality in a piece of art through portrayal of things as they appear in the real world. Characters might behave in ways that correspond to actual human behaviors, nature might appear in ways that reflect real-world locations that are recognizable to the reader. Through this representation, the reader can believe and sometimes participate in the reality created by the poem.

Non Sequitur: A thought or statement that is an illogical leap from that which precedes it.

Onomatopoeia: Pow! Rattle! Words that imitate the sounds they represent. Zonk! Whoosh! Zing! Buzz!

Oxymoron: A two-word contradictory figure of speech in which the first word negates the second by having opposite meanings. Listen to the *deafening silence*. That is such an *original cliché*.

Paradox: An impossible reality that appears to be true.

Parallelism: A figure of speech in which consecutive sentences or phrases have identical grammatical constructions. This is the first sentence, and it looks like this. This is the second sentence, and it's built nearly the same.

Personification: The representation of an abstract quality as having a human form. Uncle Sam is the personification of the United States. Rosie the Riveter is the personification of the strength of American women during the Second World War. The grim reaper is the personification of death.

Prose: Text not written in verse. It is built into sentences and paragraphs for everyday use.

Prose poem: A poem written in prose rather than verse.

Prosody: The patterns of sound and rhythm in a poem and the study thereof.

Pun: A joke driven by a situation in which a word has multiple meanings, both of which make sense.

Satire: The use of extreme exaggeration and irony to expose and ridicule human folly and/or corruption. Satire can be humorous, but it always attacks its target.

Superimposition: To lay one thing over another in such a way that both are still visible. One image can overlap with another by laying qualities of one thing over the second. If you have an image of a bird and an image of a boy you can superimpose the bird over the boy by giving him feathers, literally or figuratively.

Syllogism: A rhetorical device that applies deductive reasoning to a series of statements in order to arrive at a logical conclusion. Aristotle's famous example goes like this:

All men are mortal,

Socrates is a man,

Therefore, Socrates is mortal.

Note that poems are not bound to strict deductive reasoning. A poem can use the syllogism in its classic form to come to a logical conclusion, or the poem can forsake logic and move toward an illogical deduction.

Synecdoche: Representation of a thing by one of its parts. A bird is represented by a wing or a feather, an automobile by its steering wheel or its snow tires.

Synesthesia: The mixing or confusion of the five senses.

Trope: A commonly used theme or rhetorical device. A secret identity is a common superhero trope. A walk in the woods is a common nature poetry trope.

Verisimilitude: The quality of appearing true to life.

Verse: A poetic composition, any grouping of words into a poetic form. (Often used to refer to lineated poems, as opposed to prose poems.)

Ethos

Ethos is an aspect of rhetoric that is largely about character and how writers portray themselves on the page through persona. Whenever we write, we strive for credibility with our readers, an attribute which depends greatly on the situation. A student writing a paper for class might want to appear hard working, intelligent and engaged with the course content. A person writing a letter to ask their parents for a loan might want to appear desperate yet responsible and definitely loving and respectful toward their family. A person writing a note to ask for a date might want to come across as being fun to hang out with for a couple of hours, at least. When the text manages to create a credible persona for the reader, we say that the text has achieved "high ethos."

Ethos appears in poems in a couple of different ways, the first being the intent of the writer. If the poem is hateful or tries to injure someone emotionally or spiritually, then the writer's intent might come into doubt. Poems attempt to build empathy with their subjects; poems that lack empathy cannot create connections with the reader. This kind of ethics is important to writers, not in the sense that everyone has to come from the same moral foundation or write with the same point of view, but more that without creating empathy, the poem risks being unable to emotionally connect with the reader.

Sometimes, the poem's purpose is to convey an ethical belief in a way that the reader can experience it as an emotional response. Protest poems, for example, exist in opposition to a person, government, or ideal. The poem attempts to transform ideology into emotion—the ideology is felt by the reader emotionally, which delivers the poem's ethical information. "The Gun Joke" by Jamaal May, for example, plays with the language of jokes, but as the reader progresses through the poem, it becomes apparent that there is no joke here. The poem resists being funny, and combined with our expectation of humor, delivers the poem's ethical information.

Every poem has a speaker, which is different from saying that every poem has a writer. In creating a speaker, the poem's voice takes on a persona that may not be the same as that of the writer. That voice might be ironic or passionate or self-deprecating—whatever the quality it takes on, the voice is what delivers logos and pathos information to readers in a way that they can receive and understand it.

Pathos

Pathos is an appeal to the emotions of the audience. Nearly every movie and television show ever made is geared to make the audience laugh, cry, or feel some emotion. Many of the most famous speeches contain appeals to logic powered by the credible character of the speaker. Dr. Martin Luther King, Abraham Lincoln, Ronald Reagan, Barack Obama—these orators deliver arguments based on logic and character, yet their speeches are also driven in great part by the way they inspire and call to action through an appeal to emotions. Through pathos, a prose writer uses emotional language to establish common ground by appealing to common systems of morality and values.

Readers of prose are used to parsing out the text's logos; however, a poem's aim is often to create pathos for the reader. If logos is the realm of the human brain, then pathos is its counterpart in the lizard brain, as poems appeal to our base desires and emotions. If the purpose of logos is to move the reader from the poem's beginning to its end, then the purpose of pathos is to move the reader internally—logos moves the reader's eyes across the page and pathos moves the reader's heart or stomach at the end, leaving them feeling all squishy inside.

The Poem's Rhetorical Construction

These three points—logos, pathos, and ethos—make up the foundation of the poem's rhetorical construction. Some poems might seem to be rooted more in logos while others seem to lean more heavily on pathos. Still others might seem to be more interested in creating characters and exploring the mind of a particular speaker than anything logical or emotional. Regardless of how they appear to be working, however, poems always use all three.

For example, Patricia Lockwood's poem "Rape Joke" seems to be very much grounded in logos. It offers end-stopped lines and unlineated paragraphs that convey information about and reactions to sexual assault. It almost appears as though we are reading prose. Yet the poem also asks the reader to walk in the shoes of a rape survivor with the use of the second person point of view. This in turn creates the poem's ethos—by walking with (or *as*) the survivor, we are asked to experience the life of the survivor as figures in the poem deny and make light of the experience of sexual assault. The poem goes on and on relentlessly until the reader is ready for the poem to end. But it doesn't end—that's part of the poem's pathos, the emotional weight that the reader cannot escape. Taken one step further, the reader can walk away from the poem, shut the book without reading to the end, but for the survivor, there is no escape. If you can see the rhetorical triangle at work in the poem, you should be able to see how the poem has been built to elicit an emotional response and create empathy for rape survivors who live in a culture that forgets about sexual assault or refuses to take the experiences of survivors seriously.

6

Kairos

Simply put, Kairos is the time and place for the poem. We should start by talking about normal linear time, what the ancient Greeks called Chronos: the forward-moving flow of time that we measure with our timepieces and the way the sun or moon moves across the sky. Aristotle talks about a second kind of time: Kairos, which is less about the movement of time and more about fixed points in time. That is, there is a time and context at which point an argument might be most effective. It's this notion of the perfect time and context that has resulted in some of the most famous speeches in history: Abraham Lincoln's Gettysburg Address, Winston Churchill's "We Shall Fight on the Beaches," Dr. Martin Luther King Jr.'s "I Have a Dream"—these are memorable not only because they are well-crafted speeches, but also because they were delivered at pivotal moments in history when the audience was receptive, the message relevant to the world. The Kairos was right.

Because a poem is a rhetorical structure, it's subject to Kairos in terms of both when it was written and when readers encounter it. We can examine the role of Kairos in poetry in a few ways: the first is how poems are products of the times and cultures in which they are created, conforming to the norms of a given time and place. Another is how poems gain meaning through the events of the day, how Kairos arises from Chronos to give power to a poem. And sometimes the poet discovers the right time for the making of a poem.

Kairos: Poems as Artifacts in Time

This might seem like a no-brainer observation, but here it is anyway: an artist is affected by the environment in which they live and make art; how that art is received by its audience is greatly affected by the environment in which it is consumed. For example, when the Beatles appeared in the United States for the first time in 1964, they showed off a new sound that revolutionized rock and roll. When twenty-first-century listeners hear "Love Me Do," however, it sounds much less like a cutting edge rock song because it's now an artifact of the past—this doesn't make it a less compelling song, necessarily, just one that is an artifact of the past that sounds old fashioned to contemporary ears.

To continue with our Fab Four example: if you listen to any song from the Beatles' album *Abbey Road*, released in 1969, it sounds like a completely different band than the one that sang "She Loves You." The band evolved past the sound of "Love Me Do" into more complex music. So much happened in the United States and the world in those years: the British Invasion, the summer of love, social unrest in reaction to the Vietnam War, a rise in popularity of psychedelic drugs—the change in context and culture sparked a change in the art of the time broadly and for the Beatles in particular.

We can make this observation about art in general, actually—scholars have been making a living at this kind of thing for decades. The effect of colonialism on the European novel. The financial hardships of Mark Twain and the effects on his novel *A Connecticut Yankee in King Arthur's Court*. The world changes; it exerts social and environmental pressures on an artist; their work shows the effects of that pressure. Or it happens to whole groups of artists and the result is an artistic or social movement. Think, for example, how postmodernism is a reaction to modernism, how modernism is a philosophical response to romanticism, how Tobey Maguire made that one Spider-Man movie with Kirsten Dunst, and now we are deep into a cinematic super hero revival in America with no end in sight.

Kairos is crucial when it comes to the study of poetry as literature. A poem like "Adonais" by Percy Shelley, for example, is rooted in Greek mythology and Shelley's admiration for fellow poet John Keats, for whom the poem is written. The poem is what it is because Shelley is a brilliant poet, to be sure, but the poem is also guided by the conventions of the day, steeped in the Romantic tradition with an obsession for classical tragedy and Greek ruins. Formally, it's in pretty strict iambic pentameter with hard end rhymes throughout, which was the way of verse at the time. Part of what makes that poem difficult for modern readers of poetry is that "Adonais" is not a poem of our time. It's not as immediately accessible to a reader in terms of language, content, or form because those things belong to another era. So studying "Adonais" isn't simply a matter of studying the poem's text—it's also a matter of studying history and culture in order to fully appreciate how the poem created meaning in the Kairos of the moment.

If we have trouble reading or relating to a poem like "Adonais," that says less about the poem's quality and more about how far we are from the Kairotic forces that made that poem what it is. We could say the same thing about the poems of Emily Dickinson, Walt Whitman, Phillis Wheatley, Countee Cullen, Edna St. Vincent Millay, and so on and so on. Conversely, imagine getting into your time machine and heading back to deliver a poem such as "Triple Sonnet for Being Queer in a Family of Straights" by Dorothy Chan or "Cascade" by Rajiv Mohabir to Shelley and his friends—

these poems are full of contemporary language and are in response to contemporary concerns. Think about how much you would have to explain for the poems to make sense to Shelley. They might not even be recognized as poetry.

And although Kairotic difference accounts for some of the ways people are alienated from poetry, it's also a way into learning to read these poets. Learning how these texts came to be under the influence of Kairos is one way of discovering new authors and new ways of thinking about poems.

Kairos: Poems as Timely Artifacts

One of the most powerful things about a poem is its ability to reach a reader and move them emotionally. Sometimes the poem's arrival at the right time and place can greatly enhance the poem's emotional power. Sometimes, the emotional power of a poem isn't solely about the writer's reaction to their environment or their era. It's also about whether a poem arrives at a moment when the reader is particularly ready to receive it.

Imagine encountering a poem like "The Role of Elegy" by Mary Jo Bang shortly after the passing of a loved one. Or reading "Aubade with Bread for the Sparrows" by Oliver de la Paz after spending a morning alone in your quiet house. These poems connect with readers not because they are vague and general enough to fit any situation, more that the poems' specific emotional content allows the speaker's specific experiences in the poem to resonate with a reader's own experiences. This might seem like splitting hairs, but so often people praise a poem by calling it timeless or by exclaiming that a poem has "stood the test of time." What this means is that the poem has benefitted from Kairos repeatedly, whether that means a publisher made it available to readers in a book or that the poem speaks to a particular condition that reoccurs, or even that people continue to read the poem over and over online. The poem's reception is influenced by what the reader knows, what the reader has experienced, and what the reader might need at a particular moment.

This isn't to say that an artist has no say as to how their work will be received in terms of timeliness. A writer's topicality can go a long way toward helping a poem find its time and place for a reader. For example, Danez Smith's poem "alternate names for black boys" went viral right around the time that eighteen-year-old Michael Brown was killed by a policeman in Ferguson, Missouri. To be fair, Smith has had their fair share of viral attention on their work, from "Dear White America" to "Dinosaurs in the Hood" to "alternate names." Smith's poems are sometimes accusatory or volatile in tone, always disarming and surprising as they confront racial tension and injustice in twenty-first-century America. As a list poem, "alternate names for black boys" offers us names that are not names, which allows the reader to ruminate on precisely what these names mean even though the poem declines to explain itself. This is perhaps appropriate when the #SayTheirNames campaign asks social media users and American news outlets to identify African American victims of police violence by their names in order to center racial injustice and focus on those victims' humanity. It's a poem that belongs to our times, in America in particular.

Another example: In 2015, poet Maggie Smith wrote a poem at a coffee shop in central Ohio. She called the poem "Good Bones" and has said that it was a poem that came in one sitting—just about thirty minutes—rather than over a series of writing sessions. A year later, "Good Bones" appeared in the summer issue of the online literary journal *Waxwing*, which dropped on June 15. This was just three days after the Pulse Nightclub shooting in Orlando, which saw a gunman kill forty-nine people and wound fifty-three others, an event that left many Americans feeling sickened, vulnerable, and nervous about the intersection of homophobia, racism, and gun violence that showed itself that night in America. It seemed to many that "Good Bones" hit the internet in response to the Pulse shooting, as it quickly went viral, being shared on Twitter, Facebook, and Instagram over and over.

This poem went viral, and we can actually trace the poem's virality thanks to the detective work of poet Kelli Russell Agodon for *The Seattle Review of Books*. Agodon traced the poem's virality back to when it was shared on Facebook by poet Tarfia Faizullah where it was then screenshot by writer Shira Erlichman and posted to Twitter for her 14,000 followers. That tweet was retweeted by many celebrities, including singer Charlotte Church and journalist Caitlin Moran, who between them have over a million Twitter followers. From there, the poem took on a life of its own, being shared across the internet on various platforms with many people who are probably not regular readers of poetry. And as Agodon notes, *The Guardian* did a story on the poem for the UK on June 17, the day after the murder of Member of Parliament Jo Cox, so it was already on people's minds in Britain when the Brexit referendum came down on June 23. And then a terrorist truck attack in Nice, France, happened in July. National Public Radio dubbed "Good Bones" the official poem of 2016 as the poem became one that people turned to for solace, for comfort, for wisdom.

In the years since the poem's first publication, the poem has been translated into a variety of languages, has been turned into a short film, an interpretive dance, and was featured on the television show *Madam Secretary* (the episode was called "Good Bones" after the poem). The poem itself continues to affect people today, when anything happens in the world that leaves people feeling vulnerable and afraid. Smith has called the poem "a societal anxiety barometer." She says that she knows something bad is happening in the world when her Twitter mentions spike, which is to say that "Good Bones" is a poem that finds Kairos arising from Chronos over and over again, readers attaching meaning to it for themselves when they discover the poem's emotional resonance with them in times of trouble.

Poetry finds its way to the audience by way of Kairos—the culture and context as experienced by the reader is as important as the intent of the writer when we examine how meaning is made in a piece of art. Looking at the relationship of Kairos to Chronos offers us the perspective to recognize how historical and cultural context might affect the decisions a writer makes in creating a text, as well as how an audience might receive and interpret meaning from that text at fixed points in time. Perhaps people have wounds that are soothed by poems, pains that are exacerbated as we are assaulted by the world's ills: racism, violence, oppression, hate—and when a reader finds the right poem at the right time, it's something they can feel, either by themselves or along with millions of other readers.

Kairos: Poems in the Right Time

Just as poems are artifacts to be read and encountered in time, for the poet Kairos is a force that is very much at work when they begin to write a poem. Maybe something just happened and you *have* to write about it. Or maybe something happened years ago and this morning, something new offered you clarity on that thing and now you want to write about it.

Whatever the case, you suddenly feel the need to write. This could be a snap reaction to an experience or a slow burn between the instigating event and the poem's making. It will be different for everyone and every poem, but writers have moments when it feels like it's time to write something. Kairos. Inspiration. A moment of genius. Call it what you will, but what's happening is that the poet's powers of perception, empathy for the world, and understanding of their own emotional needs are, for whatever reason, focused on the making of a poem. It's important to be aware that while it's generally unhelpful to wait around for inspired moments like these, it's equally important to recognize that sometimes, the time is right to sit down and write.

7

The Elements of Poetry

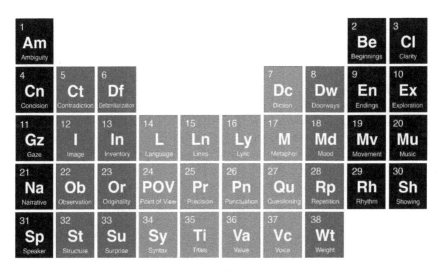

In ancient Greece, people believed that the universe was composed of four elements: air, earth, fire, and water—the essential parts of all matter. Eventually Plato added aether because the heavens couldn't possibly be made of any earthly material. This concept of breaking down the world into elements is common in other cultures, too. The five elements in Japan are similar to that of the Greeks, except that aether is replaced by the void. India, Egypt, and Tibet have similar systems in their history. The Chinese Wu Xing describes five energies: fire, water, earth, metal and wood. In the modern day, people in the West generally no longer conceive of the world as four or five basic elements. Instead, science gives us a more complex system of explaining the fabric of the universe: the periodic table. The number of elements changes as new elements are discovered and added to the periodic table, which arranges the elements into groups that all share similar chemical characteristics.

What follows are thirty-eight elements of poetry as we have conceived them, building blocks for poetry that are also essential characteristics that make poems work on the page. These elements present ways of approaching the writing of a poem and ways of thinking about how poems work. The specific function of each element will likely be a bit different from poem to poem. Don't worry about reading them straight through from start to finish. Instead, skip around from element to element to see what might be helpful to you in thinking about your poems, and as you do so, consider that poem you are working on: how might a particular element give you a path to engaging your audience? How might focusing on one element or another unlock a poem that's proving stubbornly resistant to finding its way to the page?

Remember that the poem is a rhetorical construction. The elements of poetry are the things that help the poet connect with the audience and deliver a full reading experience, working all three points of the rhetorical triangle on the way. On the one hand, as you read about each element, you might find that some of them apply in some pretty obvious ways. Elements like speaker and voice connect directly to ethos, and things like structure and lineation line up directly under logos. On the other hand, some elements like image and metaphor look like they do double duty, seemingly operating under different points of the triangle at the same time. Is the metaphor logos because it's part of an overall logical structure, or is it pathos because of the emotion that it conveys? The answer is that it depends on the poem, but more so that the poem's emotional content often arises from the specific ways that it employs ethos and logos. Studying and using these elements is less about the categorization of tools and more about how a poet can use the tools for their own end. These elements, in other words, are here to help you think about how poems work rhetorically—use them in a way that makes sense for you and the poems you want to make.

Ambiguity

If someone asks you what happened at last week's student council meeting or what your favorite sushi restaurant is, writing a poem would be a weird way to respond. That's because (as we keep insisting) a poem is not the best way to straightforwardly deliver information. If you want to efficiently communicate information, your best bet is a clearly written memo with simple sentences and bulleted lists to organize the content.

Your clearly written memo is crafted specifically to avoid ambiguity. To deliver a particular meaning with as little doubt as possible.

A poem is up to something else entirely.

Language is slippery. Interpretation is idiosyncratic. Every reader will bring their own life experiences, their own vocabulary, their own opinions and associations to bear on every word you write. The word "dog" brings to mind a different dog for every reader: a yellow lab, a greyhound, a Chihuahua, the mutt who greeted you at the front door every afternoon after school for your entire childhood.

The poet's task is not to fight this inherent ambiguity, but to embrace it. Revel in it. Explore it. Take advantage of it. A poet must dive into exactly those places in the language where meaning is slipperiest, where uncertainty is inevitable.

Language is not the same as experience. The words for things are not the things. Just as a painting of a pipe is not the pipe itself, a poem about love is not love. A poem about loss is not loss. And yet language is our medium. Language is what we as poets have chosen to use in our attempt to make sense of the world. It is our clay, our marble, our paint, our breath and brass, our wind and reed. Instead of pretending that it is adequate to the task, a poet must acknowledge its imperfections, point out those places where language falls short, where certainty is impossible, ambiguity inevitable.

For these reasons, you'll see contemporary poets openly acknowledge within their poems what they do not know, cannot know; places where language falls just short of what they're attempting to convey. Consider the redactions in the section of Solmaz Sharif's "Reaching Guantanamo," in which Sharif literally removes language from her poem; or the moment Bob Hicok describes when the speaker of "Elegy with lies" "cannot finish that story." These are moments when the poets acknowledge the limited ability of language to stand for truth. As readers, we sense truth in these poems nevertheless, but it's an ambiguous kind of truth, not easily pinned down.

Poems are not fables, to be concluded with the moral of the story delivered in a pithy phrase.

It's important for the young poet to become aware of the distinction between ambiguity and obscurity. As we mentioned in the Proceed with Caution chapter, it's easy for a poet to write a poem that deliberately means nothing, that is impossible for a reader to decipher. It's easy to use vague, abstract language that obscures the subject matter of your poem; it's also not a great idea. So ambiguity must be productive ambiguity; it has to help the reader experience your poem. This is where precision comes in; even as your poem explores complex and ambiguous facets of the human experience, your language choices must remain careful, focused, and intentional.

See Also: Clarity, Contradiction, Diction, Language, Metaphor, Precision, Syntax

2

Be

Beginnings

Beginnings

The most important element of a poem is how it begins. (In a few pages, we'll tell you that the most important element is how a poem ends, but for now, we want you to believe that how it begins matters more.)

The beginning of a poem does essential work. There is much required of a poem's first few lines. A reader comes to a poem cold, with no knowledge of the world the poem is observing or interpreting, with no sense of the poem's mood or tone or sense of syntax, with no preconceptions about the journey they're about to undertake. Working in conjunction with the title, the poem's first few lines establish what has been called a "lyrical contract" with the reader. Readers are smart; they pick up on everything. Within those first few words, readers begin to determine not only what world the poem is creating, but also the poet's stance toward that world. That shapes the reader's relationship with the rest of the poem.

Once the lyrical contract is in place, the reader expects it will be fulfilled. It would be exceedingly strange for a poem that opens with the speaker declaring, "Me and Maw, we ain't seen Paw since them hens got out they cage" to end with that same speaker observing, "Once more, our nobler selves had prevailed even as we stared into the vulpine abyss of our own souls." This is obviously an extreme (and ridiculous) example, but it illustrates the importance of consistency of voice.

You are free to violate the lyrical contract. Thwarting reader expectations is part of the work poems do. But it is essential that when you do so, you do so intentionally, with full awareness both of the expectations you established and of the effects of dashing them. That means you must play close attention to how your poem begins and what those opening lines give your reader.

The beginning of a poem is structural, as it does things like introducing a poem's "plot," in so far as poems have plots. Think about the arc of a narrative; a story begins with a problem, a conflict, some sort of catalyst to kick-start the events that follow. So, too, must a poem offer a catalyst, though it need not be a narrative catalyst: an event that leads to other events. The poem must begin immediately to justify its existence, to persuade the reader to continue reading.

Look at the first three lines of Anders Carlson-Wee's "Dynamite": "My brother hits me hard with a stick / so I whip a choke-chain / across his face. We're playing . . ." In these three lines, a sentence and just the first two words of the next sentences, we are dropped in medias res into a moment of high action and violence, but then quickly discover that the violence is a kind of play. The plot of the poem is set into motion; a straightforward approach to syntax is established; and we are introduced to the theme of violence and play in the relationship between these two siblings. That's a lot of work happening in fewer than twenty words.

Narrative poems typically begin with a plot point; more meditative poems often begin by explicitly establishing that the poet is thinking about something, as in Tracy K. Smith's "I think of your hands." Beginnings like this quickly give us the object of contemplation and the point of view of the poet doing the contemplating—a starting place from which the poem can spiral and move in unexpected directions. Providing that concrete starting place is critical; it grounds the poem for the reader and offers at least a momentary sense of stability.

Ada Limón's "Downhearted" takes the bold opening gambit of announcing its intentions quite plainly:

Six horses died in a tractor-trailer fire.
There. That's the hard part. I wanted
to tell you straight away so we could
grieve together.

Limón gives us what appears to be the central conflict of her poem—the death of these horses in a fire—and then breaks the fourth wall to address the reader directly, explaining why she started the poem with that observation. This immediately expands the project of the poem, letting the reader know that this isn't simply the story of the horses, but of the poet trying to make sense of loss. Readers are dropped directly into the world of the poem with that declarative opening sentence; then we are pulled into the mind of the poet as she tries to make sense of the fire. In this way, Limón's skillful opening establishes the poem's conflict: the tension between bad things happening and our attempts to process them.

Other poems begin more mysteriously. Traci Brimhall's "Ars Poetica" opens with an unexplained "It," leaving us to work to figure out what the missing referent might be. Evelyn Araluen's poem begins with an intimate image and blank space, creating a stutter that echoes the poem's title. Tarfia Faizullah's lovely opening lines—"Let me break / free of these lace-frail / lilac fingers disrobing / the black sky"—establish a lyrical sensibility and a mood more than any particular sense of plot; it bears mentioning, however, that Faizullah has already given us a descriptive title and an epigraph establishing the poem's mode, plot, and setting—thus freeing her opening lines from that duty, allowing her to move quickly into imagery and a prayerful request.

Beginnings are hard. (Everything about writing a poem is hard.) Worrying too much about catalysts and lyrical contracts can make them even harder.

The worst thing is to let this paralyze you—to stare at a blinking cursor while you agonize over figuring out the perfect first lines. It's more important to plunge ahead and write. Getting the beginning just right can be a task for the revision process. You won't know if the beginning is the right one until you see where the rest of the poem ends up anyway.

See Also: Endings, Narrative, Structure, Titles

3

Cl

Clarity

Clarity

This might seem a little counterintuitive, the notion of clarity as an essential element in poetry. After all, we've already pointed out (repeatedly) that a poem is not the best mechanism for the straightforward delivery of information. The elements section begins with ambiguity, for goodness' sake, celebrating the slipperiness of language. This would seem to imply that poetry values the opposite of clarity.

And yet clarity, too, matters. Sometimes poets need to be able to say exactly what they mean. The opposite of clarity is not ambiguity or mystery, but obscurity. It's easy to obscure meaning, to write deliberately difficult-to-interpret lines of poetry. The challenge is to honor the complexity of human existence and the slipperiness of language without resorting to vague phrases or abstractions, without using your language as a blanket to be thrown over your subject matter.

If you look at the poems in this anthology, you'll find that there's rarely much lack of clarity regarding what a poem is about. Precisely what each poem means may be less than clear, and each poem has its own layers of mystery or ambiguity, but the poets are not using language to deliberately hide their topics. Craig Santos Perez and Billy Collins, for example, are both quite straightforward in their poems, though both are tackling large, abstract notions such as the fragility of the natural world for Perez and the very nature of poetry for Collins. In fact, it is the clarity and concreteness of these poems that allows the poets to explore such vast ideas. A poem about something obscure and abstract that is itself obscure and abstract will tend to drift aimlessly, leaving readers no place to stand confidently.

Even a poem as lyrical, challenging, and associative as Gary L. McDowell's "Tell Me Again about the Last Time You Saw Her" is quite clear in its language use; each sentence or segment or image is on its own clear—the poem's sense of mystery comes from the juxtaposition of these moments, which readers must interpret for themselves. In McDowell's poem and perhaps in all poems, clarity works not against ambiguity but hand in hand with it.

See Also: Ambiguity, Concision, Precision

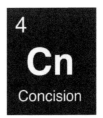

4

Cn

Concision

Concision

Don't waste words.

Tempting as it is to end this section there, forgive us a few thoughts on why concision is an important element in poetry. First, it's important to note that not all poems use concision in the same way. Concision is not always the same thing as minimalism. Poems can still be expansive, lush in their language choices, even at times wordy.

Why concision? It's part of the project of much of poetry—not all, but probably most: the stripping away of excess to get to the essence of the subject matter. For a reader, there's great pleasure to be found in reading something that feels so carefully put together, so lovingly crafted, that not a single word could be removed or replaced. For a poet, there's pleasure in creating such a piece.

Contrast the language choices made by Monica Youn in "Quinta del Sordo" with David Kirby's in "Teacher of the Year." Youn's poem is exceedingly spare and focused; Kirby's is conversational and meandering. Youn's poem may be more what comes to mind when we think of concision, but even so, Kirby's poem does not waste a word. You measure concision not by word count, but by the value each word brings to the poem. Each word has work to do.

Concision is made possible by precision and closely related to clarity. The way to get the most out of each word in your poem is to ensure that each word is the best one for the job.

Sometimes you need those less-powerful connecting words: articles (a, an, the), conjunctions (and, but, or, for, so, yet), prepositions (to, for, from, etc.), and so on; like punctuation, these words help keep sentences and lines moving. But sometimes you don't. Perhaps not in the drafting stage, when you are exploring and working merely to get words onto the page, but later, as you begin to revise, you must interrogate each word: subject each word to a rigorous job interview to determine whether it deserves its place on the page.

Words like "however," "therefore," and the like—conjunctive adverbs— are used in prose to indicate the logical connections between ideas: to show that a clause contrasts with the preceding one, say, or is a conclusion drawn from the previous sentences. In poetry, these words should be used with caution. Most often, the poet should simply offer images and ideas and trust that the reader sees the connections between them. The act of juxtaposing two images next to each other in a poem creates the logic that binds the ideas together. There is, then, no need to spell out that logic with an adverb. An argumentative essay or legalistic brief needs to leave no room for doubt, so it uses these words to hold the hand of its reader as they walk together from premise to conclusion. A poem should always leave room for doubt.

Our first drafts are almost always full of hesitations, false starts, clumsy repetitions, and overexplaining. It's natural. Some of this comes from the process of exploration we undertake as we draft a poem, still working ourselves to figure out where the heart of the poem lives. Some of it comes from our understandable desire to make sure our reader "gets it," so we explain, re-explain, and repeat ourselves. This is the writing process. What matters is that during revision, we remind ourselves to trust that our best images do not need explanation.

There's a famous line variously (and almost certainly inaccurately) attributed to Michelangelo and several other famous artists about how to create a great sculpture of say, a horse: "You start with a block of marble and remove everything that doesn't look like a horse." The poet's goal is the same.

See Also: Clarity, Precision

5

Ct

Contradiction

Contradiction

One of the ways poems embrace ambiguity is by openly contradicting themselves. If the project of a poem is to explore the ways in which the world is unknowable, it's inevitable that part of that exploration includes reversal, reconsideration, contradiction. We've suggested that a poem must always be about at least two things; sometimes those two things are in opposition to each other. And yet both can exist. Think of how often there is laughter at a memorial service, as someone shares a fond, funny memory of the person everyone is there to mourn. That laughter might exist in contradiction to the grief, and yet both can exist simultaneously, the mind and heart capable of holding two diametrically opposed feelings at once.

The world is complex. Human experience is never just one thing. Poetry must reflect this, and sometimes that means the poet must contradict something said earlier. Jeannine Hall Gailey's Wonder Woman dreams of her father shooting a doe, but also of herself shooting the doe. In the world outside the poem and outside the dream, the world we live and breathe in, both things could not be true at once. But in a poem as in a dream, two contradictory truths can exist together. In this way, the poem forces the reader to experience them both at once: "each moon claiming the other false," as Gary L. McDowell writes. Similarly, Li-Young Lee can tell readers in a single line that "nothing and anything might make this noise."

The lesson here is clear: one simple way to create ambiguity and lend your work the kind of complexity you seek is to be willing to overtly contradict yourself from time to time. Part of being a good, thoughtful human being who learns and grows throughout life is being willing to change your mind about things; the same is true of a good, thoughtful poem.

The caution here is that the contradiction must be meaningful, complex, well-timed. Like any poetic move, it can be gimmicky if done for its own sake, or done too often. A successful contradiction means that both sides ring true. Our relationship to the poem's truth becomes more fragile after the contradiction. This is the project of poetry—navigating a fragile relationship with truth. Contradiction can be a key part of that,

These are the moments you should be looking for when you aim to introduce contradiction into your poems: those times when you passionately believe both sides of an argument; when you want two things to be true at once, even if the rules of the physical world would seem to suggest they cannot.

See Also: Ambiguity, Surprise

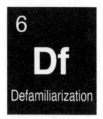

Defamiliarization

Defamiliarization is the transformation of everyday things into something a bit stranger. The poet takes something familiar, and through playing with images, with metaphors, with changing values and other elements, creates an unfamiliar experience for the reader. This is crucial, because strangeness is an important quality in poems.

The strangeness that is the result of defamiliarization contributes to the idea that poems are hard to understand. Strangeness obscures meaning simply by being strange. Even if it doesn't obscure meaning, strangeness at least forces the reader to slow down and take stock of what's happening on the page. So why make the effort to move the poem out of the realm of that which is familiar and more immediately understandable?

Partly, you do this because with strangeness comes additional value, and with that additional value, the poem can have more density and more clarity at the same time. When Billy Collins says that we can drop a mouse into a poem in "Introduction to Poetry," that's a moment of intense defamiliarization. The comparison is between the poem and a maze, a metaphor that posits the poem as something to lose a small animal in—the reader might be confused for a moment, but can make the connection between poem and maze with relatively little effort. Similarly, the way Eileen Chong uses numbers in "My Mother Talks in Numbers" presents the woman in this strange numerical way that also serves to create a specific portrait. These metaphors defamiliarize their subjects, but defamiliarization works in the end to bring additional value to the poem, clarifying its meaning for the reader.

The other part of why a poet might want to defamiliarize is that poetry is more fun that way. Collins presents the mouse in the maze, a leap from the beehive in the previous stanza—just one quick moment and then it's off to the maze. Then after the maze, the poem leaps again and has people looking for light switches in the dark, an image that puts the reader in the maze along with the mice and whatever else lurks there. And Chong's variations on the mother on her list catch the reader off guard from item to item, asking us to reconsider the metaphor each time we see it. By leaping from stanza to stanza, from line to line, these defamiliarized moments provide us with constant surprise in the poem.

Another reason to think about poetry as an act of defamiliarization is that when you set out to write a poem, you want to write the poem that only you could write. You want the final product to be original. That means you need to write the world as you see it, to focus on finding unusual, fresh, unfamiliar ways of expressing your ideas. An image that has been defamiliarized is not going to be cliché—just the opposite. We've all read about things that are white as snow; we want the ones that are white as plump kitchen trash bags on the side of a highway or white as the painted cinderblock walls of the hospital where someone we love is ailing. Give us something we haven't seen before, in other words. Look, we all tend not to trust ourselves, especially early in our writing lives; we worry that our poems are too weird, our ideas too idiosyncratic. But that's just what readers of poetry are after! Be your own strange self on the page. Lean into the weird. Your poems and their readers will thank you for it.

See Also: Clarity, Image, Observation and Interpretation, Surprise, Value

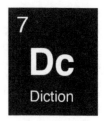

Diction

Diction, simply put, refers to the words and phrases you choose in a piece of writing. It's natural to think of poems as having elevated diction—that is, somewhat formal or lofty—but that's not always true. In fact, most contemporary poems fight against this expectation. A poem's diction can be conversational, informal, sarcastic, gritty, raw, and, yes, even poetic. Diction is closely related to voice, and voice is determined by a poem's speaker.

Here's an illustration of the same idea rendered three different ways:

- A cold wind was blowing in the pasture.
- A frigid gale swept across the forlorn prairies.
- It was dang freezin' out there in that field.

These convey essentially the same message, but they differ widely in diction. The first is fairly straightforward, not calling attention to itself in any particular way; the second more elevated (perhaps even to the point of being pompous); and the third is far more conversational and indicative of a particular speaker.

Attempts to force a particular diction on a poem can backfire. For example, if you try to spice up your vocabulary and reach for a more elevated diction by clicking the thesaurus feature in your word processor, your storm can become a squall or a tempest or a disturbance, any of which might seem more poetic but might not be the right word. Sometimes it's okay for a storm just to be a storm. Along those lines, it's risky to lower your diction deliberately. You don't want your speaker's voice to be a terrible Hollywood caricature of the person they're supposed to be. Throwing in "maw and paw" and a couple of "ain't"s and "y'all"s won't make your Southern characters seem more authentic; it will make them seem like cartoons and stereotypes. This, surely, is not the effect any good poet seeks.

For most young poets, the best strategy is to start writing without worrying too much about diction. At least in first drafts, write in a voice as close to your own everyday voice as possible; use your normal vocabulary and frame of reference. As you write more and more poems, and get deeper into the revision process, you can begin to experiment with diction. But as you can see in the poems in this anthology, even established, successful poets tend toward a more moderated diction; most of the poems in this collection avoid either artificially high or unnaturally low diction. A poem doesn't become a poem because you throw in a lot of multisyllabic vocabulary words; it's possible to craft a rich, evocative, complex poem that doesn't include a single word you'd need to study for your college-admissions tests.

Additionally, it's helpful to remember that a poem's diction doesn't have to be a fixed characteristic. Just because the poem started out conversational diction, it doesn't have to remain that way throughout. As you become comfortable modulating your diction, you can use it to control the tone and mood of your poem; you can experiment with voice; and you can use diction to shape the meaning of your poem.

One diction-related question young poets often have is about profanity. Can I swear in my poems? they ask, hesitantly and perhaps somewhat hopefully. Well, in a vacuum, the answer is yes, go right ahead. Some of the poems in this anthology use words that some might consider profanity. But we don't always write in a vacuum. If you're writing a poem for your high school English teacher and there's a school policy against profanity, maybe save the swearing for some other poem. It's also important to think about why you want to swear in a poem. A well-placed naughty word can call attention to itself in compelling ways. It can reveal voice or be good for a laugh at the right moment; it can make a poem's tone more conversational, mimicking the speech of everyday people, because let's face it, some people swear.

Look, for example, at how Maggie Smith begins her poem "Good Bones" with the diction of a poet and parent, and how it deliberately and purposefully moves the reader from the language of clever poetry toward that moment of profanity at the end—the emotional charge comes as much from this change in diction as anything. Likewise, if you are thinking about using profanity in a poem, ask yourself how it works with the rest of the poem's diction. How might the swearing work in concert with or in counter to the language in terms of the diction? Because if you're swearing to shock your reader, that's a bad idea. Swearing just isn't that shocking, particularly when it is included at the expense of more evocative, richer language. The risk is that the swearing ends up feeling gratuitous or worse, like abstract language that fails to move the reader.

Writing poems means paying heightened attention to the language you choose and how you use it; diction is a tool you can use to establish and disrupt the poem's language with the aim, as always, of connecting with and moving the reader.

See Also: Language, Syntax, Precision, Voice

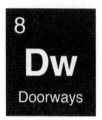

8

Dw

Doorways

Doorways

Every line you write in a poem, every fresh image, every new word—they all create new possibilities for where the poem might go next. As soon as you include an idea or item or image in a poem, you create a doorway. The more specific, the better. A flower is a decent doorway, for instance, but something like African Violet or Snapdragon is better because specificity gives us sharper images to play with. As a writer, you will find that you spend a lot of time creating doorways on the page, and then more time opening up those doorways to see where they might take you.

For example, even the familiar line "Roses are red" offers the writer two doorways: roses and red. What happens next in the poem depends on which doorway the writer opens—and how. How big are those roses? Whose roses are they and where are they growing? What breed of roses are they: American Beauty? Dark Desire? Little Buckaroo? As for red, consider what else might be colored red out there in the garden: a rusty trowel? A bulldog's tongue? The beginning of a sunburn on the speaker's neck? Opening either one of these doorways offers us so many options to move ourselves forward into the poem where we will undoubtedly create more doorways. In some ways, what you're doing is reckoning with the consequences of what you've started. Okay, now there are roses in your poem, what are you going to do about that?

Note that a doorway can also provide opportunities for lateral moves too, using the original image as a foundation before moving off into a different direction. What is rising or has arisen (a play on the word "rose")? Is there something to read (a play on the word "red") out there in the garden? Are there things that are red in the speaker's past or future? Doorways aren't restricted to simply making literal moves—by moving laterally, the doorway can create opportunities for figurative moves, allowing for more metaphor and the creation of more associative meanings. In Dorianne Laux's "Lighter," the lighter itself first appears as an example of something small and worthless that might be stolen—and the poem immediately goes through the doorway, and the lighter becomes the poem's central object, leading to metaphors about darkness and light, fire and cold.

By opening doorways and following them to see where they will lead, a writer can create networks of connected portals that help her create and discover the territory the poem wants to cover, systems of corridors that help a writer discover what material exists in a poem, and that help a reader make literal and figurative connections throughout the poem. When you have many doorways opening into the same corridor, you might find that you are on your way to creating metaphoric unity.

Yet, perhaps the most helpful thing about creating doorways for yourself is that when you get to that point in the poem where you're out of material or don't know what to write next, you can look back at the poem to see what unopened doorways you have left for yourself. If you are creating doorways adventurously, you end up leaving yourself an exit plan when you hit a dead end.

See Also: Exploration, Metaphor, Movement, Precision

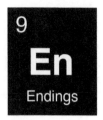

Endings

How a poem ends is the most important thing about that poem. (Yeah, we told you a little while ago that beginnings mattered most, but we were wrong. Endings matter more.) Readers are most likely to remember the end of the journey; the poem that lands its final punch is a poem that will stick with us.

If you think of a poem as a feat of gymnastics, which seems an apt enough metaphor what with all the leaping and turning, you realize how important it is to stick the landing. All the handstands and giant loops and flyaways you do while you're up there spinning around on the uneven bars of your poem don't mean nearly so much if you end up stumbling or flat on your face when you come down. So, yes, stick the landing.

But how? How do you stick the landing? That's always the question. The answer, as always, begins with reading. Look at the final lines of every poem in this anthology to see how these poets have chosen to end their works. Read 1,000 other poems and see how those poets ended theirs. (You might think 1,000 is a hyperbolic number, an exaggeration. It's not. If anything, it understates the number of poems you should read.)

The ending of a poem often provides one final turn. One final surprise. Sometimes an ending provides a kind of closure, putting the subject at hand to rest. More often, though, the final lines of a poem open things up, redirecting the poem's gaze outward, as Karen Skolfield does with her final directive to the reader to "watch where the birds go." Similarly, Catie Rosemurgy expands her tangible list of "Things That Didn't Work" to, essentially, everything: "Any shape or line whatsoever."

The epistolary form of Solmaz Sharif's poem suggests a kind of ending, offering the traditional closing of a letter, "Yours," but one final redaction, of the letter-writer's name, leaves the poem open and uncertain. The reason most poets eschew closure is likely that close can make it appear the poem has solved its problems, answered its questions—and any poem worth its salt is grappling with problems too big to solve, questions that have no clear-cut responses. As we've said earlier, poems are not riddles or mathematical equations; they're slipperier beasts.

Poets often use repetition as a closing strategy, returning to a line, phrase, or image from earlier in the poem, as Mary Jo Bang does when she closes by repeating the opening line at the end of the final line. We call it coming full circle. But as with all use of repetition, the simple fact of repeating is not enough; the words must carry new weight, land with a new kind of force when we revisit them. The journey the poem has carried us along has changed our thinking, and now Bang's phrase "the role of elegy is" feels less definite, less declarative, and more of a question. In this way perhaps, the ending offers the opposite of closure; a poem that appears to have begun in certainty ends in ambiguity—and, thus, nearer to true wisdom. Or consider that Maggie Smith's "Good Bones" has an ending that people have quoted over and over: "This place could be beautiful, / right? You could make this place beautiful." These closing lines end in repetition, perfectly capturing a pleading sense of both despair and hopefulness.

We encourage you to resist the urge to explain yourself in the final lines of the poem. It's a natural tendency, and many other forms of writing ask you to do just that: conclude with a conclusion that makes your point perfectly clear. But you should trust your images and lines to have done the work that would make such a conclusion redundant. If the poem leads the reader off a cliff, better to end there, in mid-air, than to explain that there will be a fall and that the landing will hurt.

See Also: Ambiguity, Repetition, Structure, Surprise, Value

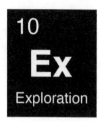

Exploration

Robert Frost famously said, "No surprise in the writer, no surprise in the reader." This quotation is a good reminder to be open-minded in the writing process, to think of drafting a poem as a process of discovery, more exploration than explanation. While poets usually begin the writing process with at least some idea of what they want to say or what they want to write about, often they won't know what they're writing about, or what point they're making, until the end. The poem must be able to follow the language where it leads. The poet must be open to surprising themselves in order to create surprise in the reader. The poem must be allowed to explore.

Think of the writing process as a voyage into some uncertain sea. The important work will happen once you get past the part of your journey that has already been mapped and into territory where you are uncertain of what's next. This is when your poem leads to true discovery. It can be unsettling—even downright scary—to venture into a poem without knowing where it's going, without knowing what the poem is about, but that's the fun of making poems. Only by loosening the grip on the plans for the poem can the poet discover what the poem itself wants to be about.

In his important book *The Triggering Town*, Richard Hugo offers an example of a poet who wants to write a poem called "Autumn Rain" but quickly runs out of meaningful things to say about that subject. We've all written these poems: "September Frost," "Summer Breeze," "Spring Flowers," and so forth. In order for the poem to avoid devolving into a bundle of clichés and sentimental observations, it must move beyond its initial subject matter. If your mind's made up about what you want to say in advance of writing, the poem is likely to fall flat; if you have a particular closing line in mind from the beginning of the process, the reader is likely to feel the strain of the poem being forced toward that line.

Much of this has to do with a poem's movement, and where it finds its leaps and turns. Often the best of those sudden jolts come at moments of peak exploration: when the poet abandons, at least temporarily, the primary subject and enlarges the poem by bringing in something new. Sometimes a poet achieves this through sound, sometimes through sensual association, sometimes through a seemingly random jolt from one topic to the next. Eileen Myles offers an example of this last one when her speaker, while looking at mountains below from an airplane, observes "how absurd to think / of Diet Coke / killing me." Suddenly the poem becomes larger than an observation of the majestic peaks; it becomes a musing on mortality and on the mundanities that fill our time and mind. By leaving the initial subject—the mountains—it expands the poem's scope. Karen Skolfield makes a similar move when her speaker abruptly departs from the landscape of a desert island: "It's the wrong time to think / of all the houseplants I've neglected."

Both of these poems call attention to the seemingly odd movements of their speakers' minds, but this is how the human mind works: one subject reminds, for whatever reason, of another, and then the two become connected, part of a single thought. Skolfield and Myles make this explicit in their poems, but other poets make the same kinds of moves as well. Another example: in "Stutter," Evelyn Araluen begins by looking at a photo by photographer Pixy Liao before allowing the poem's lyrical urge to carry the poem into a larger meditation about the body.

It is common for young poets to mistrust the wandering of their own minds, to think they need to reel in their consciousness to keep the poem on track, to mistake the desire for concision as a demand for a single-minded focus. But, as Hugo says, "It is impossible to write meaningless sequences." Once a poet has put two images—or two ideas, two anecdotes, two words—next to each other, the reader trusts that they belong there and begins to find connections between them, no matter how seemingly unrelated they might be according to the rules of ordinary logic. Poems operate with their own logic, and all poems make this claim to the reader: everything is here because it belongs here.

One of the reasons we read poems is to connect with the poet. When a poem truly engages us, we experience the pleasure of watching another human mind at work in the world. We see the world through someone else's eyes, and the poet's language becomes our own. In this way, exploration allows that surprise the poet felt in the writing process—that joy of discovery—to be felt by the reader as well.

See Also: Doorways, Movement, Surprise

Gaze

Gaze is a way of describing the relationship between the poem and its subject. The verb to gaze means something along the lines of "to look steadily and intently," and poets are doing just that as they move through the world and observe what's happening around them. When those observed events and experiences are rendered in language in a poem, they are transformed by the poet's gaze.

Think of gaze as the direction or angle from which the poem moves the reader's attention. A poet can gaze up at the subject and elevate it, putting it on that proverbial pedestal for admiration and worship. The poet can gaze down, treating the subject with scorn or derision. The poet can gaze inward at the self or outward and away from the poem's subject. Gaze defines the writer's relationship to the subject; at the same time, it establishes the relationship between the subject and the reader. This work means that like the other elements in this book, gaze is a rhetorical tool that should be used by the poet with care and intention.

Some distance between the writer and the subject will always exist, and sometimes that distance can distort the subject. In his book *The Rise and Fall of the American Teenager*, for example, Thomas Hine explains how adults, unable to understand teen behaviors and appearances, categorize and classify kids according to how they appear from an outsider's point of view. Hine calls this "the adult gaze." Kids have been called goths, Millennials, Gen X-ers, and Zoomers not because they all got together and made the decision to call themselves those things, but because some adult somewhere made up the label to sort and define the younger generations, effectively reducing them to fit the labels created by the adult gaze. Gaze often becomes about power differentials, as it observes and transforms the subject in ways that reinforce oppressive ideologies. The adult gaze labels the teens and forces them into a classification because adults are the dominant group over the teens, economically and socially.

Another common way of thinking about gaze, particularly as it is used in art, is "the male gaze," a concept introduced by film critic Laura Mulvey in the 1970s. In film, the male gaze occurs when the camera focuses on a woman in ways that objectify her the way a heterosexual man might gaze at a woman. The shot might trace the curve of her hips, linger over her cleavage, or close in on her wet lips—robbed of her status as a human being, the woman is reduced to an object that seems to exist for the camera's viewing pleasure, the male's gaze.

Because poetry is driven by images and the transformative power of metaphor, it can be easy for a poem to unwittingly adopt a problematic gaze—the poet means for the poem to say "I'm lonely and I like that person," but through its clumsy language choices the poem ends up inviting the reader to join the poem in objectifying a woman. Or the poet might mean to make a joke about cheap Chinese food and unwittingly blunder into a poem that plays on tired racist tropes, reducing a culture to stereotypes for a quick laugh. When writers fail to traverse the distance between the viewer and subject, it can be difficult for them to find empathy or any kind of commonality.

This is not to say that writers who make poems with problematic gazes are necessarily bad people. Sometimes it's a matter of being blind to the connotations a particular phrase or image has to groups outside of the writer's circle. Or the writer might be so mired in the images made popular by a dominant or oppressive way of thinking that they don't realize that they reduce and demean their subjects. It's inevitable that a poet will one day churn out an early draft of a poem in which the gaze reduces the subject rather than creates empathy. Knowing that there is such a thing as gaze is the first step to controlling it. As a poet you'll want to avoid what might be for some a natural tendency to gaze down or outward at those unlike them; instead, be aware of the effects of your gaze and make a concentrated effort at creating empathy.

See Also: Point Of View, Speaker, Value

Image

The image is perhaps the building block of all successful writing, and especially so for poetry. The oft-repeated advice to "show, don't tell" generally is a suggestion to the author to include more imagery in their writing.

What is an image? The first thing we think of is something visual: an image is a thing we can see. But the image in writing is more than that: it's anything that can be perceived with the senses: So, sight, yes, but also touch, hearing, taste, and smell.

Consider this: writing is the only artform that doesn't appeal directly to the five senses. The viewer experiences a painting or a sculpture through the sense of sight. A person listening to music experiences a song through the sense of hearing. When a person sits down to eat a meal, the cuisine is experienced through the senses of taste and smell and touch. In fact, art or not, the five senses form a person's experience of the physical world. In a poem, however, there is only text, experienced through eye or ear. The transformation from word to idea and image happens in the mind of the reader.

Images—sensory details—immerse the readers in the world of your poem and allow them to move from the sensual world to your textual one. By appealing to your readers' senses, you create a palpable sensation in their minds as they read, which in turn brings your details and ideas to life for them. You want your images to be concrete and specific, as opposed to abstract. To create concrete images, use your sensory appeals; in the world, a concrete thing is something you can touch, feel, taste, smell, or see. A cement block. An egg yolk oozing through your fingers. The mossy bark of an oak tree. A field of lavender. An abstraction, in contrast, is intangible, ethereal, more concept than object. Love, grief, loss, loneliness, happiness, beauty—these are abstractions.

There are also words and phrases that can be either abstract or concrete, depending on context. The word "abyss," for instance, could be concrete if you're standing on the edge of a canyon in Arizona and referring to a particular abyss that's full of sun-blasted rocks and cacti and sand. But if you're using abyss as a metaphor to refer to some great absence, it's an abstraction, and therefore less likely to be a powerful image in your poem.

In general, you are better off populating your poem with concrete images than with abstractions. This doesn't mean poets never use abstractions.

Abstractions can be springboards to great specificity and precision, anchors to personification, or even subverted through contradiction. However, a poem that relies too heavily on abstraction fails to immerse readers in its details and emotions and risks becoming a Greeting Card Poem.

We mentioned that in addition to being concrete, your images should be specific. A bird is a concrete thing, yes, but the word "bird" itself is far from specific. Are you referring to a chickadee, an eagle, an ostrich, Foghorn Leghorn? A flower might be concrete, but white rose, sunny dandelion, purple tulip are all more specific—and therefore might be more meaningful to your poem.

Along these lines, you want to watch out for over-relying on abstract adjectives in your descriptions. If a figure in your poem has "beautiful eyes," what does that mean? Better to show us that they're pale brown and surrounded by thick, dark lashes and let us judge their beauty for ourselves. Words such as *beautiful, ugly, terrible, fantastic*, and others along these lines are abstractions, and they are also judgment words. Such judgment says more about the speaker doing the judging than about the subject being described. Sometimes, as a poet, you might want this effect; it depends on whether you're observing or interpreting and on whether you want the focus to be on the speaker's voice or on the subject itself. Bear in mind also that any such judgment is inherently subjective, beauty being in the eye of the beholder and all that. What the poet thinks of as a "modest" house might be one reader's mansion and another reader's hovel, depending on the size of the homes in the neighborhoods where they grew up. You should never assume that your judgment is "normal" or somehow universal. The best way to avoid falling into such a trap is to build your poem on a foundation of specific, concrete images and save abstractions and judgments for key moments when they serve the poem's larger purpose.

An effective image also does a great deal of work for you in the poem. The poet Natalie Diaz says, "an image is more than what we show our readers—it is story, it is history, it is emotion." By way of example, she suggests that to put an apple in a poem is to bring to that poem all of our cultural associations with the apple. Eve and the Tree of Knowledge of Good and Evil. Temptation. Snow White and the poisoned apple. Not to mention a reader's personal associations with the fruit: a stack of apples in the local grocery store, bins of them at a farmers' market, the tree in the yard of their grandparents' farm, an orchard visited in childhood. An apple is not only an apple; it is all these apples. The image is layered, complex, possibly contradictory. Building your poems out of strong, clear images will take you a long way.

See Also: Defamiliarization, Metaphor, Observation and Interpretation, Precision, Value

Inventory

In short, inventory is the things in a poem. Poems need to be filled with things so that the reader can experience the textual reality created by each poem—it's the inventory that helps the reader discover and understand the nature of that textual reality. Sandra Beasley's "Halloween" has sexy costumes, ribbons, the eyelet of a corset, shoelaces, and fish stuck in a pair of netted tights. Ada Limón's "Downhearted" keeps the inventory simple with the horses, all that blood, and those internal organs. Naomi Shihab Nye's "1935" uses the inventory of the photograph to take the reader back in time to her father's boyhood. Inventory gives these poems physicality and prevents them from drifting off into the metaphysical ether. These poems refuse to give us a full glimpse of the reality they create because that's the nature of these realities. Inventory can create and defamiliarize our ideas of a poem's reality.

It follows that the poem's inventory is important to establishing the poem's reality. A poem that lacks an inventory—a poem devoid of physical things—risks being abstract to the point of meaningless. It lacks connection to the physical world we inhabit. As a reader, you can often figure out what a poem is up to thematically by making a list of the things it contains: its inventory. A poem that contains a dusty bedroom, a faded stuffed bunny, and a pink ribbon on the carpet is creating a whole emotional world for you simply by containing these objects. A poem that contains a river-worn boulder, a fallen oak tree, and the muddy paw print of a bear exists in a different world entirely.

Inventory is also important to the writer of a poem in process as a poet works to explore and develop what is to be the poem's material, its substance. Part of the drafting process might be looking for your poem's inventory. As the poem is filled with things, the writer might discover new doorways to explore as they create opportunities to play with value and defamiliarization—in other words, each item you add to a poem's inventory creates new possibilities for where the poem might venture next.

See Also: Defamiliarization, Doorways, Image, Precision, Value

Language

For poets, language is our medium and our raw material: our oil paint, our charcoal, the colored threads from which we weave the tapestry of our poems. It's also the foundation of all the other elements in this section; we're emphasizing how important it is that poets make intentional, rhetorical use of language. Choosing to write a poem in the first place is a rhetorical act; it announces to the reader that you've chosen to privilege mystery over explanation, idiosyncrasy over universality, originality over familiarity, and uncertainty about the nature of life over simple, easy answers. You've chosen to make language the center of your creation.

You'll see lots of poets in this anthology and elsewhere make questions about how we use language an explicit part of their poems. Clearly, any poem in the ars poetica mode is doing so, but you can also see this, for instance, in Ada Limón's "Downhearted," in which the poem moves from a consideration of the language of grief—"What / is it they say, heart-sick or downhearted?"—to a personified heart enacting the behavior of a grieving person. Limón challenges our ideas about the familiar, abstract language of emotion by bringing the metaphor to life within her poem. Anders Carlson-Wee explores the power of naming in "Dynamite," as the two brothers in his poem engage in increasingly threatening behavior toward each other, and the danger they face is related to the labels they've placed on the objects around them: "I say a hammer isn't dynamite. / He reminds me that everything is dynamite." Naming a thing dynamite turns it into dynamite in the world of the poem.

We recommend that young poets begin with contemporary language because that's their natural diction. The poems we read in high school often lead us to believe that poetry is built on archaic diction and antiquated phrasings. But this is not 1600 or 1840, and we are not William Shakespeare or Edgar Allan Poe; our poems should sound as though they were written in the twenty-first century. Excise the "thees" and "thous" and "nevermores" from your poetic vocabulary. The same goes for convoluted syntax. The twisted structure of a Shakespearean sonnet—"And yet, by heaven, I think my love as rare / as any she belied with false compare"—worked 400 years ago for a poet trying to fit his ideas into iambic pentameter and a particular rhyme scheme, but when we try it now, we end up sounding less like the famous bard and more like Yoda from the *Star Wars* movies: "Anger, fear, aggression, the Dark Side of the Force are they."

One component of language is frame of reference. As with your vocabulary and sentence structure, your frame of reference will be contemporary. Our language is shaped by the culture around us, and it's just as natural for our poems to be populated with mentions of commercial Halloween costumes and pinatas and online customer reviews as it was for Lord Byron to write about the concerns of nineteenth-century high-society London or for Allen Ginsberg to fill his poems with the cultural ephemera of 1960s America. We are not suggesting that you need to pepper your poems with pop song lyrics and TikTok memes to make them seem contemporary; indeed, you don't want your poems to become name-dropping, brand-filled billboards trumpeting their currentness. But nor should you ignore the culture around you. From high culture to pop culture, from classic literature to rap music, the world around us shapes our perceptions of the human condition—and importantly for poets, it shapes our language. That means it can be fertile territory for our writing.

In this way, frame of reference is often inseparable from the language we use in a poem. Dorianne Laux can probably count on a shared understanding of the word "lighter" in her poem, but it's likely that at least some of her readers will be less familiar with the word "tenement." But if we could only use words that we were 100 percent certain our readers can define, it would severely limit our ability to use language to its full capacity. Language is vast, ever-evolving, and complex; as poets, we must face the fact that we will never master it, never fully be able to bring it under our control to do our exact bidding. Yet that is our calling and our challenge. Every word choice, reference, and allusion in a poem—indeed, every drop of language in a poem—is an invitation to the reader to consider the word or phrase and how it exists in the larger world as well as how it exists in the poem.

One bit of advice we're always giving to young poets: push on the language of your poems. That is: ask more of each word in your poem. Consider each word, each phrase, each line in your poem in relation to the elements in this textbook. Is your language doing as much work for you as it could be? Is it as concise, as precise, as intentional as it could be? Are your metaphors fresh, your images original, your lines full of density? As we've said elsewhere, language is an inadequate medium for capturing the full richness of the human experience, but since it is the medium we have chosen as poets, it's our job to push it as far as we can, to get it as close as possible to the beautiful, terrible, complex experience of being alive in a body in this world.

See Also: Diction, Music, Precision, Syntax, Value (Really, see of all them— language is all of them, language is everything.)

15

Ln

Lines

Lines

Now we've come to what verse is all about, right?

The line is the fundamental unit of the poem, perhaps the defining characteristic of poetry (setting aside the prose poem for the moment). It's how you know a poem when you see it: the words don't run all the way to the right margin of the page.

This choice to stop the words short of the end of the page is similar to the choice to write a poem in the first place. Just as the act of writing a poem indicates that prose is inadequate to the task the poet has in mind, the choice to break a piece of writing into lines suggests that the poet needs more than word, sentence, paragraph; they need another unit of meaning, another syntactical strategy. The line offers the poet a whole new universe of possibilities.

Dividing a piece of writing into lines is part of what makes poems challenging for readers. The line is inherently disruptive—that's its raison d'être: to interrupt the flow of language, to force a reset, a rest period, a starting over. The word "verse" has its etymological roots in a Latin word meaning "to turn around," as a plow turns around at the end of a row. The reader hesitates for just an instant at the end of each line before moving on to the next. It's up to us as poets to decide what happens in that micropause.

It has been said that the length of a line is related to the human breath: when a poet recites a poem, the line is determined by how much can be spoken before the natural pause for breath. This sounds lovely but perhaps a little too good to be true, because each of our capacities for breath are as varied as there are possibilities for the length of a poetic line.

The formal poetic line is a consequence of meter and rhythm, where the prosody of the language determines both length and music of the poetic line. From a writer's perspective, there's something comforting about having your line determined for you, but it presents a different kind of challenge: to make the right words fit into a preconceived form. In free verse, the line is not determined by meter or syllable count; in fact it's not predetermined by anything at all—break the line where you want! For the young poet, that freedom can be scary. If you can break the line anywhere, if the choice is entirely yours, how do you decide? What if you do it wrong? How do you know what's best?

As with every other decision one makes while writing, one never truly knows what's best or whether one is doing it wrong. So, as with most things poetic, it's best to decide there's no such thing as wrong and forge ahead.

Honing one's instincts begins with reading and re-reading (again, this is true of most every aspect of writing). The more lines of poetry you read, the more you'll learn about how they work, what they do, how some line breaks catch us short and steal our breath while others send us effortlessly ahead into what's next without our even noticing their gentle hands at our back.

Principles of Line and Line Break

Lines that end at a natural stopping place (periods, question marks, sometimes commas) are called "end-stopped." Lines that end without punctuation, where the sentence proceeds uninterrupted to the next line, are called "enjambed." Neither is better than the other. Poems where every line is end-stopped risk becoming chanty, predictable, staccato; poems where every line is enjambed may risk feeling uncontrolled, loosey-goosey, uneven. Most poems vary their lines between enjambed and end-stopped as the poet controls the flow of the language, sometimes aiming for one effect, sometimes for another.

Here are two rules of thumb for breaking lines:

- Try to end lines on powerful, evocative words: most often nouns or verbs.
- Rarely if ever end a line on an article (a, an, the), preposition (for, to, of, etc.), or conjunction (and, but, or).

You'll note exceptions to these guidelines throughout this anthology and across all poems you read, but start with this in mind. The more poems you write, the more comfortable you'll be with breaking your lines in conventional or unconventional ways.

Here are three factors or outcomes to take into account when breaking lines: pacing, meaning, and appearance.

Pacing: Poets control the pacing of a poem in part through line length. Given that each line break creates a micropause, the more line breaks you have in a poem, the slower the reading experience. Skinny poems with short lines tend to be choppier, more hesitant. Longer lines flow more easily, creating a reading experience more akin to that of reading prose. Short lines create more points of emphasis, requiring the reader to stop and reset more often; longer lines may allow more room for a lush image to exist on the page uninterrupted.

Read Monica Youn's "Quinta del Sordo" and then read Ali Cobby Eckermann's "Inside My Mother" and consider how differently paced they feel; think about how line length determines where you linger and where you speed ahead. Or look at how Kazim Ali uses end stops at the beginning of "The Return of Music" to create a halting feel as we proceed through the poem. Jenny Johnson changes pace within "The Bus Ride" by establishing a pattern of fairly long lines at first and then abruptly intensifying with the shorter lines of the closing couplet.

Meaning: Breaking lines allows a poet to create emphasis on certain words and phrases. Words that appear at the ends of lines receive emphasis, as the tiny pause that happens as the eye leaves one line and moves to the next places extra weight on those words. Words that appear atop each other at the ends of lines, especially in couplets and tercets, invite the reader to pay special attention to their juxtaposition. By using line breaks strategically, the poet guides the readers toward the elements of the poem that matter most. In "Ars Poetica," Traci Brimhall breaks one line thus:

. . . a bird startled to find

there wasn't more light on the other side
of the window.

The combination of the stanza break and the line break call great attention to the phrase "on the other side," leaving little doubt that the poem is in part about life and death, and not merely the two sides of a window flown into by a bird.

Often this kind of meaning-making can be surprising. An example: a word that seems to mean one thing at the end of the line can mean something different when you get to the next line. (But if you do so too often, your reader will stop trusting you, so you want to save the technique for significant moments in your poem.) Look at these lines from Karen Skolfield's "How to Locate Water on a Desert Island":

. . . Even science
can't make up its mind about the divining
rod trembling in the old man's hand:

That word "divining" takes on tremendous importance here because of the line break. In the sentence, the word is an adjective, part of the phrase "divining rod," which is a tool used to find water when deciding where to dig a well. But in the line? The word means something entirely different: "science / can't make up its mind about the divining." The word becomes a noun, momentarily, and calls attention to the possibility that there are questions about spirituality that science cannot answer.

Similarly, consider these lines from Eileen Myles' "To the Mountains":

when I look out
at you
how absurd to think
of Diet Coke

As a sentence, it reads: "When I look out at you, how absurd to think of Diet Coke." But when broken into lines, "how absurd to think" stands alone for a moment as you read, calling into question the very concept of human thought in the face of the mountains' majesty.

In each of these examples, it's not that one meaning is more "correct" than the other; it's not that the line takes precedence over the sentence or vice versa. Both meanings exist simultaneously; as the poem unfolds and reveals its meaning line by line, each line becomes its own unit of meaning separate from the meaning of the sentence. That is what poetry does: operates on multiple levels of meaning at once. The line is an essential tool for accomplishing this.

Appearance: How a poem looks on the page is an important component of the reading experience. Poems with fairly regular line length have a uniformity that offers a certain kind of stability, and it's common for all forms of art to consider unity as a kind of goal. Sometimes, though, deliberate disunity is part of the project of a poem, and widely varied line lengths can be a way to achieve that. If you look at Natasha Trethewey's "History Lesson," you'll see its regularity, its tercets of roughly regular line length (plus one final couplet). Compare that to "Stutter" by Evelyn Araluen, which not only varies its line lengths, but also splashes the lines across the page, fighting against uniformity at every turn. There's pleasure in either experience, and each also has a different rhetorical effect on the meaning of the poem.

Concrete poetry (also called visual poetry) is a particular kind of poetry where the shape of the poem is essential to the experience of the poem—perhaps the most famous example is a seventeenth-century poem called "Easter Wings" by George Herbert, in which the stanzas are shaped like wings. Contemporary poet Diana Khoi Nguyen does this amazing thing in her book *Ghost Of* where a poem one on page uses white space to create a kind of hole in the middle of the page—and when you turn the page, the subsequent poem is shaped to fill that exact hole. This kind of poem can be fun to play with, especially given the ease and capabilities of modern design software. The challenge is not letting the unusual shape be an excuse to be sloppy, cliché, or imprecise in your language. Attention to shape does not replace the need for attention to language; rather, shape and language work hand in hand as you create an experience for your readers.

There are some poems in this anthology that challenge our notion of the line and by so doing expand the possibilities of the form. Both Patricia Lockwood and Layli Long Soldier rely on the sentence to determine their lines, although Long Soldier breaks that pattern at the end. Gary L. McDowell uses white space within his lines to create caesura. Karyna McGlynn and Tarfia Faizullah use variations of the contrapuntal form. Hanif Willis-Abdurraqib offers a prose paragraph but uses slashes to replicate the pacing effect of the line, albeit with a different visual effect.

One thing you should do both as you read and as you write is consider each line of a poem individually. Each line is its own unit of meaning, even if that meaning isn't grammatical but evocative. Often you'll find that any single line contains, in some sense, the entire poem. You can see this principle at work in the sonnets of Diane Seuss and Terrance Hayes, as well as in many of the lines in Mary Jo Bang's "The Role of Elegy."

The line is an infinitely malleable element: bendable, breakable, and incredibly resilient. Young poets are encouraged to play and experiment with the line. Here's something you can do for practice: Find a published poem you love and retype it without any line breaks. Read it as a prose paragraph. What is lost by removing the line breaks? What, if anything, is gained? How has the reading experience changed? Then play with the line breaks. Give it short lines. Give it long, expansive lines. Try a mix: some short, some long. How does the poem change as you put it through these new incarnations? How can you manipulate line length and line breaks to call attention to different images, ideas, sections of the poem? One of the benefits to composing on a computer is the ability to quickly try a range of line lengths and line breaks (much harder to do if you're writing with, say, a typewriter or quill on parchment).

Think of the line as just another rhetorical tool in your toolbox. That means, as with every other element in this book, the prime consideration is the experience you are trying to evoke for your reader. The more you focus on the possibility of the line, the more you will gain a stronger awareness of your own particular sense of the line—and you will be more confident in how best to use the line to help you achieve the particular aims of a given poem.

See Also: Language, Prosody, Rhythm, Structure

16
Ly
Lyric

Lyric

As with narrative, you'll notice that lyric appears in this book as both an element and a mode. That's because there are poems that are driven almost entirely by the lyric impulse—poems in the lyric mode—but most if not all poems include lyric elements, even if they function primarily in some other mode. Hence, this section you're reading right now.

What do we mean by the lyric impulse? Historically, a lyric poem has been defined as a short poem that describes the speaker's feelings or emotions. They are often written in the first person and are often image-rich or musical, arising from a tradition of short poems delivered to the accompaniment of music (often an actual lyre, back when those were more common). This explains the relationship of the term to the lyrics of a song, which is how the broader culture usually uses the word.

As a poetic element, lyric also refers to how a poet handles time. As opposed to narrative time, which is largely chronological and action-driven, lyric time is determined by feelings and associations. Whereas one could make a timeline of a narrative, laying out events in the order they occur, lyric time might be more accurately described as a bubble in which past, present, and future exist simultaneously. The poem's movement within that bubble is not determined by the passage of time but by connections the speaker makes between events and emotions.

Tracy K. Smith's "Song" opens by suggesting it's interested in chronology, as the poet remembers "your hands all those years ago / Learning to maneuver a pencil," but the poem moves away from that, examining those same hands in various states: "lying empty / At night," or "How they failed. What they won't forget year after year." The poem glides among past, present, and future, and the connective tissue is not the passage of time or the narrative development of any particular story, but the emotional connection the speaker feels to those hands. This is the lyric impulse.

Smith's poem is itself a lyric poem, but even poems that appear to be more straightforwardly narrative include lyric elements. David Kirby's "Teacher of the Year" ties together its three separate narrative threads through lyric association. The pausing of time is a lyric move, placing the narrative chronology on hold to explore different concerns, possibly associative or imagistic, but also possibly musical or metrical. To be focused on writing in iambic pentameter, for example, is to be focused on the lyrical instead of the logical or chronological.

As you read poems, look for these moments of lyricism, lines and phrases where the poet moves beyond time and logic to make connections that defy narrative logic. This is arguably one of the defining characteristics of poetry. A work of prose is more commonly driven by narrative and chronology: the effects of time's passage on the characters depicted, how an action now shapes future events. (We're speaking in generalities here; there are novels and short stories that push against this definition.) But poetry concerns itself with precisely these kinds of lyric leaps: moments driven by language and feeling and sound, not by the cause-and-effect of narrative. In this way, in its lyricism, poetry represents how thought itself works; our minds are a lyric tangle of sensations, memories, and ideas.

See Also: Exploration, Narrative

Metaphor

Effective use of metaphor is essential to how poetry operates. It's at once a mechanism for poetry and a way poets access their powers of perception and creativity—in a way, metaphor is the poem's magic. There are Tibetan Buddhist monks who practice an art called throat-singing or harmonic chanting in which the human voice appears to be capable of producing more than one pitch at a time. It's kind of a miracle, or the appearance of a miracle at any rate, and it's the same thing we do when we employ metaphor to make our poems reverberate on multiple frequencies simultaneously. Remember: poems are always about at least two things and metaphor is a big part of how you access those layers of meaning.

Metaphor as Figure of Speech

You're probably familiar with this concept of metaphor: a direct comparison between two things in order to make a rhetorical point. This is often a writer's entry point into metaphor as they create analogies between two unlike things without using comparative words such as like or as. If we say, the sun is a mass of hydrogen and helium bound together by its own gravity, that's more descriptive or definitional than metaphorical—it just explains what the sun is. But something like the sun is a golden orb or the sun is a fiery chariot is metaphorical.

You probably also know the related term simile, an indirect comparison that specifically uses the word like or as in the comparison. The choice between metaphor and simile can change the meaning of a sentence significantly. It's one thing to say, as Tarfia Faizullah does in "Aubade Ending with the Death of a Mosquito," that a rising cloud of mosquitoes is like smoke; it would be another thing entirely to write that the mosquitoes are smoke. To say a thing is similar to another thing is different than saying that thing is the other thing. The distinction is not merely semantic but rhetorical. This rhetorical difference between these two figures of speech is important to note, but don't lose track of the fact that a simile is a kind of metaphor in the same way that a square is a kind of rectangle.

Metaphor as Representation

One way poets use metaphor is to describe the way one thing stands in for another. That bottle of Mountain Dew at the end of Matthew Olzmann's poem represents the love between the speaker and his spouse. The bottle is an important piece of inventory—a real physical thing in the poem—and it's this specific, physical reality of the thing that allows it to symbolize love, much in the same way that things being sold in commercials take on their own symbolic values. When one thing stands in for another, it can start to take on new or additional value. A metaphorical value.

Using one thing to represent another like this is a simple way of starting to get metaphor working in your poems. Once we substitute one thing for another, we start creating meaning through the implicit comparison. In "Jet," Tony Hoagland substitutes jet fuel for alcohol and the big sky river for the milky way. These simple substitutions of one thing for another set up the metaphorical foundations for the poem: the alcohol is the fire inside us and the river is the galaxy, metaphorically speaking, and from there the poem shifts these representations through to the poem's end.

Metaphor as Transformation

As we've argued earlier in this book, language itself is metaphor. The word "highway" is not the highway—it's a symbolic representation of the highway, a configuration of ink on paper or pixels on a screen that we've agreed will stand in for the highway. But here's something amazing: recent neuroscience studies using MRI technology have shown that reading or hearing the language for a thing activates the same part of the brain as observing that thing. In other words, when you read "flashlight," the same neurons light up the same area of your brain as when you hold a physical flashlight in your hands. What begins as representation becomes transformation in the brain. Talk about a miracle! We suspect that every poet who learns of this study lets out a triumphant cry of, "I knew it!" Poets have long taken on faith that language works this way; now we have scientific support for our hunch.

Think about what this suggests about the power of language and of metaphor. It means that a metaphor is not the same thing as an analogy. An analogy is a comparison used to make a point in an argument or when explaining something; the initial subject remains primary, with the object of the comparison serving no larger purpose other than to shed light on the original point. If someone is teaching you about photosynthesis and tells you that what the plant cells are doing when they store light is the same as when you buy more food than you need at a restaurant and save some in your fridge for later, that's an analogy. The meal at the restaurant isn't important to the lecture except insofar as it explains the scientific process your teacher wants you to learn.

But in a metaphor, the two sides carry equal or near-equal weight. When you write in a poem that your heart is on fire, in the world of the poem, now there's a fire in your poem, and your poem-heart actually is burning. Remember that the word "fire" triggers the same neurons for your reader that a literal fire would. That means you can't go willy-nilly lighting fires in your poems, thinking, "Oh, they're just metaphors."

There are two sides to a metaphor: the tenor (the original subject) and the vehicle (the new subject). In the best metaphors, these two parts each matter. A good metaphor illuminates both sides of the equation. When Oliver de la Paz writes, "Mornings are a sustained hymn / without the precision of faith," he teaches us something about both mornings and hymns; the metaphor works in both directions. The introduction of the hymn enlarges the poem; it is not merely an analogy to help us understand something about mornings. Poet Mary Ruefle, in her book *Madness, Rack and Honey*, says that metaphor is "an exchange of energy" between things. Because of this exchange, we understand not just that this poem is about faith, religion, and spirituality, in addition to being about feeding birds to start a day; metaphor transforms the feeding of the birds into a spiritual act between the speaker and the world. This is much more fun than merely thinking of it as an analogy.

Metaphor at Work

Remember that the role of metaphor is to expand or clarify a poem's meaning, not to obscure it. It would be easy to write a poem, say, about preparing for a first date using entirely an extended metaphor of a soldier preparing for battle. However, this in the end would, in all likelihood, be a shallow poem. Because the metaphor is being used to cover up the poem's true subject rather than to find some new layer of meaning in it, and because the battle language is being used more as analogy than as true metaphor, it's probable that the resulting poem says nothing new about either the task of the soldier or the original situation of getting ready for a date. (Often the young poet who writes this poem reveals the true situation in the final line or two, opting for a cheap but ineffective surprise.)

You'll often see poems that extend metaphor in effective ways. Limón's poem does this, extending the metaphor of the personified heart through the final two-thirds of the poem, transforming the clichéd expression into something weird and new. In Anders Carlson-Wee's "Dynamite," the idea that everything is dynamite is an extended metaphor. In Mark Halladay's "Trumpet Player, 1963," the song "Surf City" becomes an extended metaphor for empty promises about happiness and decadence. Sandra Beasley uses costumes as an extended metaphor for gender identity in "Halloween." Because a metaphor becomes real once you put it down on the page, it allows you the freedom to continue exploring within it.

Closely related to the extended metaphor is the idea of metaphoric unity. Because each metaphor you introduce into your poem expands the world of the poem, it's generally a good idea to rely on metaphors that seem to belong in the same world. If within five lines, a poet claims that love is an unlocked door in a tall castle, a sinking ship, a tulip on a spring morning, a minefield, and a bird's song, the reader is going to be a little dizzy. The world these metaphors create is haphazard and chaotic, and the reader's mind is being pulled in a lot of directions. There's a distinct lack of metaphoric unity here. Now, this is something you can do on purpose, if that sort of disorientation is what you're after, but do so with caution.

Metaphor and the Reader

The metaphor is a rhetorical device, and as such, the poet must consider how the metaphor works and how it contributes to the reader's experience of the poem. Faizullah's mosquitoes are like smoke and de la Paz's morning is a hymn. A swarm of mosquitoes looks like smoke if there are thousands of them flying in a dense cloud, and even then perhaps only from a distance. And the morning is nothing like a hymn, really—but it's this difference between the tenor and vehicle that makes for a good metaphor.

Metaphors are interactive—they require the reader to do a bit of work in bringing the tenor and vehicle together to create meaning. Part of what makes metaphors work is the reader's recognition of the difference between the tenor and the vehicle. If the two are too close together, then the meaning being made is too simple to be interesting. "Love is a strong emotion" or "grief is a feeling of sadness" are statements that lack the distance a reader needs for surprise. Similarly, if the relationship between the tenor and the vehicle is a familiar one, then the metaphor risks being cliché. Love is a heart or a kiss. Grief is a flower with its petals fallen off. These are predictable and obvious, and readers tend to read past them because the cliché doesn't say anything the reader doesn't already know.

It's when a metaphor offers the reader a moment of disorientation as they try to reconcile the difference between the tenor and vehicle that the metaphor gets its work done. Natasha Trethewey shows the reader minnows that become switchblades; Kim Addonizio transforms a human tongue into an oxygen tube. These metaphors ask the reader to do a bit of work to bring the tenor and vehicle together—thus creating a kind of transformation in the poem.

And as you experiment with metaphor in your poems, you might find yourself understanding the world through the connections and exchanges of energy, through an enhanced perception of what things are and how things work, a kind of magic to filter into your poems.

See Also: Defamiliarization, Image, Surprise

Mood

A poem can be wistful or mournful, nostalgic or defiant, gloomy or joyous, sarcastic or reverent, tender or blunt, or some combination of these things, or most any other emotional state. As you read the poems in this anthology, ask yourself what mood the poem evokes in you—and then try to figure out what specifically on the page makes you feel that way. That will give you a strong sense of how to establish mood in your own poems.

Mood exists in a poem at the intersection of diction, speaker, voice, all of these elements combining to set the tone for the piece. The words you choose, from whose mouth those words emerge, and the attitude behind them—it all blends together. If you think of a poem as an experience built for a reader, the poem's mood is a huge part of that experience.

Mood is also closely related to setting: the geographical and chronological location of a poem. David Tomas Martinez's "In Chicano Park" is set in a particular time and place, and the images are hard (metals and concrete), industrial, crumbling. The urban landscape helps set the tone for the poem; in turn, the mood teaches us something about the place being explored. It's a reciprocal (and rhetorical) relationship. This is true in Laura Kasischke's "Landscape with one of the earthworm's ten hearts" as well, with that lone apple tree and the winter soup establishing a particular season and setting: the mood is chilly, forlorn.

Consider the effect on the reader's mood of the snow in Traci Brimhall's "Ars Poetica" or the superheated Sonoran desert in Eduardo C. Corral's "To Juan Doe #234." The temperature serves as a sensory detail, connecting us physically to the scenes depicted in the poem and helping shape our reaction to them. Just as the weather in the real world can impact our emotional well-being, the literal and metaphorical weather of a poem shapes our mood as we read.

See Also: Image, Inventory, Precision, Weight

Movement

We mention throughout this book that sometimes the point of a poem is the journey it takes a reader on from beginning to end. This is a metaphor that implies physical movement. One comment you'll often hear in a workshop setting is that a poem "flows well," but when you ask the commenter to expand on that notion, to explain what makes the poem's flow so effective, they're often stumped. Yes, a poem can flow; yes, a poet has movement. For the reader, that movement is indeed physical, the eye flickering from left to right and back again and down the page with the poem, sometimes back up to revisit a previous word or line. What does the poem do on the page to foster such movement? Each word and phrase, each line and sentence, plays a role in taking the reader toward the end of the poem. Let's look at how a poem can move, leap, and turn.

Move: Each poem progresses logically through its subject or story, but each poem also creates its own logic. Poems move at varying rates and in a variety of directions. They move forward, backward, up and down, through narrative time or through physical space. Christina Olson's "In Which Christina Imagines That Different Types of Alcohol Are Men and She Is Seeing Them All" proceeds chronologically through a series of first dates; David Tomas Martinez's "In Chicano Park" takes the reader on a tour of a specific location. This movement can follow chronology or reverse chronology. The poem can move fast or slowly, depending on line length, rhythm, and the rate at which it delivers its images. This simple movement is apparent in Tony Hoagland's poem "Jet." The first stanza anchors us on the porch with the boys and it moves our gaze up toward the stars. In the third stanza, we are moving back down to earth, and we go so fast that we seem to be simultaneously in the sky and on the ground, in the big sky river and in the beer bottles in the grass.

Leap: A poem doesn't always proceed logically—sometimes the language jolts sideways and appears to create a kind of disjunction in time or space. Sometimes the poem surprises us with an abrupt change of subject or scenery. The poem can make a lateral move from one train of thought to one that is perhaps parallel or similar. There are big leaps and small leaps, but the leap always surprises us with some kind of change. In "Jet," we are anchored in the first stanza on the porch with the boys, but then we leap to outer space in the second stanza. Once we are there, we get those space images: asteroids, astronauts and the weird fish.

Turn: When a poem lands a leap, it often looks around to find a new perspective on things. It finds its way to a new place and then turns to discover something that it did not know before. Sometimes, the poem uses the turn to leave the speaker with a new perspective; sometimes the turn reveals something new to the reader about that which has come before. In "Jet," this happens in those final two lines. Throughout the poem, we've experienced sensory images that move up and down and leap all over the page—we are drunk with images throughout most of the poem. In that final turn, we are confronted with the speaker's attitude toward the drunkenness. There is a desperate wistfulness for drinking on the porch with the boys, an almost painful desire to be back there. When we reach those last lines, we find that they give the rest of the poem a slightly different meaning than it had up until that point.

Similarly, "Introduction to Poetry" by Billy Collins starts with five short stanzas, each of which ends in a leap to a new place, each place moving with new systems of imagery and metaphors at work. There are five leaps before the leap to the torture stanza—it begins with "but," which negates everything that came before it. All the delightful color slides and mice and waterskiing are erased with that conjunction, leaving us in that room with the chair and a length of rope—that's the biggest leap in the poem. Then the turn happens at the end when we discover what the torture is all about: extracting meaning from the poem. The leap to the torture room ruins the playful tone of the poem, and then the turn reveals that it's the quest for meaning that's to blame.

Some poems move more than leap, and some leap all over the place. Some poems end in a turn and others have multiple turns. What is constant is the poem's movement. Physically and metaphorically, the reader is indeed taken on a journey.

See Also: Beginnings, Endings, Exploration, Lines, Narrative, Lyric, Structure

Music

Poetry is descended in part from an oral—and aural—tradition. Poems were intended to be both spoken and heard long before they were written down. Even now, for many poems, how they sound when read aloud is an important part of the experience of the piece. You should read your poems aloud to yourself during the writing process; sound can be a useful guiding principle in a poem, a source of tension and association and surprise.

But poems are not songs, and songs are not poems. Song lyrics can be poetic and very often share features with poems. But even though Bob Dylan won the Nobel Prize for Literature, the distinction between songs and poems matters. This is not to suggest that song lyrics are inferior to poems in any way, merely that they are a different genre, a different form of art. Lyrics are intended to be sung, and rely on that fact, as well as instrumental accompaniment, as crucial parts of the experience. A song whose lyrics are sentimental and dripping with cliché can still be a terrific listening experience because of the human voice singing it, or the piano accompanying the melody, or the killer guitar solo in the middle.

A poem does not have a melody or a pianist or a lead guitarist. Whether spoken or written, a poem's instrumentation is its language. We're focused mostly on written poetry in this book; slam or spoken-word poetry, like a song, is primarily intended to be delivered live to an audience of listeners rather than readers, with more focus on the performative aspect. We're suggesting no hierarchy between the two; the distinction between stage poetry and page poetry is important but generally speaking, they both achieve their music through language.

Sound

One of the primary ways that poets create music in their poems is meter, but that also has a lot to do with a poem's rhythm. As we've said elsewhere, rhythm and music are difficult elements to separate, but if we consider rhythm to be the speed and tempo of sound, then a poet can consider the different ways that language creates sound.

Vowels and consonants are the basic way we categorize the sounds made by the English alphabet. This might seem elementary, but in terms of their sounds, vowels are sounds that are made by allowing breath to flow out of the mouth without closing any part of the mouth or throat. Consonants are sounds made by blocking the breath with the tongue, teeth, or palate.

Plosives are sounds made by closing the airflow off in the mouth and then releasing it with force: sounds like *p*, *t*, *b*, and *k*.

Fricatives are sounds made by squeezing air through the teeth or over the tongue: sounds like *s*, *z*, and *th*.

Nasals are sounds made through the nose while the flow of air is closed at the mouth. There are three nasals in English: *m*, *n*, and *ng*.

We don't want to exhaust anyone with a comprehensive list of technical terms, but sounds are the building blocks of a poem's music and this should be enough to at least get a poet started considering the value of how to identify the sounds of the English language. Music arises as the poet hears and orchestrates the many sounds at their disposal.

Rhetorical Devices

Isolating the different kinds of sounds in the English language uses to create words is important, but beyond that, what can a poet do with those sounds? Here are some rhetorical devices poets use to shape the sounds of language into music:

Alliteration: The repetition of consonant sounds at the beginnings of
  words.
Assonance: The repetition of vowel sounds in nearby words.
Caesura: A pause in a line of poetry, often near the middle. Sometimes
  they occur as the result of natural grammatical breaks (the end of a
  sentence, a comma between clauses) like these comma-made caesura
  from Traci Brimhall's "Ars Poetica":
    People bend over, afraid to touch her
    in case she might rise, a bird startled to find
Consonance: The repetition of vowel sounds in nearby words, like
  alliteration, though not necessarily at the beginning of words.
Onomatopoeia: Some words all resemble and recreate the sounds they
  represent. Words like crash, gargle, bludgeon, and zap create their
  own music when spoken.
Refrain: A line repeated at recurring intervals in a poem. Typically, it
  refers to a whole line, but even a single word can become a kind of
  refrain, as "Nothing" does in Bob Hicok's "Elegy with lies."
Rhyme: The repetition of end sounds in words. In formal poetry, this
  often means end rhyme, where the last lines of adjacent or nearby
  lines end with the same sound.
Slant rhyme: Also called "near rhyme," this refers to the use of words
  that do not share an exact end sound but come close. Karen Skolfield

uses this in "How to Locate Water on a Desert Island," ending lines with small and still, love and us. Closely related is the notion of eye rhyme or sight rhyme, which refers to words that don't sound the same but like alike on the page: love and move, cough and bough. This is less about sonic music and more about visual music: the suggestion of music. All varieties of rhyme—exact, slant, and sight— do more than create a sonic or visual connection between words; they also connect those words in terms of meaning. The words are yoked by the rhyme, and that yoking invites readers to make connections between the meanings and associations of the words.

Rhetorical devices like these work in harmony (get it?) with sound to make music one of the driving forces of a poem's movement. Often a sonic connection between words provides the poet with an opportunity for a leap, music offering a kind of logic for a poem that is neither narrative nor intellectual, but physical.

See Also: Prosody, Rhythm, Structure, Syntax

Narrative

Storytelling is an inherently human trait. Ever since the human species sat around campfires in ancient caves, we have shared stories: remembering experiences, showing off the power of the imagination, finding common ground with one another. People love stories and are drawn to them.

Poems are one way to tell a story. You'll notice that narrative appears not only here in the Elements section of this book, but also in the anthology section as a mode. There, we'll be looking at how narrative acts as a larger driving force for some poems—those that are driven primarily by narrative, by that storytelling impulse. But here, we want to look at narrative as an internal element of poems—another useful tool in the poet's workshed.

The essentials of narrative are captured in the inverted checkmark that should be quite familiar to fiction writers. A narrative begins with a problem, some sort of catalyst to set things in motion, followed by a sequence of events we call rising action—that is, tension rises as things move forward in time. The stakes grow higher and higher until the climax or crossroads, where tension is at its highest. Anything after that is falling action leading to the narrative's resolution.

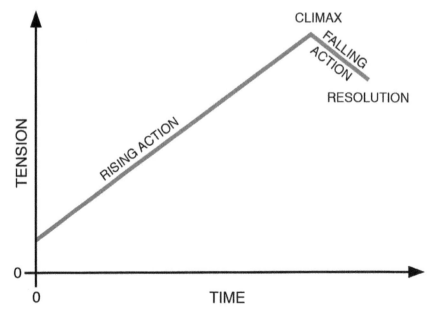

Even in poems that are decidedly non-narrative—poems that move almost entirely through sound or abstract association or some other lyrical device—the reader will impose a narrative. It's what we do; it's one of the ways we make sense of what we're reading. Laura Kasischke's "Landscape with one of the earthworm's ten hearts" is in some ways an anti-narrative: nothing much happens in the poem. Yet it feels like a narrative. The poem introduces characters and setting, and there's high dramatic tension in its stillness, so that at the end of the poem, that thumping sound feels like a climax of a series of events. Kasischke uses the components of narrative—and our predilection for imposing narrative on anything we read—to her advantage.

If you're stuck in the process of writing a poem, narrative offers one avenue for escape: create a problem, heighten the stakes until you're at a turning point, then resolve the problem. Note that "resolve" doesn't necessarily mean "solve" here; the most complex and interesting problems—those most worth writing about—are often unsolvable, and poems that wrap up things too neatly (". . . and they lived happily ever after") risk being cheesy, sentimental, overly simplistic.

As an element, narrative has as much to do with how a poet handles time as it does in providing an external structure. Narrative time—as opposed to lyric time—is concerned with chronology and how events unfold through the passage of time. So those moments in your poem where you explore the relationship of past to present are narrative moments; narrative posits chronology as a meaningful explanation for how the world works. We understand the present better by examining the past.

David Tomas Martinez's "In Chicano Park" is not a narrative poem, exactly, as the poem itself exists more in lyric time (that bubble of past, present, and future), but it most definitely includes narrative elements, exploring the passage of time as cause and effect in this landscape. We sense the passage of time and the existence of story in these lines: "men walking the streets to work / look longingly towards their doors."

In a similar fashion, Jeannine Hall Gailey's "Wonder Woman Dreams of the Amazon" slips effortlessly between meditative and narrative modes: "I capture Nazis / and Martians with boomerang grace," clearly a narrative moment, is followed by the dreaminess of "When I turn and turn, the music plays louder." The capturing of Wonder Woman's enemies occurs in narrative time while the turning and the music happens outside of time. Narrative is not the mode of the poem, but it is an element within it.

See Also: Lyric, Movement

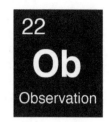

Observation and Interpretation

When we write, we make a choice, sometimes subconsciously, between two ways of delivering the subject to the reader: observation and interpretation. Each approach suggests a different relationship between text and subject.

Observation

When a writer is conveying to the reader what is literally happening, they are writing an observation. This can involve hard data from the five senses and isn't necessarily accompanied by explanations or filtered through any kind of interpretive lens. In portraying the world in objective terms, the writer is able to deliver to the reader a simple who, what, when, where, and how of a situation. The reader gets the straight-up facts with no fancy bells or whistles to enhance the experience beyond relaying the literal events or objects being described. Clarice set fire to the living room. She dropped a lit match into a garbage can, stepped back and laughed. The garbage can was full of all our contracts with the corporation. These are three observations made about Clarice and the things that she has done.

Interpretation

Writers are always making observations about their surroundings and once those observations are on record, they transform them through interpretation. Interpretation filters the word through some kind of consciousness, that of a writer, speaker, or character. Interpretation is figurative material, often involving metaphors or similes, that works to explain or contextualize observational information. Clarice was beautiful like the ravenous night. She struck a match and cackled like a night bird as the flames threatened to engulf the whole room. The garbage can held our papers, our tethers to the evil corporation. There is much interpretation at work here: beauty is subjective, the night is not literally ravenous, a match strike is a figure of speech, the night bird is a simile, and so on.

These things seem pretty straightforward, but sometimes telling them apart can be tricky. For example, the fire was big—well, compared to what? Size can be a subjective measure, but this might not be a helpful distinction to nitpick. Or I feel angry, like I have a crocodile's heart. Is that an objective declaration of feeling, or a comparison of anger to the impossibility of having a reptile's heart? In this case, it's an interpretation of the objective declaration, and knowing that helps the reader to understand that the crocodile is angry and not hungry or sad.

Poems may tend to rely heavily on interpretation, but there can also be a lot of power in the observed moment. The observations Craig Perez Santos makes about the family gathering in "Rings of Fire" are metaphorically interpreted as those fires burning all over the world. Similarly, "History Lesson" by Natasha Trethewey depends on the careful observation of the details in that photograph so that the tiny interpretations can work—the flowered hips, the sun cutting the Gulf and the minnows like switchblades. These interpretative moments are important in that they say a lot about the mood of the poem's speaker as they defamiliarize and provide additional value not just to the girl in the photo, but also to the woman who snapped it.

Conversely, poems like "Quinta Del Sordo" by Monica Youn and "Stutter" by Evelyn Araluen appear to be almost completely interpretations of the painting by Goya and the photo by Liao, respectively. We don't get any straightforward observation of the artwork itself because description literally isn't the point—that's more the realm of catalog captioning than that of poetry. However, by creating an interpretation of the artwork, Youn and Araluen transform Goya's and Liao's visual works into their own textual art.

A poet doesn't necessarily have to privilege one of these methods over the other. That is, a poet who only works in observations risks becoming dry and uninspiring, while a poet who only works in interpretations risks overwhelming the reader with figurative language or perhaps leaving the reader confused. Each depends on the other—to observe the world is to interpret it, surely. In your poems, think about how interpretation and observation work together to transform your subjects into an experience for the reader.

See Also: Defamiliarization, Image, Value

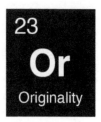

Originality

One of the hardest things for a young poet to do is learn to trust themselves. But when you can do that—when you can believe in your own voice and your own experiences, when you believe that you have something to say about the world—you will unlock a new level in your poems.

Sometimes, our earliest writing experiences happen in school, where we learn to sand off the rough edges of ourselves and play it safe with our writing. Standardized-test culture encourages us to write toward some imagined homogenous middle; we are rewarded for writing that is most like that of our peers. But poetry asks for those rough edges to be left in; poetry, it might be said, is only and exactly those rough edges.

American essayist Phillip Lopate, offering advice to beginning writers of creative nonfiction, says that young writers are often limited by two separate and contradictory but simultaneous fears:

- "I am so weird that I could never tell on the page what is really secretly going on in my mind."
- "I am so boring, nothing ever happens to me out of the ordinary, so who would want to read about me?"

He's talking about nonfiction, to be sure, where the words on the page are often drawn straight from the life of the writer, but the same fears can be stumbling blocks for young poets as well. We want to make sure our poems look like other poems; we worry that our own idiosyncrasies are both too weird and too boring. But here's a secret: no one is boring. You are not boring. And if you're weird, well, so much the better. Lean into the weirdness. Make it the centerpiece of your poems.

As readers of poetry, we don't come to the page to find what's familiar or easy. We come for something we've not seen before. This is why young writers are urged to avoid cliché. Push past what's expected; push past the initial language that comes to mind precisely because it is familiar. Mark Doty says we read poetry in part to be brought into "intimate proximity to someone else's sensations"—to watch someone else's mind at work on the world. For the poet to deliver such an experience, they must be willing to reveal the workings of their own mind. To dig deeper than the surface of their thoughts, to explore their own ideas, imaginings, and associations.

This might sound like a huge, daunting task, but you can make it more manageable by starting with small moments in the language of your poems.

If a toad in your poem hops out of sight, can it pulse or slide or ink instead? If the ground outside is white with snow, could it be blue or braided or limp with snow instead? Look for any and every opportunity to defamiliarize your imagery and your ideas. Don't worry too much about whether you're making perfect, logical sense. Poems are allowed to make a different kind of sense. Richard Hugo says, "In the world of imagination, all things belong," and your poem is a world built from your imagination. That unlikely description, that noun being used as a verb, that out-of-place adjective— they belong because you say they belong. The reader will accept that. Will be drawn to it, even. Making your poems new is more important than making them make sense.

Another thing: we know what we've said about imitating other poets, but the process of imitation ends in the goal of originality. There is so much to learn about writing poems by imitating the moves you see in poems you love, and so much less to learn about writing poems by copying the poems other people have written. We have a whole chapter about this so we won't belabor this point, other than to point out that imitating poems is a way of getting a glimpse of the relationship between poet and poem, but at the end of the day, writing your own original poems should be your goal. Strive for originality and you'll likely learn more from your imitations.

We all see the world from our own subject position. No two people have exactly the same sets of perceptions. Even our own family members have different roles within the family unit, different experiences outside the unit, and different memories about even the biggest moments in the family history. The person sitting next you in class may share some of your background or demographic identity, but far from all; you've read different books, heard different songs, eaten different foods. Our experiences are ours and ours alone. So take advantage of that in your poems; as we said above, trust in yourself. Your end goal should be to write the poems only you can write.

See Also: Defamiliarization, Voice

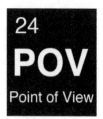

Point of View

Often, writers look at point of view as a fiction technique, but the point of view matters in a poem, too. It seems pretty straightforward, those three technical points of view that you might already know: first, second, and third person, each distinguished by the pronouns used to represent the main characters. But more than pronoun use, more than the perspective of the speaker, point of view is key to the reader's relationship to the poem as it's being read, as it offers the reader an anchor in the poem. Point of view offers the reader a seat, a specific vantage point from which to experience the poem. Understanding precisely what point of view is and how it's used in poems is key to getting the most work out of it.

Third Person

The third person point of view is the realm of they / he / she / it. What matters most here is where the reader's seat is in the poem; in the third person, it's outside the poem, or at least outside the characters in the poem. The reader might be up close, so close that the sensory detail is overwhelming. Or the reader can be far away, across the street, on the other side of town or on the surface of the moon. Positioning your readers outside the poem yields greater opportunity for objective observation and quantitative information. Sometimes a poem's point of existing is to bear witness, to look at something and acknowledge its existence. This isn't to say that the third person is necessarily an objective point of view; the third person can be highly subjective. But sometimes, with distance comes clarity, and third person is a good way of creating distance in a poem.

First Person

When I write in the first-person point of view, the reader's seat is inside the poem along with me. It's an intimate place to sit—so close to the speaker and all those thoughts and emotions and interior noise. There are two kinds of first-person points of view in poems.

Singular: First person is the realm of the "I." When I write in first person, the poem uses my perception as the filter through which it relates to the world. As a result, the poem has an inherent subjectivity in its voice. My observations are made through my intellectual / cerebral / emotional lenses. The stories I tell are my stories, which can sometimes include stories about other people from my perspective. Note that there might be a difference between me (the poem's writer) and the speaker—but in terms of point of view, it's more important to notice how close the reader is to the I, how the reader takes a seat and is surrounded by my interior thoughts and feelings. Just as I might use third person to find objectivity, I might choose first person to discover the beauty of subjectivity.

Plural: We can also choose to write in the first person plural, the "we" voice. However, when we are using a "we" point of view, we should know who we are. If we are using a universal we, then the point of view includes everyone everywhere. Or if the we is a smaller group of people, then the effect is the same, but at that point, the poem might have to explain who the members of the group are. If the "we" consists of just the speaker and the reader, then the poem becomes a much more intimate place as the speaker makes an appeal for unity with the reader. One mistake young writers sometimes make is failing to fully consider who's included in their "we," and conversely who is excluded. If you write, "we all hate liver and onions," and it's clear in context that the "we" means you and your siblings, it's fine. But if your "we" is ambiguous, you leave room for readers to object that they, in fact, adore liver and onions. Obviously, this is a fairly innocuous example, but if a poem is dealing with bigger or more sensitive issues than one's taste in entrees, care with the perspective is warranted.

Second Person

The second person is the realm of the you. Writers often gravitate to the second person because the pronouns seem to place "you" in the poem, which offers the illusion of closeness. This sense of immediacy a reader might feel toward a poem or its speaker can be a powerful tool in engaging the audience and getting them to feel what you want them to feel. However, it's important to consider why you might use the second person, as well as which second person you want to use. There are many ways to implement a second person point of view—that could be why the second person is so often misused in creative writing.

Second Person as the Reader: Sometimes in a poem, the you is actually the reader, like one of those "choose your own adventure" books where the reader is the main character of the story. It's tough to put the reader in the poem, though—maybe you are in love with a woman but the reader doesn't share that sexual orientation. Or maybe you drive too fast on the freeway and the reader is like, "Hey, wait a minute—I drive the limit." It's not an impossible feat to pull off, but if a poem is a rhetorical structure, putting the readers' seat at the very center of the poem is a heavy-handed way of trying to get them to respond emotionally. "You feel sad," you write, and the reader says, "No I don't feel that."

Second Person as Directed Voice—Specific: While the third person places the reader's seat outside the poem and first person places the reader's seat inside the poem, then the second person is more interested in addressing its voice outward at the reader. Maybe you are explaining how to perform a task or how to get to a certain place. Or perhaps you want to make a direct connection with the reader during a particularly heated moment near the end of the poem, your gaze swiveling from the subject in the poem to the reader to move them closer to the poem.

Alternatively, you might want to address someone or something other than the reader. Maybe you are writing a poem to Abraham Lincoln or Marilyn Monroe or the people in your third-grade school picture. Or maybe you are directing your voice at something inanimate like a shipwreck or your childhood neighborhood or your favorite rock band. Regardless of who the voice is directed at, the directed voice knows, or at least has a pretty good idea about, who it is addressing. To not know this is to direct your voice at nothing or no one, which isn't a very good rhetorical strategy. See the Apostrophe section of the anthology for examples of this kind of second person in which the you being addressed is specific and made explicit.

Second Person as Directed Voice—Universal You: Sometimes you don't want to talk to a specific person. Instead, you want to direct the voice at the universe, at all of creation. This use of directed voice without any specific target in mind is fine in poetry, but it's often the result of a writer not thinking enough about whom they want their poems to address. A common workshop question is, "Who is the *you*?" Maybe the *you* is no one; maybe it's everyone. Sometimes that vagueness works, but more often it's better when it's a particular you and the reader is in on who it is.

Second Person as Displaced First Person: In short, this point of view is the speaker talking to the speaker. There are so many reasons for talking to yourself. You lack confidence and need to talk yourself through an ordeal. You did something stupid and you are embarrassed or angry at yourself and you wish you could take it back. You feel guilty about something or you can't admit something about yourself so you try to talk yourself into accepting or denying the whole situation. If the first person puts the reader's seat inside the poem and third person puts the reader's seat outside the poem, then the displaced first person removes the speaker from the poem's center and directs its voice at itself.

Writing in the second person sometimes draws criticism as a cheap trick to give the illusion of immediacy to the reader—and teachers used to say it was "against the rules" of formal writing. You should feel free to ignore that criticism. You know that there are no rules, and besides, now you understand the nuance of writing in the "you" voice. Just as it is with first person or third person, the point is to wrangle as much work out of the POV as you can.

See Also: Gaze, Speaker, Voice

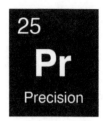

Precision

The childhood taunt of "sticks and stones may break my bones but words will never hurt me" is right about sticks and stones, but it vastly underestimates the power of words. The ability to use language effectively is a great power, and everyone knows what Spider-Man says about great power: It brings with it great responsibility. This is the responsibility of the poet: to know language well and to use it with precision.

What you want from your poems when they're done is that not a word appears out of place and that each word is doing the work you want it to do. This requires attention to detail and care with language. This can come during the revision process, but at some point, you'll need to interrogate each word in your poem to be sure it's doing what you want it to. This is related to concision, but it's not just about using as few words as possible; it's making sure the words you do use are the right words.

You'll need to develop a keen awareness of the difference between denotation and connotation. Denotation is what a word overtly means—the dictionary definition, essentially. Connotation refers to meanings associated with the word, the social, emotional, or political overtones a word may carry. As a poet, you are accountable for both. Consider the differences, say, between being called skinny and being called slender: similar denotative meanings, but different connotative associations, right? Or, imagine for example, a young poet who titles a poem about becoming a parent "Choice" without considering that word's implications in the societal debate about abortion rights. Perhaps the poet had another choice in mind entirely, and perhaps the poem itself makes pretty clear that some other choice is being explored. That does not free the poem or the poet from the inevitable associations some readers will make.

Similarly, words' meanings change over time. This may be self-evident, but it's important to remember. You are writing poems in the twenty-first century; you don't get to pretend the word "gay" doesn't have a different meaning now than it did in the "gay '90s" of the late nineteenth century. If you call women "ladies" in your poetry, you're probably going to have some explaining to do about why you sound like an old-fashioned male banker from the 1920s. If a word in your poem has multiple meanings or particular social implications, you get them all. Typically, we don't get to walk around with our poems and explain that we meant A but not B. So choose your words with care.

See Also: Clarity, Concision, Language, Value

Punctuation

How tempting it is for many young poets to think that writing poetry frees them from the tedium of comma rules and other nonsense having to do with punctuation. And sure . . . kind of. Alas, it does not free you from knowing the standard conventions of written English; it merely frees you from following those conventions. Ignore the conventions if you wish. But do so from a place of knowledge; your disregard for what we've been taught are the rules ought to be intentional.

Look, all grammar and punctuation rules are made up and somewhat arbitrary. There's no moral imperative to use the comma before the conjunction in a list of items such as Moe, Larry, and Curly; it's just a convention some people have agreed on in order to facilitate communication and clarity. In straightforward prose writing, punctuation should be essentially invisible, not calling attention to itself but serving to guide the reader through the sentences as seamlessly as possible. Periods signal when one clause ends. Commas indicate pauses, slight shifts in thinking. Question marks indicate . . . well, questions. You know how it works. Anyone who reads a lot becomes intuitively familiar with most punctuation conventions, even if you might not remember precisely whether or not the comma belongs inside the quotation marks.

As a poet, you can get away with using punctuation in unconventional ways. But you should do so with an understanding both of the convention you're flouting and of the effect your choices are going to have on your readers. Punctuation, like all the other elements of your writing, is rhetorical. Its presence in a poem has an effect, whether it follows the rules your twelfth-grade teacher drilled into your head or not. Punctuation can help shape both the meaning and rhythm of a poem; they are an important component of syntax.

Our aim here is not to teach you all the significant rules of grammar; there are plenty of handbooks for that. What's important for a poet is start with learning the rules—but move beyond that to understanding why they are so. It's not enough to memorize where commas go and which nouns to capitalize; it's equally important to know how these rules are intended to aid you in communicating your ideas. That way when you start sprinkling your poems with semicolons and dashes and someone asks what the heck you're doing, you can whip out your poetic license and explain that you're challenging the reader's expectations about the syntactical relationship between ideas.

We talk elsewhere in this book about how a well-chosen line break can create double meanings in a poem. That's an important rhetorical move that is somewhat dependent on how the poem uses punctuation. The different meanings of the line and sentence can be much more difficult for the reader to parse without effective punctuation to mark the clauses and pauses in the sentence.

If you look at the poems in this book's anthology with an eye specifically toward how they use punctuation and capitalization, you'll see that most of them are pretty standard in their adherence to convention. Many of the poems in this book's anthology follow pretty standard punctuation rules; in such poems, the job of the punctuation is to be as unobtrusive as possible—periods to indicate the ends of sentences, capital letters to indicate the beginning of the next, and so forth. The poet uses punctuation to provide clarity and straightforwardness; what is challenging in the poem comes from language choice, thematic complexity, and the use of lines and line breaks.

But other poems do things differently. For instance, Gary L. McDowell's "Tell Me Again about the Last Time You Saw Her" and Eileen Myles' "To the Mountains" each forgo punctuation entirely, leaving the readers to negotiate pauses and stops on their own. McDowell uses white space on the page and capital letters that suggest the beginning of a new sentence; Myles relies largely on line breaks and concision to create clarity. Layli Long Soldier's "38" explicitly acknowledges that it will be following the convention of beginning sentences with capital letters and "ending each one with appropriate punctuation such as a period or a question mark, thus bringing the idea to (momentary) completion." And Evelyn Araluen uses wide spaces line by line like she's inventing her own kind of punctuation for the poem. In this manner, the poet places the act of writing in order to shape understanding front and center in her poem.

You'll notice that most contemporary poets tend toward sentence case when it comes to capital letters, capping the first letter of sentences and proper nouns. This is a shift in convention from, say, seventy-five years ago, when most poets, writing in metrical verse that determined line length by syllable count, capitalized the first word of every line, regardless of whether the sentence called for. Some poets still do this, as Mary Jo Bang does in "The Role of Elegy"; her choice gives the poem an old-fashioned formality on the page, which seems appropriate to the poem's project. As with most poetic choices you'll make, there is no right or wrong here—there is only the choice you make and the effect it has on the reading experience. (Whatever you do, don't capitalize the first word of every line solely because autocorrect does it for you.)

Oh, and one last thing to mention in this section. We ask one thing of you in particular: please, for the love of Emily Dickinson, learn the difference between a hyphen and a dash. The two marks are not interchangeable. All poets should know this distinction.

See Also: Lines, Precision, Rhythm, Syntax

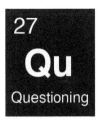

Questioning

What happens in your mind when, as a reader, you come across a question in a poem? Do you automatically fill in a response? Do you expect the poet to provide an answer at some point in the poem? Are you frustrated if there is no such answer to be found? Do you think of the question as a rhetorical device, employed to help the poet make some point about the world? Do you ponder the question for a while after the poem is finished, wondering what the best response might be? Can a poem ask too many questions? Is a poet obligated to provide answers?

It's our job—our calling—as poets to question the world around us. Sometimes that means, quite literally, asking questions in our poems. It's one way we can introduce productive ambiguity into our language. Often, a question serves as a method for drawing the reader into the world of the poem, a sort of forced interaction. As an indication of how integral the act of questioning is to poetry, more than a third of the poems in this anthology contain at least one explicit question, which is pure happenstance, as we did not set out intentionally to find poems with questions in them.

In conversation, we use the phrase "rhetorical question" to refer to a question asked to make a point or raise an issue rather than in expectation of an answer. If you're walking into the dining room reading a text on your phone in one hand with your coffee cup balanced precariously on the edge of your soup bowl in your other hand and you end up spilling your coffee or soup, and your friend says, "Well, what did you think would happen?" your friend isn't literally inquiring about your thought process but making a point about your poor planning. That's a rhetorical question. Well, in poems, all questions are rhetorical: the poet and reader are (likely) not in the same place, so the poet cannot expect an answer. That means the question is in the poem to make some kind of point.

Questions serve to emphasize that a poet is exploring the world rather than revealing it, illustrating that the poet, like the readers, does not have all the answers. Oliver de la Paz asks two consecutive questions in the middle of "Aubade with Bread for the Sparrows": "What's left / but to watch the daylight halved by the glistening ground? / What's left but an empty bag and the dust of bread / ravaged by songsters?" There's a bleakness to the questions, a longing, and a sense that the speaker wants some kind of optimistic answer that is not forthcoming.

When the question is asked not to the general reader but to a particular recipient the poem has established, it offers a kind of intimacy, two characters interacting with each other on the page. Solmaz Sharif asks several questions in her letter poem, and as readers we understand that the recipient of the letter would be expected to provide the answers in reply; the questions here drive home the intimacy of the epistolary form and simultaneously emphasize the invasiveness of the redactions, which remove significant words from the heart of the questions. Naomi Shihab Nye similarly asks a question of the addressee of her poem, who is not there to reply. Sometimes, the best questions to ask in poems are those that cannot be easily answered; to answer would be to shut down the poem, to limit its possibilities. Better, then, to ask and continue asking.

See Also: Exploration, Surprise, Syntax, Voice

Repetition

Repetition is one of the first poetic elements we learn. When we first start writing poems in elementary school, we very often use repetition as a way to provide a poem with structure and music. Music scholar and author Elizabeth Hellmuth Margulis has suggested that, in fact, repetition is the very essence of music; that songs have choruses because a listener gains pleasure from hearing something again. Consider how often we listen to our favorite songs, Hellmuth suggests; there must be pleasure in the act of revisiting, of rehearing.

There's a kind of comfort in familiarity, and the second time we encounter something we approach it differently, more generously. It's similar to the way standup comedians use callbacks within a routine, and so often the biggest laughs come when the comedian pulls back out a phrase or line from an earlier joke.

We encourage you to move beyond the simple repetition we used in those third-grade poems; when a poem returns to language it has already used, the image or phrase should look different. The meaning should be shaped anew by the time we encounter it again. When you bring a poem full circle by repeating an earlier image at the end, the image should carry a new emotional impact.

There's no question that repeating a word or phrase changes our understanding of it. We've all had that experience of writing or saying a word or phrase so many times that it begins to look or sound weird. Margulis suggests having someone repeat a word to you over and over for a few minutes: lollipop, lollipop, lollipop, lollipop, lollipop, lollipop. As we repeat (or re-read or re-hear) the word over and over, the sound of it becomes divorced from its dictionary definition; the syllables become simultaneously more familiar and more strange. This is called the "semantic satiation effect," and it's probably about as good a metaphor as there is for what a poem is doing.

A caution: Watch out for inadvertent repetition in your poems. There are words and phrases we fall back on out of habit, and it's important to watch out for overusing them. If the afternoon light is dancing across the surface of the lake in your first stanza, perhaps the clouds should be doing something other than dancing across the sky in your second stanza—unless the repetition of dancing is part of the point. In that case, you want to make sure that whatever you're repeating deserves it; that your "chorus" stands up to the increased scrutiny it faces by appearing repeatedly in your poem.

In our made-up example, you could for sure find a better, more surprising verb than dancing.

Margulis likens repetition in music to rituals such as those performed in religious ceremonies, say. Rituals may be either physical or verbal, and by their nature are participatory both for the actors and for those observing them. The repetition of ritual behavior gives the action a larger meaning. That is, the flipping of a coin before a football game does more than decide which team receives the ball first; it also links the football games to all other games that have begun the same way; it signals to the crowd and the players that the game is about to begin. The action has a practical purpose, but it's also ceremonial, decorative, meaning-making. The repetition of the act enlarges it. The same is true of repetition in poetry: the words have one purpose within the sentence or line or syntactical unit, but when the poet repeats them, they become larger, more meaningful.

One of the effects repetition can have is a sort of numbing effect. When Patricia Lockwood begins each sentence with the same clause—"The rape joke is"—we begin to grow desensitized to the phrase. The phrase, at first shocking, becomes familiar, which is part of the project of the poem, to explore the place of that phrase in our culture, to consider the oxymoronic nature of the idea of a "rape joke" in the first place. Repeating the same words at the beginning of a series of clauses is a particular kind of repetition called anaphora, from the Greek for "carrying back." It lends emphasis to the repeated words and often has the effect of creating a sort of litany or an almost religious sort of recitation. It often forces a strong rhythm on a poem. A similar role is played by epistrophe, which refers to the repetition of words at the end of a series of clauses, lines, or stanzas.

Another way poets often use repetition is to establish expectations only to thwart them by later breaking the pattern. It's a pretty standard way to achieve surprise in your poems.

See Also: Endings, Music, Rhythm, Surprise

Rhythm

Rhythm refers to pattern and to pacing. It's an essential part of music and poetry; it's also innately human. Think about the rhythms of the body: our breathing, our pulse, our cycles of sleeping and waking. There can be comfort in rhythm, in patterns, in that it can create predictability, stability.

In a song, rhythm is often created through percussion—drums, cymbals, and so forth, create the beat and tempo. In a poem, there is no instrumentation other than language, both spoken and written; percussion is replaced by the sounds and patterning in the syllables of each word. In many kinds of formal poetry, a certain rhythm is inherent in the form, the poem moving to the beat created by the pattern of stressed and unstressed syllables. Free verse poems have rhythm too, although it may not be as uniform or predictable as a fixed form. What's important is to think of rhythm as fulfilling a rhetorical function: it's part of how you shape your reader's experience with your poem. There is no one rhythm that poems should be striving for, necessarily; each poem establishes its own patterns of sound and beats.

It's difficult to separate the poem's rhythm from its music because those things are intrinsic to one another, each one enhancing and perpetuating the other. But consider rhythm as the method by which a poet controls the poem's pace and speed: how quickly do you want your readers to advance through each line? Where do you want the readers to linger longest? The more you develop a sense of your work's rhythm, the better able you will be to make use of it.

For example, certain things will make the poem feel faster. Short lines, short words, hard plosive sounds, and simple language are things that can increase the speed at which your readers can traverse the body of the poem. Conversely, longer lines, bigger words, fricatives, and nasals might slow the poem down. Longer, more complex words might also slow the poem down as the reader spends more time reading and pondering the words' meanings.

And rhetorical devices: sometimes repetition seems like it's something that would speed a poem up. Alliteration combined with plosive sounds can make spoken language faster; at the same time, alliteration with fricatives can slow the flow of language. This is in part how tongue twisters work: listen to how "Peter Piper picked a peck of pickled peppers." The plosive sounds make the sentence move fast, faster than one's lips might be able to handle, while at the same time "She sells seashells by the sea shore" places all of those fricative sounds in the way, forcing the tongue to slow down in order to say the phrase with the proper distinction between s and sh.

The word "rhythm" comes from the Greek for "measured motion," and that's a helpful way for a poet to think about it. This is in part why it's a good practice to read your poems aloud during the writing process. Perhaps your poem is best served by an easy, smooth rhythm; perhaps you want a more halting poem full of interruptions and starting over. Maybe your poem needs to upshift and downshift, getting faster and slower in different places. Hearing the poem spoken allows you to hear the patterns and points of emphasis in your poem, to better understand its rhythm and to help it find the motion that suits it best.

See Also: Music, Prosody, Syntax

30

Sh

Showing

Showing and Telling

If you've ever taken a writing class or read a book of advice about writing, it's almost certain that someone has advised you to "show, don't tell" in your writing. In general, this is excellent advice, encouraging the use of image over abstraction, of evoking rather than merely explaining. The job of the poet is not simply to tell the reader that the cherry trees are in bloom, but to show those trees in all their light and brilliance. Bring the blossoms to life on the page through sense details: colors, smells, and sounds.

However, sometimes telling is perfectly appropriate. Sometimes a deftly handled abstraction is every bit as effective as a beautifully rendered image. It's important that a poet not rely exclusively on telling or on abstractions, to be sure. But a poem that is entirely image and sense description risks being contextless and static; it risks failing to explore the implications of its subject. What you want for your poems is to find just the right balance between showing and telling. Alas, there's no simple formula that can tell us just what that balance is: 75 percent show, 25 percent tell, and voila! No, each poem requires its own negotiation between these two elements.

Consider these lines from Ross Gay's "Ode to Buttoning and Unbuttoning My Shirt," which came after the poet has skillfully evoked the tactile sensation of buttoning a shirt: "in terms of joy / this is not something to be taken lightly." There's nary a concrete, specific detail in these lines; clearly, they tell instead of showing. But this move is effective because it enlarges the poem; it shifts from observation to interpretation. By making a straightforward assertion about the effect of the experience, the poem practically dares us to disagree.

You'll see lots of poets use that strategy: making plainspoken claims about the nature of the world. Such telling moments can be effective because there is a comfort in reading such certainty; sometimes we like being told what to think, we appreciate the possibility that we've just read a bit of wisdom we can carry with us. Often such moments are the most-quoted lines from a poem.

As a reader, though, you are always faced with the question of how seriously to take these claims; often these moments are undercut, or at least complicated by the images around them. It's as if the speaker is making a pronouncement to try it out, to see if it still feels right after saying it aloud. Perhaps the poet is stating the claim as a kind of hypothesis which the rest of the poem then tests: poem as scientific method.

What we're asking here is for you to reject the oversimplification that showing is good, telling is bad. Each has its place; each is an element of poetry, with its own rhetorical effect. The more you read and the more you write, the better skilled you will become at deploying each to maximum effect.

See Also: Image, Observation and Interpretation, Surprise, Value

Speaker

There is a tendency for readers to think of poetry as "true." That is, the speaker of any poem is the poet herself, and what happens in a poem happened in real life. The belief is rooted in the way many of us are taught poetry: that each line should be parsed for its relationship to the speaker's life or to historical events. A teacher tells his students biographical details of Emily Dickinson's life so that we can know what her poems are "really about."

This notion is mostly hogwash. It's also, frankly, a bit insulting to both poet and audience. It discounts the role of imagination and empathy in the writing process, suggesting that all a poet does is dress up actual events in fancy language. It limits the reading experience to finding clues that point to the poet's life story. So repeat after us: The speaker is not the author. The speaker is not the author. The speaker is not the author.

Once you've accepted this, it has implications for you both as a reader and a writer of poetry. As a reader, not treating every poem as confessional means you don't need to know the poet's life story to engage with the poem. Instead, what you engage with is the words on the page. The poem itself should contain everything you need to have an experience with it. Yes, sometimes knowing something about the poet can shape your reading experience in particular ways, even enriching it, but it should not be necessary to the poem. As a poet, it frees you up to invent and fabricate, to fit your story to the language, not the other way around. The speaker can be you, or not you, or partially you and partially an invention. Yes, you can lie in your poems!

There's no doubt that sometimes a poem invites the reader to think of it as autobiographical. In Patricia Lockwood's "Rape Joke," for example, attracted a lot of attention when it was first published in an online journal, *The Awl*, and most responses tended to assume the author was writing from personal experience. Lockwood mentioned this reaction in interviews, and told *The Rumpus*: "Part of the purpose of a poem like this is to take the target out of yourself and put it up on the wall. It's a method of distancing, of detachment. . . . Making an object out of your suffering allows you to be objective about it." In other words, Lockwood's personal experiences are one thing, and the poem is something else. They might overlap, certainly— many of our best poems are drawn from our most powerful life experiences, whether positive or negative—but they are not the same, and the degree to which they overlap isn't important to the reading experience.

Sometimes the speaker is the author. That's fine, too. But note that even when you are writing about yourself and the details of your poem come straight from your life, you are still creating a version of yourself on the page. The word "persona" comes from the Latin for "mask," and every speaker you create is in some way a mask. Backing up from poetry for a moment, think about the many masks we wear in our everyday lives. The person you are when you're on a first date might not be exactly the person you are when you're having Sunday dinner with your grandmother, and that in turn might not be the person you are when you're in a diner having coffee and pancakes with your best friends at 3:00 a.m. on a Friday night. There's nothing wrong with having these various personas; such code-switching is part of having different relationships with different people.

Similarly, the self you present on the page in a particular poem is merely one facet of yourself. If you're writing about an argument you had with your father about politics, you might not draw much on the version of yourself that collects military memorabilia or binge-watches *Gilmore Girls*. Or maybe you do mention those versions, but you don't spend much time on the self that spent hours drawing horses in third grade or played goalkeeper for your seventh-grade soccer team. You get the idea. We all contain multitudes, as Walt Whitman observed, and no poem is going to represent all of them—which means you are making choices about the self you present on the page, which means that self is a persona. Even when the speaker is the poet, the speaker is not the entire poet.

Sometimes, the speaker is not the poet at all. Sometimes, as in the persona poems in this anthology, the poet openly inhabits another character, whether real or invented, and uses that voice as a lens through which to explore the world. Writing in a full-on persona can be a freeing experience, allowing a poet to let go of the burden of being oneself for a while and explore the world incognito. And once in a while, approaching a subject as if you were someone else entirely allows you to be even more truthful than usual about how you see the world.

See Also: Gaze, Language, Point Of View, Voice

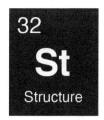

32
St
Structure

Structure

Not all poems are formal poems. But all poems have structure. A poem is a built thing—a work of art made from language. And to be built, a thing must have structure. Just as a building needs its load-bearing walls, ducts for heating and cooling, entrances and staircases, floors and ceilings, poems need the components that give them shape.

Without structure, a poem would be a random arrangement of words on the page, and although some poems may appear to be random, that seeming randomness is almost always orchestrated. Structure—how a poem looks on the page, how its lines connect to one another—is just one part of the rhetorical construction of the poem overall.

Poems can look however the poet wants them to look. There are no rules, and the only limits have to do with the size of your page and the capabilities of your pen or word processing or design software. Some poems rhyme and some don't. Some poems have long lines, some have short lines, and some poems look more like paragraphs than lineated poems. Some poems look as though they have been split in half, some in thirds, and some are scattershot across the page. Sometimes the poem's structure has an obvious rhetorical connection to the poem's theme or subject, and sometimes it's not so apparent.

Just as you do with your images and your ideas, we encourage you to experiment with your poems' structure. Try things. Play.

Useful Vocabulary

What follows is a list of terms poets use to describe a poem's structure. Can you write great poems without knowing any of these words? Sure, maybe. But knowing them will help you have more efficient conversations about the mechanics of a poem's structure and the work that a poem's structure does.

Caesura: An interruption or break in the middle of a line that breaks it in two. Often, poets create caesura with punctuation to signal a pause in the rhythm of the line. Other poets sometimes force caesura with white space on the page, as Janine Joseph does in "Move-In."

Contrapuntal: A poem that is made up of two independent poems placed side by side like Tarfia Faizullah's "Aubade Ending with the

Death of a Mosquito." When done with care, such a poem can be
read across both poems or down each one individually, creating an
intricate overlapping of meanings.

Couplet: A two-line stanza, often rhymed.

Dropped Line: A line break with the subsequent line indented
so that it appears in the horizontal position it would have
been in had the line not been broken. The effect is that it looks
like the line
                    drops down after the break
                                          like this.

Epigraph: A phrase or quote from another source that works as an
introductory element at the start of a poem. Typically appears under
the title, often italicized or in a smaller font than the poem.

Formal Verse: Poetry that follows a pattern of rhythm and rhyme
(usually a fixed or traditional form).

Free Verse: Poetry that does not follow a fixed pattern of rhythm or
rhyme.

Line: A unit consisting of a string of words on a single line. The smallest
structural unit in a poem.

Prose: Text that is composed without line breaks and operates in
sentences rather than lines.

Prose poem: A poem that is written in prose rather than traditional
lines. Most commonly (though certainly not always) looks like a
standalone prose paragraph.

Prosody: The system of a poem's rhythmic and sonic structures and the
study of poetic systems.

Quatrain: A four-line stanza.

Quintet: A five-line stanza.

Rhyme Scheme: The rhyming pattern of a poem. A's rhyme with A's and
B's with B's. If the rhyme scheme is ABAB, then there are four lines
with lines one and three rhyming together and two and four rhyming
together. If it's ABAB CDCD, that means the first four lines have an
ABAB rhyme scheme like above, and the second four lines have a
similar rhyme scheme but with different rhyme sounds. ABAB CDCD
EFEF just extends the above pattern. And so on.

Sextet: A six-line stanza.

Stanza: A unit consisting of a series of lines in a poem.

Section: A unit consisting of a series of stanzas in a poem. Sections are
usually marked with a number or a letter or a subtitle of some kind.

Tercet: A three-line stanza. Sometimes called a triplet.

Verse: A metrical structure.

See Also: Line, Movement, Music

33

Su

Surprise

Surprise

One of the things we want most as readers is to be surprised. We approach the page craving something different than we expected, something we didn't even know was possible. We read in order to expand our notion of what is possible. When reading poetry, that applies to language: we want poems to use language in ways that are surprising, fresh, original. We want to encounter phrases that we've never seen before—and yet that still hit home, that give us that feeling of yes, this is exactly how to express that idea.

One of the things this means is that poets should avoid relying on clichés. This is not new advice, and this is probably not the first time you've been told that. But it's worth spending a second on why clichés damage your poems. Some clichés become clichés because they are overused; we use them in our everyday communication as a shorthand for complex ideas. But as shorthand, they lose the precision poets demand from their language. They become an abstraction of an idea rather than the idea itself. Also, many clichés fall into the easy, expected emotion of sentimentality, which is basically the antonym of surprise: "The sun will come out tomorrow," "Love is blind," "If you love someone, set them free," etc.

We don't mean surprise here as in a big twist at the end of your poem like the one at the end of an episode of the cartoon *Scooby-Doo*, when the heroes pulled off the mask and we learned that the museum curator had been the bad guy all along. It's easy to change the rules without notice, to reveal in the last line that the poem we all thought was a love poem was about your family dog, or that your speaker has been dead the whole time. This is the cheapest form of surprise, and even if you pull it off, it harms your poem because it works only the first time we read it. There's no reason to revisit such a poem once you've learned its big secret. This is the opposite of what a good poem should do, which is to invite and reward multiple readings.

The twentieth-century film director Alfred Hitchcock made distinction between this kind of easy surprise and what he termed suspense, a far more meaningful storytelling device. Surprise is blowing something up at the end of a scene when the viewer has no idea the explosion is coming; suspense is when the viewer knows full well the explosion is coming but must wait out the scene in anxious expectation. This second version of the scene is more satisfying and more complex. For a poet, this means don't be coy. Writing that poem about your dog is a risky move because we all love our pets but no one else much cares; if you do insist on writing about Fido, it's far better to let us know up front that this is the subject of the poem. That forces you to deal with the subject head on and do the challenging, meaningful work of making your reader care, rather than ducking that task by withholding the important information until the end.

Philosopher Kenneth Burke referred to form in art as the establishment and fulfillment of desires in the audience. From the first word a reader encounters, that reader begins to form expectations about the poem that follows. Your job as a poet is to be aware of these expectations and to manage them. Sometimes you'll meet them, sometimes you'll thwart them. You never want your poems to be predictable, but sometimes you want the poem to feel inevitable. The best moments in any poem are those that are both surprising and inevitable.

See Also: Metaphor, Value

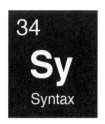

34

Sy

Syntax

Syntax

If diction refers to the words we choose, syntax is the order in which we put those words. How we build our sentences, in other words. The line might draw most of the attention, but the poetic sentence is also essential to writing successful poems.

Let's back up: What is a sentence? Many of us were taught some definition like these in elementary school: "A sentence is a complete thought." Or, possibly, something along the lines of "a sentence is a grammatical unit that features a subject and verb and can stand alone."

The first definition is, unintentionally ludicrous: How can thought ever be complete? (In some ways, this perhaps is the very nature and beauty of poetry: the attempt to set down a complete thought in language pitted against the impossibility of that task.) The second definition feels pretty close to truth, but leaves us at a loss when we come across a fragment that seems to do the same work as a sentence but lacks the grammatical bona fides. Besides, what does it mean to stand alone? Surely nearly all sentences gain strength from the sentences around them.

In the end, trying to define a sentence with any clarity, concision, or certainty becomes a slippery, near-impossible task. We end up with something like this: A sentence is almost any word or series of words that starts with a capital letter and ends with a period (or question mark, or exclamation point). And sometimes poets forgo the capital letters or the punctuation, rendering even this broad definition inadequate.

Let's back up again: What is the purpose of a sentence? Harkening back once more to our early language arts classes, we might hazily recall being taught the four types of sentences: declarative, imperative, interrogative, exclamatory. These four types help us identify sentences by the work they do: make a statement, give a command, ask a question, make a statement with more-than-usual gusto. Now we're getting somewhere. As poets, we should always be asking of our language, "What work are you doing?" We've discussed how words in poetry do different kinds of work and evoke multiple layers of meaning. So, too, must the best poetic sentences do double (or triple or quintuple) work. Statements, commands, questions, emphatic statements; this is the stuff of effective syntax.

It doesn't matter all that much to our life of writing poems whether we can successfully provide that perfect definition of a sentence. What matters is how we use the sentence. It's a way of grouping words that work together. This grouping is how we make meaning. This is syntax.

Many poems take a fairly standard approach to the sentence. Many poets use fragments that aren't technically sentences grammatically but serve the same purpose. All three list poems do this effectively, for instance. Bob Hicok's "Elegy with lies" also relies on fragments that give the poem a sense of constant interruption and re-starting. Reading through this anthology you will see immense variety in the approach to the sentence. You'll find long sentences (even, in the case of Ross Gay's poem, a sentence that meanders the entire length of the poem) and short sentences. Patricia Lockwood and Layli Long Soldier turn to the sentence as its own sort of line. You'll see a variety of approaches to line-sentence interplay, sometimes even within single poems.

Many young poets have the idea that a tortured syntax can make their language seem more poetic: "Toward thee, I send this kiss," or the like. Some of this comes from reading too many rhyming poems where the poet twisted their words in order to get the right words at the ends of the lines. If you're doing this, you're doing your poems and your readers no favors. In the end, as with the other elements in this book, you must bear in mind that syntax must be purposeful. As you write and revise, be mindful of the way arranging your words creates meaning and shapes both voice and rhythm. Be aware of whether your syntax eases the reader through the poem or creates a stumbling block. You don't want your syntax interfering with your poem.

See Also: Diction, Language, Music, Repetition, Structure, Value

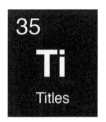

35
Ti
Titles

Titles

Titles can be hard to write. No sugarcoating it. But they're so important. The aims of a title are manifold:

- They must get our attention. Imagine a reader browsing the table of contents in a literary journal or an anthology; the title offers that reader the first indication of what a poem might be up to and whether they might find it interesting.)

- They must entice us to read more. A successful title engages the reader's intellectual or emotional curiosity.

- They must be meaningful in their own right. Again, the best titles are themselves a line of poetry (even if a short line, sometimes a single word), offering a kind of weight and gravity all their own.

- They must stand the test of time. Like a poem itself, a good title should pay off more with more reflection and re-reading. Even when we revisit the title after completing our initial reading of the poem, it's nice to find something fresh waiting there—the meaning of the title evolved somehow by the experience of reading the poem.

Imagine opening a poetry journal and seeing this table of contents:

Based on the titles alone, most readers are flipping straight to page 6. Matthew Olzmann's title is clever, thought-provoking, and unexpected. It gets your attention and immediately raises questions about the poem that will follow it. How is this going to be a Mountain Dew commercial? What's going on with that disguise? Is this a love poem or isn't it? What makes the title successful is more than ostentation, however. All of these questions are not answered simply once we've read the poem. Rather, the reader is left to ponder their nuances and complexities.

Titles matter not just because they help your poem stand out in a table of contents, but also for how they help guide the reader. A good title contributes to the reading experience of a poem and helps shape meaning. Olzmann's title fits that bill, too—it offers a frame for the poem, a kind of reading context that helps you understand what you're getting into as you begin reading. Then, once you've finished the poem, you can return to the title with fresh understanding. If the aim of the poem is to help us see the world in a new way, our experience with the title is a microcosm of that: we see it one way before we read the poem and another way after. In other words, a successful title can't be merely flashy, like a clickbait headline that promises more than the story delivers. The title needs to set a high bar for the poem— and then the poem has to clear that bar with ease.

Too often, young poets fall back on abstractions for their titles: "Grief," "Joy," and so on. This is not a good approach. Often it reveals a conceptual problem with the poem itself: you're taking on too much, trying to explore a vast abstract concept instead of focusing on specific experience, images, details, language. Or sometimes such a title sits atop an otherwise successful poem and completely undersells it. In that case, you just need to rethink your approach to the title.

As with all things, the key to a strong title for your poem is to think rhetorically. What experience are you trying to create for your reader? How does the title help you shape that experience? Also as with all the elements in this book, the key to writing better titles is to read more. The more titles you read, the stronger your sense of what titles can do will become. Let's look at some of the poem titles from this anthology and explore what they teach us about titling strategy:

Title as Mode: Some titles serve as a seemingly plainspoken label of the poem's form or mode. There are sonnets called simply "Sonnet" and sestinas titled "Sestina." In this anthology, you'll find Traci Brimhall's "Ars Poetica" and both Li-Young Lee's and Kiki Petrosino's "Nocturne," among others. There's something almost defiant in the simplicity of these titles, and the poems themselves are far from simple. It's as if the poets use their titles to lure us in with the idea that the world can be so straightforwardly represented, but the poems belie that notion.

Narrative Title: Sometimes the title itself tells a story. Examples include Karyna McGlynn's "I Have to Go Back to 1994 and Kill a Girl," Tarfia Faizullah's "Aubade Ending with the Death of a Mosquito," and Christina Olson's "In Which Christina Imagines That Different Types of Alcohol Are Men and She Is Seeing Them All." In each of these cases, the title does a lot of the narrative heavy lifting for the poem, thus freeing the poem up to be lyrical and evocative. As readers we get the plot, as it were, from the title, while the text of the poem moves more associatively than chronologically.

Title as Topic: Natasha Tretheway's "History Lesson" and Sandra Beasley's "Halloween" are examples of apparently simple titles that provide a brief frame for the poem that follows. They are evidence that a title need not be long or complex to be compelling and evocative. Notice that Beasley never explicitly mentions the holiday in her poem; she doesn't have to, because the title has done this for her.

Title as Evocative Detail or Phrase: Often, a poet chooses a compelling word, detail, or phrase from their poem to use as the title: Maggie Smith's "Good Bones," Anders Carlson-Wee's "Dynamite," and Jamaal May's "The Gun Joke" employ this approach. It's a form of repetition, and doing so calls particular attention to that detail, creating a familiarity when readers encounter that part of the poem and strongly suggesting that the detail in question is doing work on both literal and metaphorical levels.

Title as Necessary to Understanding the Poem: Sometimes the title provides a kind of frame that the poem needs in order to make sense at all. List poems in particular rely in this kind of title: Gabrielle Calvocoressi's "Glass Jaw Sonnet" and Catie Rosemurgy's "Things That Didn't Work" both use the title to establish the connection between the listed items within the poems; without the titles, these poems lose most of their meaning. The same is true of the found poems, ekphrastic poems, and the self-portraits, wherein the title provides important guidance for the reader.

These are not the only titling strategies, obviously. Sometimes the title serves as the first line of the poem, leading right into the text grammatically. Sometimes the title offers a kind of mystery that doesn't make sense until the reader finishes reading the poem. Sometimes the title argues against the poem. Some poets find a title in lines they've cut during the revision process. For many poets, the title comes early in the writing process, perhaps even before the poem itself. For others, titles are most often added very late, after the poem is otherwise complete. When you're in this situation and stuck, try writing twenty-five titles for your poem, each doing some different kind of work. You might not be fully satisfied with any of those twenty-five, but you'll begin to get a sense of the possibilities and of which approach might be most meaningful.

See Also: Beginnings, Value

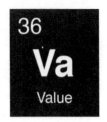

36
Va
Value

Value

In the chapter on revision, we describe the practice of putting each word in a poem on trial for its life. What we mean is that for each word—and each phrase, each image, each line—in your poem, you should be asking: What is the value of this word? What does this phrase, image, or line bring to the poem? What work is it doing?

All words have rhetorical value; that is, they contribute to the overall project of the poem and the particular experience it builds for a reader. To change any single word in a poem is to change that experience, perhaps minimally, perhaps fundamentally. Value can be measured in different ways: mechanical value, ornamental value, or associative value.

Mechanical Value

Mechanical value has to do with what a word or phrase does for the syntax and structure of a poem. Some words we use because they are kind of like syntactical glue holding a sentence together. Articles such as "a" or "the" and conjunctions such as "and" or "but" or "or"—we use these words because they make our sentences easier to read. They have mechanical value. But it's fair to ask what additional value they bring—and could the line or sentence work without them? Or could we change them to increase that value? Consider the difference between, say, "the cow in the field" and "this cow in this field." The words "the" and "this" have the same mechanical value, holding the phrase together, but the word "this" also brings a sense of familiarity and particularity that changes the meaning at least slightly. Different rhetorical value, in other words. You could also consider cutting the articles entirely, changing the phrase to "cow in field," which has a different feel altogether.

In Tony Hoagland's "Jet," the word "wish" in the first line has a mechanical value in that it sets up the structure of the poem, which explores the implications of the wish. And of course, it's doing rhetorical work as well. To open a poem with a wish is to foreground the speaker's yearning: the wistful nostalgia felt for the back porch, the old friends, and the alcohol. You want such doubled value from your language; one way to make your poems concise and precise is to look for places to cut language that does not have this heightened value.

Ornamental Value

Sometimes we want our poems to be pretty. Or ugly. Or harsh, or discordant, strident or subdued, loud and angry, or quiet and mournful. We choose words and images for the ornamental value they bring to a poem: how they sound when read aloud, the mood they establish. Back to "Jet": the sky becomes the river, which becomes an "effervescent gush" all sparkly and fluid, and then in the next stanza, we're watching fireflies light up the grass. The image of the night sky is now superimposed over the grass, and for the reader, part of the pleasure of the poem is the immersion in these images.

Of course, in Hoagland's poem and in any poem, such ornamental moments are not merely decorative. They have rhetorical value as well. Sometimes you'll hear "flowery" used as a criticism of a poem's language, and that's generally a comment on word choices that are more decorative than purposeful. The tulips are beautiful flowers, the sunshine is a pleasant sensation, and the gargoyle's grin is delightfully mischievous. The flowers are on the table at supper time: they look nice, but they might take up room on the table that might be better used as a spot for the gravy boat or the sweet potatoes. Sunshine feels nice, particularly when it's cool out and you are sitting near the window. And that gargoyle perched on the side of the building is better than looking at a blank wall. There is sometimes a tendency in young writers to want to use flowery language and images, but these things can be purely ornamental: if they exist to adorn the poem without adding enough additional value, they don't do enough work. Cut them or find a way to make them more valuable.

When something in a poem connects with the reader in a way that appeals to logos, pathos, and/or ethos, the poem is doing rhetorical work. The parts of the poem are working together toward the goal of the poem's overall rhetorical construction. When the ornamental quality of a thing also does rhetorical work, that's an indicator that there is good, efficient poem-making happening on the page. The tulips on the table hide a hole in the table cloth. The sunshine in the window is a relief after the long Michigan winter. And that gargoyle—it serves as a ward against evil spirits.

As an example of a moment that does both ornamental and rhetorical work, see the long paragraph that Aimee Nezhukumatathil builds in the middle of "One-Star Reviews of the Great Wall of China." It creates a wall in the poem about the wall, but it also does rhythmic work with those long sentences in the middle of so many short ones. Or see the way the lines in Tarfia Faizullah's "Aubade ending with the Death of a Mosquito" get split into two columns; this creates a contrapuntal reading experience—each column can be read as a separate poem, making it three poems in one. It looks cool, and more meaningfully, it also creates three completely different reading experiences for the reader.

Associative Value

Not all value is inherent; sometimes it comes from external associations. A comic book with the first appearance of Superman is worth a ton of money because it is rare and because comic collectors covet it. That boomerang your grandfather carved when he was eleven reminds you of the time he tried to teach you how to whittle and you had to get five stitches in your thumb. That dragon insignia tattooed on your shoulder blade has a Chinese cultural significance rooted in strength and luck. These values are not inherent but associative, having to do with each item's connections to other things in the world.

Likewise, the significance of a piece of language may come from how it connects with other language. Allusions do this overtly, offering specific, intentional references to people, places, or events that tie a poem to the larger world. Craig Santos Perez, for instance, refers to specific places in the world and specific acts of violence that have occurred at those places. As readers, we know that the Yemen and Iraq in the poem are also the Yemen and Iraq in the world we inhabit; these words have important, political associative and rhetorical value.

Words can accrue value from the surrounding material. See, for example, the way the sniper in Jamaal May's "The Gun Joke" takes on the value of fire—the house is on fire and snipers fire guns. Or maybe it's the other way around. We are waiting for gunfire throughout the poem and then when the firefighters appear, they are immediately in opposition to the sniper. This sort of comparative value is recursive, each word adding value to the other—and through that value, each changing the meaning of the other.

A common complaint about associative value you'll hear in workshops about any cultural reference or allusion, whether it's to the myth of Sisyphus or *Hamilton*, the Iran-Contra scandal, or *Call of Duty*, is a reader saying, "It took me out of the poem." However, this is often the point of this kind of allusion. It is deliberately intended to connect the poem to a particular event or figure or concept who also happens to exist outside the poem, whether in the world we all live in or in some other work of art. Some readers will recognize the allusion immediately and be able to engage with all the work it does in the poem. Others will have some familiarity with it, or be moved to go and look it up, and engage on a different level. Still others won't know the reference and won't look it up, which leaves them either to do the best they can to understand the reference based on context clues in the poem or to read around it.

See Also: Concision, Image, Inventory, Metaphor, Movement

37
Vc
Voice

Voice

Find your voice, many young writers are told, but it's not always clear just what that means. It's a metaphor, because the advice-giver does not mean the physical human voice, with its particular range and volume and timbre, but the voice on the page. The task of "finding your voice" can be a daunting one indeed for a beginning writer. Hard to find your voice if you have only a vague sense of what that means in practical terms.

Try this: If you make a Venn diagram featuring circles for diction, syntax, and speaker, voice would be the intersecting area of those circles. The words you choose, the order in which you put them, and the personality of your poem—that's voice.

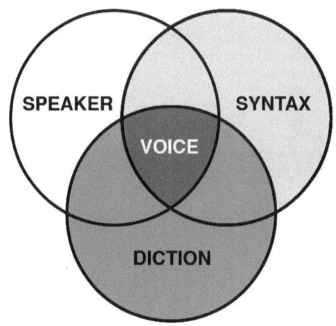

Voice is an important element of poetry, to be sure. But if you're being yourself on the page, it's not something you need to stress out over. Our advice? Don't worry about it. Focus on using language with precision; aim for concision; balance clarity of expression with the ambiguity of the human experience. That's plenty to wrestle with for now. Then worry about finding your voice later—like, much, much later, say after you've written 200 or 2,000 or even 20,000 poems.

In the meantime, pay attention to what voice looks like on the page as you read. First, try to describe the voice of the poem you're reading. Does the speaker come across as confident, wise, happy? Sad, resigned, strong, caring? Uncertain, open-minded, passionate? Then try to pin down specifically what it is in the language that gives you that impression. This is part of being a rhetorically savvy reader, part of reading the way a writer reads.

A voice can be wry and matter-of-fact like Billy Collins's speaker in "Introduction to Poetry." It can be tender and verging on desperate like Solmaz Sharif's letter-writer in the section from "Reaching Guantanamo." But how do these poets render these voices? Collins uses everyday vocabulary and straightforward, declarative sentences of a similar, medium length, combined with almost-silly physical images (dropping a mouse into a poem, waterskiing across its surface). Sharif asks lots of questions and discusses intimate personal details (and the withholding of those details with the redactions only emphasizes their importance).

Subject matter also influences voice. Collins is writing about a teacher's mild frustration with their students; Sharif is writing about the devastating effect of military action on a family relationship. Each of these topics fits exactly into the described voice. That's because voice is a way of getting to know the speaker, and what concerns us, what moves us to write—subject matter, in other words—these are closely connected to who we are and how we choose to express ourselves in the world.

Voice is not some ethereal concept that can't be easily defined; rather, it's simply the cumulative effect of how the various elements of poetry come together on the page. The more you learn to pay attention to these elements as you read and in your own writing, the more confident you will become in manipulating them to good effect in your poems. That's when you'll find your voice.

See Also: Diction, Language, Point of View, Precision, Speaker, Syntax

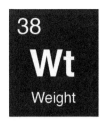

38

Wt

Weight

Weight

This element has to do with the emotional weight a poem has for the reader. When the poet Robert Bly named the six powers of poetry, the aspects he thought crucial for a good poem, he called one of them "psychic weight." In his essay "What the Image Can Do," Bly refers to an "adult grief that makes the poem feel heavy." This requirement that the poem have a heaviness isn't necessarily a prescription that a poem has to be about heartbreak or sorrow or the world's pain. In most contemporary poetry, the poem exhibits weight to some degree, and we can examine weight by talking about its gravity and levity, its heaviness and lightness.

Gravity

As gravity in the real world keeps our feet planted on the earth, gravity in a poem helps the reader feel grounded; the emotional heaviness allows readers to anchor themselves in the poem's content. In poems like "Two Guns in the Sky for Daniel Harris" by Raymond Antrobus, the gravity is right there in front of our noses. This poem centers gun violence and loss from its very title. But not every poem makes its weight so apparent from the outset.

Sometimes a poem seems to have an obvious gravity, but when we look hard at it, we discover a moment in the poem where the gravity becomes distinct and more nuanced—a center of gravity, of sorts. Anders Carlson-Wee's "Dynamite" is a short narrative poem fraught with a violent game played by two brothers. At first, the violence seems to be the poem's gravity, but then that final line drops—the boys do such grievous harm to one another in the game with dynamite, and then that last line tells us that everything is dynamite. The ambiguity of "everything" brings us and our propensity to hurt and be hurt into the game. Layli Long Soldier's "38" is a difficult poem because of the subject matter, which appears to be all the gravity a poem needs to give it weight. But then the poem goes on. And it goes on and it becomes more uncomfortable as it goes on, until it becomes clear that this unending experience is part of the poem's real, more powerful weight. In this sense, we can identify the weight around which the poem moves, or the weight to which the poem cannot help but move toward.

Lightness

Weirdly, a poem's gravity is perhaps most noticeable when it's absent. Poems that lack gravity sometimes lack emotional depth. Some humorous poems deliver a single and sometimes predictable emotional (funny) experience; we call it light verse for a reason—there's no gravity! Light verse is often humorous or cute as it makes rhymes and curtsies with its tongue planted firmly in its cheek. Most limericks are light verse, and so are nursery rhymes and many greeting cards. They are light because they lack gravity—they are emotionally one-dimensional, missing the weight that creates an emotional experience for the reader outside of that which is singular and predictable.

And yet it would be wrongheaded to say that there is no room for lightness in a poem. The converse of heaviness is lightness but what that means is that the poet can control the poem's weight. Gravity is not a constant value as moments of levity can provide a reader with moments of respite in an otherwise heavy poem. Or a bit of humor might emotionally disarm the reader before a bit of heaviness is delivered. Lightness can help create and accentuate gravity in the poem, helping the poet to create weight in the right place and the right degree. Dorothy Chan's "Triple Sonnet for Being a Queer in a Family of Straights," for instance uses an almost flippant tone to explore a quite serious issue: levity and gravity working together.

All of this is different from saying that a poem ought to be primarily about an emotional experience, as writing about emotions can result in melodrama. The poem's weight creates significance through pathos, so the writer has to be careful—if the rhetorical moves to deliver moments of gravity are too overt, the sentiments being evoked with too heavy a hand, the reader might see the rhetorical move more clearly than they feel the emotional response, in which case the poem is likely to fail to deliver because its gravity is a false gravity.

See Also: Mood, Value

Beyond the Elements

8

The Poetry Workshop

If you are enrolled in a poetry-writing class, you'll probably participate in a poetry workshop sooner or later. A workshop is a group conversation during which writers critique one another's work. It's generally a conversation led by the workshop leader, and in most cases, the writer remains quiet and listens to the discussion. It's like a test drive for the poem during which everyone takes it out for a spin and then reports back on how the poem handled in bad weather, how well the poem accelerated on the freeway, and what kinds of funny sounds rattled under the hood at a stoplight. The workshop is a way for writers to come together and explore poems, offering one another encouragement, commiseration, and support through the common language of poetry.

Having your poem workshopped can be a nerve-wracking experience. Sharing your work is already hard, and now people are going to discuss it in front of you. Keep in mind that the workshop is supposed to be helpful, and that feedback is intended as a gift. Also, keep in mind that in your first workshops, the people discussing the poems might themselves still be learning how to respond to writing and poetry. Sometimes workshop participants might lack the experience, knowledge, or background to be able to offer useful feedback for the writer. Some young poets don't have enough confidence in their ability to respond to poems. This lack of confidence can lead to people in the workshop holding back and a quiet room—without much in the way of help for the writer. Here are some things to remember about the workshop, both so you can be prepared to have your poem workshopped and so you can be a good workshopper.

Three Levels of Understanding

If the workshop is to have a conversation about a poem, that means that workshop participants must have read and understand the poem enough to have an intelligent, sustained conversation. The workshop leader will generally keep the conversation moving in a productive direction without too many unhelpful digressions or pointless repetition, but a successful poetry workshop needs everyone involved. You should begin by working to understand each poem on three separate levels.

First Level of Understanding: I Like It / I Don't Like It

The most basic way of reacting to a poem is at the level of whether you like it. Liking or disliking a poem requires little thought about anything other than the self. Maybe you don't like poems about horses or you don't like poems with pop culture references. Maybe you don't like poems at all, in which case you should probably put this book down and go do math problems or something. Deciding that you like or dislike a poem requires little critical thought about the poem itself; in fact, it can be a quick choice made before even one word has been read. The kind of understanding that stops at this level isn't a helpful way of reading a poem for a workshop. It's entirely okay if you don't like a poem for whatever reasons you have for disliking it (not every poem connects with every reader, nor should it need to), but when you're asked to read a poem in a workshop, you have a responsibility to move past your personal preferences and read the poem with care and attention.

Second Level of Understanding: This Is What the Poem Means

Readers are interested in a poem's meaning. If it means nothing, then there isn't much point to reading it, much less talking about it. So naturally, as we read a poem, we try to make meaning out of what the poem offers up—isolating and analyzing symbols, looking for metaphors, connecting the poem to sociopolitical contexts, all in service of trying to figure out what the poem is trying to say to us.

Understanding what a poem means isn't restricted to the ideas it is trying to convey, however. A workshop might also focus on the emotional journey a poem takes, pointing out the moments in the poem that elicit emotional reactions from readers. Or it might investigate the different questions that the poem raises, either explicitly or implicitly. To accomplish this, a reader might make comparisons to other poems, consider the genre if there is one, or even look up words, their origins, and their alternate meanings. All of this is to say that a poem is doing *something* on the page, and this second level of understanding is where the reader can grapple with that something. If we can't discern a poem's meaning or what we think it's trying to do, we might end up talking in circles with nothing specific or important to say about the poem.

This second level of understanding is the general realm of most classes in literature and/or poetry appreciation, where the focus might be more on interpretation than on craft. Interpretation is worth considering in a workshop, to be sure, but consideration of a poem's meaning is a waypoint in the conversation, not the ultimate destination.

Third Level of Understanding:
This Is How the Poem Has Been Built

Once you have an idea of what a poem means or what it is trying to do, you can start thinking about the third level of meaning: how the poem works. The elements of poetry in this book provide the writer with an idea of the many different tools and building blocks for crafting a poem, and they also offer the reader a way of thinking about the choices the writer has made. It's these choices in syntax, diction, concrete imagery, sound, and so forth that are at the heart of a creative writing workshop as the group talks about how the poem accomplishes what it does. How do the images in "Self-Portrait as Mae West One-Liner" by Paisley Rekdal create a different emotional response in each line of the poem? How does sentence structure in "Aubade Ending with the Death of a Mosquito" by Tarfia Faizullah interact with the contrapuntal structure? How does the length of "Rape Joke" by Patricia Lockwood serve to enhance and complicate the poem's emotional effects? If you can't get past the first and second levels of understanding, any conversation you have about a poem will likely be limited in what it can accomplish. If you can enter a workshop conversation with an eye toward a writer's choices and how those choices shape the readers' understanding of and experience with a poem, that conversation becomes more useful for you and everyone involved.

The Two Conversations

In almost every workshop, there are two conversations happening simultaneously, the first being for the writer of the poem being discussed. The primary goal of this first conversation is to help the writer understand how a particular poem is working and how to revise it into a better poem. The group focuses its attention on the text, not the writer. The individual reactions of the workshop participants are intended to be helpful to the writer in terms of isolating problems, offering different readings, and generating possible ideas for revision. Additionally, the workshop leader usually offers commentary and criticism to help move the conversation into the places it needs to go so that the writer can get the best feedback possible to consider in that poem's revision—and, importantly, beyond, as they work on their future poems

Some young poets make the mistake of assuming that there is nothing for them to learn unless their poem is on the table. You don't have a poem being workshopped—why even show up, right? But a workshop meeting is not just an advice-giving session about one poem—it's a learning experience for everyone in the room as new knowledge is created through the exchange of ideas. There is a second conversation happening concurrently with the first as the group formulates ideas not just about how the poem being workshopped works, but about how poetry works. Sometimes, people are actually thinking about their own poems, using the poem being workshopped as a kind of sounding board against which they test their discoveries, which can feel disrespectful to the poets whose work is on the table. Being conscious of this mechanism, the way that the workshop sometimes talks about a poem as a way about talking about other things, can help everyone understand what is happening and give the poet and poem its due respect while being able to explore what there is to learn about poetry and other poems.

These two conversations—one for the writer and one for the room—work in tandem to create a rich, complex learning experience for all participants. Getting feedback on your poem can be a way of understanding your poems outside of what you dreamed up on the page. Learning how to respond to a poem is an important part of your development as a poet who strives to grow a deep relationship with poetry.

About the "Gag Rule"

Traditionally, the workshop operates under the "gag rule." The authors of this book aren't necessarily huge fans of the gag rule, either as a metaphor (it's awful!) or as an absolute practice. What it means is that, in many workshops, the writer is required to remain silent while the group talks about their poem.

There are valid reasons for this approach. When the writer is a silent participant, it allows them to observe the conversation that surrounds the poem, taking notes about what was said in order to have a record for later. The group has a conversation about what the poem is saying, or what it's trying to say, and the writer gets the chance to see how the conversation aligns with their writerly intentions.

In addition, the silent writer feels less pressure to defend the poem. While ideally there should be nothing to defend because the conversation shouldn't be an attack, sometimes as the conversation unfolds, the writer notices things they wish they could change or feels embarrassed about something in the draft. If the writer is allowed to interject apologies, explanations, or disclaimers into the workshop, they can disrupt the exchange of ideas and possibly obstruct the conversation for the room before it has a chance to develop.

However, there are also good reasons that some workshops might choose to do away with this rule. Sometimes the workshop leader might want to open the discussion with questions from the poet. Or the poet might begin by describing their writing process and what they hope the poem achieves. In this way, what the poet wants becomes a frame for the conversation, making the feedback more likely useful to them. But note that this example could privilege the conversation for the writer over the conversation for the room. If the writer fully sets the parameters for the discussion, the conversation might not develop naturally, and it might keep the discussion focused on micro-level issues having to do with a particular line or phrase and less about more substantive macro-level issues.

Silencing the writer can become problematic, too, when the workshop is not a homogeneous group. When the workshop is made up of people from varied backgrounds, people of different races, cultures, gender identities, sexualities, social classes, and so forth, the conversation can become one in which the group tries to isolate problems in a poem rooted in experiences they may know nothing about. And let's face it: the workshop is rarely a homogeneous group, nor would you want it to be in most cases.

The problem is exacerbated when most of a class is from a similar demographic and a few writers bring a different perspective and lived experience than the majority of their classmates. If a young poet is the only Japanese American in the workshop and he brings in a poem about the internment of American citizens during the Second World War, the workshop might read it and know nothing about this. Someone says "teach me more about the historical event." Someone else says "try to make the food more exotic and Japanese." Someone says, "take out the Japanese words because I don't understand them." A silenced writer would be unable to tell the workshop that the poem is not a history lesson, that Japanese food is not exotic, and that the Japanese words are the words of his grandfather who refused to speak English after the war. In this scenario and cases like it, the so-called gag rule interferes with both conversations, preventing the writer from getting the feedback they want and the room from delving deeper into a conversation about a poem from an unfamiliar viewpoint.

The goal of a healthy, productive workshop should be to balance the two conversations. Give the poet room to share their hopes and dreams for their poem and to ask questions about readers' experiences with their words; at the same time, let those readers' experiences guide a conversation about how the poem works on the page. Regardless of how a particular workshop leader wants to proceed, it's up to that leader and everyone in the room to decide on ground rules to ensure that both conversations—for the poet and for the room—receive the appropriate attention.

Tips for a Good Workshop

A poetry workshop is a collaborative activity that depends on the willingness and generosity of the people in the room to work. The workshop leader should frame the discussion with care and best practices, and then it's up to the group to create an environment in which a conversation about poetry can be good for the writer as well as the room. Here are some tips to help you make your workshop the best it can be.

Make the Workshop a Safe Space

Being part of a workshop means that you have entered into a community that values safety, both in terms of being a writer and a reader. A young poet has to believe that their work is safe in the hands of the workshop, that no one will needlessly tear it down, and that no one in the room is judging their talent as writers or their worth as human beings. Similarly, each member of the group has to feel as though their contributions to the conversation are welcome and respected even if they are viewpoints with which some might disagree. Writers need this kind of safety in order to feel free to unashamedly write the poems they want to write. The group needs this kind of safety so they can respond critically without being afraid of hurting someone's feelings. Safety comes from trust, so as you workshop, consider the different ways in which you and your peers might work to inspire trust in one another.

Be Nice

This should be obvious. Most people don't engage in creative writing to make enemies. It's a lot more fun to make friends. At the least, you should want to avoid hurting anyone's feelings. Remember that you are engaged with another person's hard work, and being overly critical doesn't help the conversation reach the writer. Some people claim to be straight shooters, throwing out harsh comments in the name of "calling it like they see it." Really, those people are just jerks. Don't be a jerk. It's good advice in life, and it's good advice in your poetry workshop.

Be Forgiving

We have all said things before that we wish we could take back. Maybe it was a joke that didn't land right or a statement that sounded more harsh than intended. Even if the workshop is safe, someone might say something that comes across as cruel. If it happens over and over, maybe there is a pattern of behavior that needs to be addressed. However, more often than not, people don't say things in workshop with the intent of being hurtful. It's better for the workshop to try to forgive people when they misspeak rather than hold a grudge and try to take revenge when it comes time to workshop that other person's poems.

This means taking criticism in the way that it is generally intended. The things people say about poems in workshop are aimed at helping the writer understand the different ways the poem engages with readers. Workshop is meant to be helpful and supportive, so when your work is being covered in class, try to accept the feedback as such. Keep in mind that like you, your classmates are doing the best they can to make sense of poetry, both as readers and as poets. A comment that strikes the wrong note is more likely to come from a place of inexperience than a place of malice.

Be Generous with Your Critique

Being nice is good for the workshop atmosphere, but it's just as important that the writer understands how the poem is working for readers. Generosity means assuming that the writer did the best they could with the draft in front of you—and that they have the talent and drive to make it better with revision. Generosity means pointing out the strengths of a poem as well as areas that might offer opportunities for improvement. Generosity means reading the poem carefully, more than once, and being willing to think about the poem in specific terms, using the elements of poetry as a foundation for commentary. Don't be afraid to dig into someone else's poems and grapple with the different ways they work on the page or in the air; consider how the text creates meaning and how reading it aloud generates music and rhythm. You respond to your classmates' poems with generosity because it makes you a better, more thoughtful reader and a valuable member of the workshop community—and also because the workshop will respond in kind when it's time to look at your poems.

Try to Read the Poem on Its Own Terms

It's tough to step outside of your opinion about the things you like and dislike in the world. If I don't like poems about professional wrestling, then it might be difficult to read a poem about Hulk Hogan without flinching. Or if I don't know anything about contemporary pop music, I might have to work pretty hard to figure out how to respond to a poem that relies on Beyoncé lyrics. But as poetry workshop participants, the benchmark isn't whether or not we like the poem.

Taking this one step further, when you encounter a poem outside your own worldview or experiences, it's important that you don't try to force it to conform to your own worldview. A poem by a young man who has recently come out as gay to his parents or a poem by a young woman from Mexico using Spanish language and slang offer up experiences that might not be immediately accessible to straight, white audiences. The easy route here is to ask the poems to conform to the "normal" standard set by the workshop, which could be detrimental to the poem and frustrating for the writers—it devalues the writers' experiences and disrespects the work they have done to bring the poem to the group.

Instead, consider this question: What is the poem trying to do? Only after understanding the answer to that question can we ask the follow up: How might the poem do what it's trying to do better than it is now?

Describe the Poem instead of Prescribing a Fix

The workshop metaphor implies that the task at hand is to "fix" a poem, the way you'd repair a broken lawnmower engine in a real-world workshop. There are a couple of problems with this approach. It's not that you shouldn't have an opinion about what should be done to a poem—in fact, when you encounter poems in workshop that don't seem to be quite working like they should, you should be thinking about how you might proceed if it was your poem because that's one of the ways we learn how to write poems.

But in a workshop, it's not your poem to rewrite in your voice with your vision and aesthetic. The poem belongs to its writer, and the writer alone gets to decide what happens in the revision process. By simply prescribing fixes to a poem, you imply that (a) there is something wrong with the poem and (b) that "something" is a problem that can be solved like changing the air filter in your car or checking the dictionary for a spelling error. This turns the conversation into a troubleshooting session that is more about telling the writer what to do rather than engaging with the poem.

If, however, the members of a workshop can root their discussion in describing how they perceive the poem and what they think it's trying to do, then the writer gets a better idea of how the poem is being read by the people in the workshop. As different readings emerge in discussion, the writer can start to formulate possibilities for themselves. Note that this doesn't mean that you can't offer suggestions as to how you might see the poem's revision going, but it's important that this kind of thing is rooted in being a conversation about possibilities for the poem's bright future rather than diagnosis and corrective surgery. Workshop readers don't get to make demands of the poet or to say definitively what a poem "needs" in order to succeed.

Listen and Take Notes

The writer should try to avoid becoming defensive during the conversation about their poem. There might be an instinctual need to rise up from the chair to defend one's artistic vision, but that isn't helpful. The poem has to go out into the world and live on its own without its writer to stick up for it and explain its brilliance. So think of workshop as a test of how well the poem can live on its own, and instead of arguing with your workshop, take notes about what they say so you can remember the conversation later. Take notes about the positive things people say as well as the negative or constructive suggestions. We all tend to forget the positive feedback, but we need to know what we have done to good effect as well as what we could do better.

You might even want to take notes when it's not your poem being workshopped. By doing so, you'll be using the workshop conversation to make yourself a better reader, both of your own work and the work of others. Write down everything. You never know what will be helpful to you when you begin to revise.

Give Praise

There's an unfortunate tendency to think of honest feedback as being "brutally honest," but giving someone feedback on a poem is more than calling out what isn't working. Make it a point to highlight the moments in a poem that you found most engaging, elements you saw that you'd like to see more of, and lines that you found yourself thinking about later. Not only does this make it easier for the writer to receive criticism, but it's also part of trying to understand what the poem is trying to do and talking about how it goes about trying to achieve its goals.

Write on Other People's Poems

Don't be afraid to write on the hard copy of someone's poems, assuming it's allowed in your particular workshop context. Making marginal notes can be part of being an active, engaged reader. Where are you confused about the poem's meaning? Where does the poem make you feel some kind of emotional response? What suggestions do you have about things like line breaks, image, or metaphor? This kind of marginalia can help you remember what your experience was like the first time you read the poem, as well as what you wanted to say to the writer at that moment, and it can help the writer understand how the poem is affecting its readers.

Remember That the Poem Is a Draft

In order to write a good poem, sometimes a writer has to start by writing a truly awful draft. If a poem seems as if it's appropriating another culture, as if it's being disrespectful to people of color, or as if it's too grounded in the male gaze, then the workshop should cover those things. If the poem's metaphor is askew or if the language is overwrought, or if there is embarrassingly too much sex, then the workshop can explore those things, too. Ideally the writer will sense such missteps on their own and change course before the poem makes it to workshop. The important thing to remember is that the poem is a draft and a young poet needs to be allowed to make mistakes in drafts in order to learn how to circumvent them in the future.

These poems are drafts. Sometimes that means they don't work. A young poet isn't a terrible poet or person because she brings hastily done drafts to class for workshop. She is no less talented or skillful than anyone else in the room—instead, think of her simply as a young poet who brings some rough drafts to workshop and wants to make those poems better. The job of the workshop is to help the poet become aware of how their poems land in the world so that they can learn from that in future poems.

Processing Workshop Feedback

After a workshop, you will have lots of stuff to look at. There might be notes from each person in the workshop, copies of your poem with marginalia, and likely some kind of feedback from the workshop leader. There will be so many opinions and comments from your peers that it can become overwhelming. As you look at your materials post workshop, consider the following tips.

Don't Simply Look for Consensus

One of the things that frustrate young poets after a workshop is the multitude of voices offering feedback, all those people talking and none of them agreeing on what is best for the poem. It's okay if the advice you receive is in conflict with itself. The goal of a workshop isn't necessarily to reach consensus about how the poem works, and you are probably going to find lots of conflicting opinions afterward. If everyone agrees that the end rhymes are distracting from the imagery in the poem, that might be something you should look at. But a workshop is not an election in which the opinion receiving the most votes determines what you do with your poem. To look for consensus above all else is to turn the complex and nuanced conversations of the workshop into a search for poems that appeal to a lowest common denominator, and that's not helpful to anyone.

Filter the Workshop's Voices

Part of being in a workshop is learning who you want to listen to in terms of taking advice about writing poems. The worst thing you could do is go through all the advice your workshop has given you and try to incorporate every single thing each member of the group has said. This doesn't mean that you should just look for voices that you agree with or voices that confirm what you are already thinking about the poem. Instead, think about the voices in the workshop that you trust, the voices who are the most thoughtful in conversation, and try to listen to those voices first.

Look Past the Advice

You're going to get a ton of advice in workshop. Some of it will be tweaks to language, and some of it will suggest changes that might alter the identity of the poem as you understand it. Don't just take advice blindly. Think about who gave the advice and why taking that advice is the best thing for the poem.

Most importantly, think about why the advice was given. Advice is given in reaction to a problem perceived by the reader, so it's important that you think about what that problem might be. If someone is suggesting that you could cut the third stanza of your poem because it repeats information from stanza two, but you think it's doing some other work entirely, the real problem might be that your language lacks precision. Understanding what someone saw as a problem in your poem might help you understand whether the advice is helpful to your vision of the poem. Knowing the problem might even lead you to an easier solution than the workshop suggested. Or you might decide that the problem isn't actually a problem at all.

Get Some Distance

You don't have to leave a workshop inspired to immediately get to work revising your poem. Sometimes, sure, you're fired up and ready to go. But it's sometimes helpful to put the poem away for a bit before trying to revise. A week, two weeks, a few months, a year: this is why it can be important to take notes during workshop so you have a record of what was said and how the conversation went. With distance, sometimes you can get some clarity on how people were responding to your poem and you can more objectively consider what the workshop comments mean for you in the revision process.

Coping with an Unsuccessful Workshop

One day, you might have a workshop that isn't satisfying. Maybe the workshop focused too much attention on one thing and the conversation was repetitive. Maybe the workshop got off topic and the group spent time debating something other than your poem. There are lots of reasons that a workshop can feel like it was unsuccessful, and usually the best thing you can do is talk to your workshop leader.

The workshop leader might not be aware that you are feeling like the workshop didn't go well, at which point it might be helpful to talk to that person and voice your feelings. Generally, a workshop leader wants to know when participants feel like their workshops weren't useful and will want to do what is needed to get the workshop working for you and the rest of the group.

If you are nervous about approaching your workshop leader, take another workshop member with you for moral support and to corroborate your feelings. You don't have to storm into the room and gang up on the workshop leader—in fact, never gang up on anyone because it puts them into a defensive position and you won't find your audience receptive to what you have to say. Workshop leaders want the workshop to be a positive experience for everyone involved, and if you talk to them about your negative experiences, they will generally want to talk you through your problems and get the workshop back on track.

Or if you feel like the workshop isn't working for you and your poems, it might be that you are in the wrong workshop with the wrong people. This is a problem if, say, you're enrolled in a semester-long college course with nothing to but grin and bear it for 16 weeks. In this case, you need to focus on what you can do to get something valuable from the experience. Focus on being a better reader of other people's work. Focus on writing the poems you want to write despite the workshop's feedback. And continue to listen. Don't shut off the possibility that some of the feedback can be meaningful, even if much of it is not.

Thoughtful, active workshop participation will help you become a stronger reader of other people's poems. Being a stronger reader in turn makes you a stronger writer. You become more aware of how language works, and you gain a keener sense of the effects various rhetorical elements have on readers. The more poems you read, the more you understand what a finished poem looks like—and what a poem looks like when it has rough edges that perhaps still need smoothing. These new ways of seeing poems are things you then take back to your own poems. When you can begin to anticipate what your classmates are going to say about your poems, that's an indicator that you have begun to hone your awareness of audience—and how your poems will interact with readers once you send them out into the world.

9

Revision

One of the most common questions young poets have about writing poems: How do you know when a poem is done?

The flippant answer is also, in this case, the true answer: you don't.

It's possible to revise and revise a poem and never be sure when you've reached the right place to stop. Indeed, it's possible to make a poem worse by revising it. It's also true that some poems come out pretty darn close to right the first time. Such poems are rarer than we'd like and should be considered gifts from the Muses (or, at least, a reward for all the hard work you've done wrestling with poems that refused to cooperate). For most poems, revision is going to be an essential stage in the process.

The trick is that when a poem is finished, it appears inevitable. On the page, the poem looks to its readers as though it must have emerged fully formed from its maker, like Athena sprung from Zeus' skull. This is the point. This is what you're working toward. That appearance of effortlessness. The cliché about not wanting to know how the sausage is made applies here; the reader doesn't need to know about the effort it took for a poet to get the words in their final order.

But effort is required. Revision is very much part of the deal. With rare exceptions, the poems that look inevitable on the page arrived in that place only after passing through numerous revisions. In her book on writing, *Bird by Bird*, Anne Lamott famously describes the "shitty first drafts" a writer must create in order to get to stronger, more polished writing:

> The first draft is the child's draft, where you let it all pour out and then let it romp all over the place, knowing that no one is going to see it and that you can shape it later. You just let this childlike part of you channel whatever voices and visions come through and onto the page. [. . .] Just get it all down on paper, because there may be something great in those six crazy pages that you never would have gotten to by more rational, grown up means.

For the young poet, this should be a freeing concept: not only is it permissible for our first drafts to be crude or confused or subpar, it's practically required.

Remember that your favorite writers write junk, too. Many of your favorite poems probably started as incoherent, half-formed thoughts.

Revision = Re + Vision

The question, then, is how does one get from here to there? How do you transform your initial pile of words into the poem you want them to be? The first step toward a successful revision process is being able to turn fresh eyes on the initial draft: to re-vision, in other words.

Once upon a time, Albert Einstein famously said, "the significant problems we have cannot be solved at the same level of thinking with which we created them." In a similar vein, the poet Mary Oliver writes in *The Poetry Handbook*:

> One of the difficult tasks of rewriting is to separate yourself sufficiently from the origins of the poem—your own personal connections to it. Without this separation, it is hard for the writer to judge whether the written piece has all the information it needs—the details, after all, are so vivid in your mind.

It can feel impossible to figure out how to look at the poem with fresh eyes, to achieve Einstein's new level of thinking so that you can find the new poem in the old one. But much as writing a poem in the first place is an act of seeing the world in a new way, the revision process requires being willing to see the poem itself in a new way, being willing to see the first draft as raw material with which to work.

The revision process can be—should be, even must be—every bit as imaginative and playful as the process of creating the original draft. The same sorts of invention activities that we use to get started on a poem belong in the revision process as well. It's essential not to think of revising only as editing: tweaking a word or two here or there, adjusting a few line breaks or punctuation marks. The revision process can and should be far more immersive than that, at least as focused on the big picture of the poem as on the small-picture details.

Copy editing and proofreading can be done all along, and are essential to the process; a poem with typos or even small errors in grammar or word choice is sunk. But making micro-level changes is decidedly not the beginning and ending of revision.

Letting Go Is the Hardest Part

We all get unreasonably attached to our first drafts. Once we've written something down, changing it is hard. There's a reason William Faulkner said that writers must be able to "kill your darlings." Often it is our favorite line or phrase that most needs to be done away with, or it is the piece of the poem that was its initial catalyst.

The challenge is in letting go, not only of the shape and content of the first draft on the page, but also of the initial impulse that got you started on the poem. The poem you wanted to write, the poem you thought you were writing, the mindset you had while writing—it might no longer matter. What matters is the material on the page. You have to learn to listen to the language, to let it go where it wants to, even if it's not where you first thought you'd end up. In fact, especially then. A poem that achieves exactly what you first set out to achieve, says exactly what you wanted to say—well, that's often a poem that fails. It's said that the end of a poem must be both inevitable and surprising, and "both" is the key word there. One without the other is lost. A poem that knows where it's going and heads there directly, as if with blinders on the whole way, is sure to fail.

William Wordsworth's oft-quoted definition of poetry as "the spontaneous overflow of powerful feeling" does us no favors when excerpted this way. Young poets who are resistant to revision lament the loss of that spontaneity and protest that revising a poem takes away something magical that can happen only in a first draft. But Wordsworth continues, positing that a poem "takes its origin from emotion recollected in tranquility" and that writing a poem requires a poet to "think long and deeply" in order to make sense of those powerful feelings. In other words, a poem must capture that spontaneous magic, but it must additionally temper that spontaneity with the kind of reflection that happens later, during the revision process. What you thought the poem was no longer matters. Your revising self owes your drafting self nothing; your focus must be on the poem in front of you and not on what you now think you probably meant when you first sat down. It's okay if the poem changes. It's okay if the poem ends up being something you never intended to write. In fact, it's probably inevitable.

Revision is work, and hard work at that. It's also where the magic happens. So don't let our natural aversion to work dissuade you from engaging in the process, and don't let fidelity to your original ideas become an excuse for not pushing your poem as far as you can push it.

Revising the Almost-Good-Enough Poem

Sometimes you know your first draft is junk. Maybe you had to write the poem in the twenty-five minutes before it was due in class. Maybe you were distracted by a fight with your roommate or a call from your mother or a midterm chemistry exam and simply weren't in a good place to write poetry. Those first drafts are usually pretty easy to let go of, and the revision process is pretty easy to jump into—really, it's just continuing what you started.

What we're talking about here are the harder ones to take on. The poem that is pretty solid. Maybe even good, or at least almost good. Maybe even good enough to earn an A in class. And yet maybe not great. Maybe not fully the poem it should be. This is when letting go of that initial draft is the hardest, when entering the revision process can be the most daunting.

Often, our resistance to revision is about fear. Fear that we're not capable of making the poem any better. Fear that we'll do a lot of work and the poem still won't be great. So, yes, revision requires a certain amount of courage. Willingness to fail and to flail about in the poem for a while. Willingness to plow ahead even if you're not sure what the result will be. It also requires a kind of faith in yourself as a writer, a trust that you are in fact good enough to get the poem where it needs to be eventually. Even if you feel you haven't yet earned that faith at this early stage of your writing career, have faith in the process. Trust that revision works.

And don't settle. Don't settle for almost good, or good enough. Don't settle for a poem that will get you an A. Making an A in a poetry class isn't all that hard. You know what's hard? Writing a poem that will change the way someone else sees the world. That's what you should be aiming for.

Save Your Drafts

One of the great things about writing poems in the twenty-first century is the ease technology brings to revision. Want to see how your poem looks as a prose poem? A tall, skinny poem with three-word lines? A contrapuntal poem? You can try any of them, try all of them with a few clicks on your keyboard. You can print out every version and compare them. Now imagine how challenging that would be on, say, a typewriter, if you had to type out each version one at a time? Or rewrite them all by hand with your giant feather-tipped quill, working by candlelight?

Changing your poems on the fly with Microsoft Word or some other word-processing software is exceedingly simple. This simplicity, though, should not be considered a substitute for careful consideration—Wordsworth's deep thought. Just because you can make a poem contrapuntal by hitting tab every so often doesn't mean it's right for the poem. You still need to think about the relationship between form and content, the connections or deliberate disconnections between the shape of the poem on the page and the words it's employing.

Some poets still handwrite their initial drafts and then move to a computer for revising and finalizing. Others compose on the computer from the beginning. Some poets draft in notebooks, either collecting lines and fragments, or writing out near-complete drafts. Young poets should try each way to figure out what works for them. Writing a poem out by hand creates an entirely different relationship with your words than does typing them into a blank document. Even if you're more comfortable composing on the computer directly, consider handwriting drafts at some point in the process. Something about making your body physically involved in the process of creating the poem can trigger some new way of considering the poem. Composing directly on a computer blurs the line between writing and revising, as you're continually backspacing, changing, deleting, cutting, and pasting. Writing a poem out by hand is more linear, more one stage at a time. Either way has its costs and benefits.

One other thing technology offers that's an incredible boon to the poet: the ability to save every draft. You should save and save often. If you find yourself taking out a line that you rather like but no longer need in the current poem, save it somewhere. Create a file just for such murdered darlings, and then when you're stuck on the next poem, you'll have a file full of potential starting places.

In addition, for the young poet who does not want to revise a piece they've become attached to in its initial form, this is a great way to free yourself: save the original draft. Tell yourself this new document doesn't matter; you're just playing. You'll know that the original draft is back there, safe and sound in its own file and that nothing you do now can affect it. That frees you up to play, to dabble, to pull apart and reassemble, all with impunity. With such freedom from the worry that you'll somehow harm the original poem, you will quite often find that you like where you end up.

Read to Revise

As with starting your poems, reading can often be an essential part of the revision process. In fact, you can deliberately make it so by using successful poems as your own troubleshooting guide. All the challenges we face as we revise poems have been faced by other poets, and we can learn from how they navigated the hurdles. Stuck on the last line of your poem? Read the ending of every single poem in this book, and you'll see dozens of possibilities for how to end a poem. Want to end on an image, a question, a philosophical comment? Look for poems that do so and figure out how they made it work. The same process can help with first lines, line breaks, formal structures, thematic considerations. This kind of purposeful reading can be superproductive. It leads you to see all previously existing poems as models, as examples of how poems work.

Reading before you begin revising can also help you get into the right frame of mind for the work. Even reading poems that are nothing like your own, or nothing like the one currently in front of you, can remind you of what poems can do, what they can be, what effect they have on a reader. If you often find yourself sitting down at your appointed revision time but simply staring at your drafts, unable to get started, consider starting each revision session by reading for ten minutes. Read poems that are old favorites or poems that are new to you. Read poems you love or poems that challenge you. This is a great way to transition from "life mode" to "poet mode," from the self that's thinking about what's for dinner or the cable bill or what's going on next weekend to the self that's ready to buckle down and make art.

Revision Techniques and Exercises

Revising is hard work, and every poem you write will require you employ different strategies for revision because they are different poems with different structures and different goals. There isn't a universal system for doing revision, and you shouldn't trust anyone who insists that there is—but here are some activities that might help you get out of that same old level of thinking you used to draft your poems so you can get down to some serious revision.

- **Distance:** Give yourself some space from your poems. Often, the revision process—and that letting go—demands a fresh perspective. If you're struggling with a poem, put it away for a while. A week, a month, six months. Longer, if necessary. When you come back to it, you'll be a different person, and it will be easier to turn an objective eye on what isn't working, what could be stronger. (Note that when you're writing a poem in the context of a class, this isn't always possible. End-of-semester deadlines are sure to get in the way. Nonetheless, at the least consider this a call to avoid procrastination; the earlier you write your poems, the more time you'll have to work on them—or to set them aside before returning to them with clear eyes.)

- **Immersion:** This is the exact opposite of the previous technique! Print a copy of your poem and carry it around with you so that you can pull it out and read it whenever you get a free moment. Post a copy over your desk. Use a copy as the bookmark for the novel you're reading. Just as when you read the same word over and over, it can begin to appear so strange it doesn't even seem like a real word anymore, so too can your poem begin to feel strange through this intense contact. As you spend more time with your poem, your relationship with it will evolve in unexpected ways and you will begin to see new possibilities.

- **Inversion:** If you're not sure what to do with a poem, try rewriting it in reverse order: that is, last line first, next-to-last line second, and so on, ending with what had been the opening line. A couple effects are sure to result: First, you'll find grammatical and syntactical oddities in the new ways the lines connect. Some will be nonsensical, but others might be compelling and offer new insight into how your words are working together. Second, your poem will take on a new kind of logic. No longer will the story proceed from beginning to end, or the argument from premise to conclusion. Inverting the order of things can lead you to surprising new connections between ideas and images. That surprise is what you're after. If inverting doesn't get you where you want, try printing out the lines, cutting them apart, and then shuffling them into random new orders. The point here is not that turning a poem upside down or inside out will magically lead to a new, finished piece of writing, but that it will help free you from your original intentions; that it will help spark some new way of seeing the language and the ideas.

- **Write between the Lines:** On your word processor, put an extra return between each line of your poem—then write new lines that fit into those spaces. Focus less on stretching out these new lines to fit grammatically and more on making new thematic or narrative or imagistic connections between the original lines. The point is not to end up with a bloated, wordier version of the original poem, but to stretch your conception of the poem into something new.

- **Cut It in Half:** Try writing the exact same poem in half the number of lines. What is lost? Was it necessary? Maybe it was; if so, put it back in. At least now you know you need it, right? Trying to cut a poem by more than half. What happens when you try to take out 70 percent of the words? That's the aim here: Try stuff and see what happens. You'll learn something about your poem every time you do.

- **Poke for Soft Spots:** This one is essential for any revision process. You know how when you go for a dental examination, the dentist or the hygienist takes one of those pointy instruments and jabs it into each tooth one at a time, checking for soft spots? You need to do the same thing with each word in your poem. Check for abstractions that should be replaced with concrete, specific images. Check for clichés that should be excised entirely. Check for words you've unintentionally used more than once. Check for expected moves or familiar phrasings—if your frog hops, could he slide or pulse or plod instead? If you find yourself using phrases you've read or heard before, rewrite them into something more original.

- **Read to Yourself:** Read your poems aloud to yourself. Listen for words that don't sound right next to each other. Pay attention to places where you stumble; that's often a sign the line or phrase isn't quite right yet. Do this often, with every draft.

- **Read to Someone Else:** Find someone willing to listen to you. It doesn't have to be a fellow poet; sometimes it's better if it's not. Ask what they heard, what they noticed as you read, places where their attention waned, places where they were most engaged. Ask where you sounded most confident.

- **Have Someone Else Read It to You:** Give your poem to a friend so you can listen to your words in someone else's mouth. Listen for moments that don't sound like you think they should, or moments where your friend's voice falters or stumbles—take a look at these areas for possible revision.

- **Write It from Memory:** After you've been working on a poem for a while, try rewriting it from memory. It's best to do this when it has been at least a couple of days since you've looked at the poem. Then compare the two versions. Which parts match between the two versions? Which phrases are better in the original? Which came out better in the new version? If you forgot some parts, ask yourself why. Are they necessary? Or did their omission hurt the poem?

- **Write as Someone Else:** Ask yourself: "How would _____ revise this poem?" It would be quite a different poem if Maggie Smith wrote it than if Layli Long Soldier did, right? So pick a poet and try to channel their voice, their vision, their sense of form. Rewrite your poem through that lens. Try doing this with multiple poets; try it with both Maggie Smith and Layli Long Soldier. In the end, you'll have to make the poem your own, written in your voice and capturing your particular vision of the world, but trying on someone else's point of view for a while can teach you a lot about your own.

- **Stretch to Fit:** Similar to trying out another poet's voice, it can also be fruitful to stretch your poem over the framework of another poem. Try writing it, say, in the split lines of Karyna McGlynn's "I Have to Go Back to 1994 and Kill a Girl"; that would force you to pay attention to those places where the form places emphasis. Alternatively, reimagine your poem in a series of narrow couplets or a numbered list. Any of these forms would draw attention to different components of your poem, asking your language to fit into new molds. Just as imitation can be inventive, can be a starting place for writing poem, it can also be a valuable part of the revision process.

No one of these revision techniques or exercises should be expected to be a magic pill that you can swallow and wake up with a new, perfect poem. You might try several of them with any given draft before hitting on the right one. Sometimes, no exercise will yield the result you're seeking, and the poem will need to be revised painstakingly, a word or phrase or line at a time. Sometimes revision will lead to an entirely new poem, which is its own kind of magic when it happens, but that original draft will still be there, waiting for you when you're done.

There is no one-size-fits-all approach to revision, just as there is no one-size-fits-all poem. The key is to remain inventive, imaginative, playful. Be willing to do the work that the poem demands. Accept the false starts and dead ends as inevitable parts of the process.

Back to the question that opened this chapter: How do you know when a poem is done? The answer comes from knowing that you've invested yourself fully in it; that you have explored and exhausted as many possibilities for the poem as you can imagine; that you have read enough poems and written enough poems to recognize a poem when you see it.

10

Proceed with Caution

There are so many ways a poem can go wrong, just as there are so many ways cooking a meal, building a deck, and going on a first date can go wrong. It's okay when a poem goes wrong, but it's sometimes a good idea to understand where the pitfalls are ahead of time. No one wants to discover they have cooked a meal that is just a dry piece of leathery meat. No one wants to be the dude who built the deck made entirely of cheap lumber that is falling apart after a single winter. No one wants to be the person who took someone on a first date that ended alone at the Burger King drive-through at 7:30 p.m.

So here are some poems for you to beware of.

The Poem That Is a Tricky Riddle

There was that time in tenth grade when your English teacher dropped a bunch of Emily Dickinson poems on your desk and said, "Figure these out—good luck!" Sure, poems are mysterious. But what you're trying to do is to create an emotional or thought-provoking experience for the reader, and an impossible guessing game isn't a particularly satisfying or rich experience. It might be fun to tease the reader with clues as to what the poem is about: the sound of a traffic jam in the sky, a snowy gust across the lawn, the fading sunlight to the right—oh, the poem is about geese flying south for the winter! Maybe it's clever, maybe it's not, but in choosing to focus on creating a riddle for the reader, the young poet might miss the opportunity to write a poem that says something interesting or complex or original about migrating birds. Shoot for clarity and honesty. Otherwise, the poem is driven solely by the reader's need to figure out what it's about—and once the riddle is solved, the reader will be done with the poem forever

The Poem with the Surprise Ending

Oh, it's from the dog's point of view! Oh, the speaker has been dead all along! It's the easiest thing in the world to change the rules at the end of the poem, or to withhold some key bit of information until the dramatic reveal, but that's not fair to the reader—imagine if you were watching a detective movie and at the end, everyone but our hero takes off their masks to reveal that everyone is a robot. Or a romantic comedy that ends with a twist: Mr. Right is a serial killer and the whole movie has just been a plot to lure our girl into his trap. It's also not a good idea. A poem needs an element of surprise, but not to the point that the poem is dishonest and tricks the reader. Poems that over-rely on a big twist might be fun to write, and they might be fun for the reader once, but they lack staying power and the emotional or intellectual richness that the best poems must offer. Poems that depend on their surprise ending do not reward re-reading.

The Poem That Is All Feelings

Poets can be inspired by their strong feelings about the world, their children, their significant others—this is ripe territory for finding a poem. However, sometimes the poem sits on the page and announces, Hey, everyone, I have feelings. Sometimes the poem tries to force an emotion on a reader, or it tries to convey more emotion than is possible given the poem's content. If a young poet wants to write a poem about the boy who broke her heart (the cad!), she should totally do that, but the poem can't be simply about her feelings. She can write a poem about grocery shopping at night, about something that happened at the bus stop, about going to a costume party in order to trigger an emotional experience for the reader—but if all she does is say, hey, I have feelings, the reader might end up not caring.

The Poem That Is Open for Interpretation

Sometimes a writer might decide that the poem is going to mean whatever the reader wants it to mean. The poem is going to mean everything, which means it's about nothing. A writer may want their poem to be accessible to a wide audience, but remember that universality is achieved through the particular. A poem about kittens drowning in a lake will elicit more grief and sympathy than a poem that is about grief and sympathy. Write about something singularly concrete and real, and the reader interpretation part will follow.

The Poem That Was Written
for Me and Me Alone

Writing is about communication, regardless of whether it's poetry. Sure, many people write poems for themselves and there is nothing wrong with that. But art doesn't happen in a vacuum—the power of art is in how it communicates to its audience, not in what it means to the creator. If all you want to do is write poems for yourself, then why take a poetry class? If nothing anyone says about your poems matters to you, then maybe think about why you want to write poems and whether there's any point in letting other people read them.

The Poem That Tries to Be a "Poem"

Sometimes a writer can't escape all those classes where they read Shelley and Byron and Wordsworth, and there is nothing wrong with liking those poets. But when a contemporary writer starts using archaic language to describe ancient ruins or feels like they have to start waxing up their flowery language to describe their pottery, they might be thinking more about what poems used to be centuries ago and less about what poetry is today in our present moment. It's okay to write a poem using your own conversational language, and it's okay to write about regular everyday things instead of objects you see in the museum.

The Poem That Rhymes Because the Poet Thinks Poems Are Supposed to Rhyme

Look, there's nothing wrong with rhyme. Handled skillfully, it can add music to a poem; it can enhance meaning and emphasize sonic connections between otherwise unrelated words. It can move a poem forward or force pauses in certain places. However—and this is a big however—rhyme for its own sake can overwhelm a poem. It often leads to expected language choices or tortured syntax as the poet strains to get "above" at the end of the line below the one that ends with "love." Or maybe the poem becomes a game of expectation, as the audience is more interested in anticipating the rhyme than anything else. Much contemporary poetry has moved beyond end rhyme as its main musical driving force.

The Cheesy Poem

We've all read these poems; we've all written these poems. Everyone was in seventh grade once. These are cheesy, schmaltzy poems that tackle big issues like love and sadness. They are super emotional and rely on cliché turns of phrase. They rhyme love with dove, soul with hole, trusted with busted. There might be a broken mirror or a sad song on the radio. There is emotion dripping from the page like a drop of blood sliding eternally down a shattered shard of glass. You get the idea.

The Greeting Card Poem

A greeting card is intended to appeal to as many people as possible—it's written in order to get people to buy it, and it does so by being deliberately vague, by emphasizing generic ideas and concepts over a particular narrative or image. A greeting card aims to say something broad about grief or love or a stay in the hospital that applies to as many situations as possible. A poem, in contrast, cannot be all things. A poem should not try to tell all love stories, or be appropriate for every funeral. While it's true that some poems have a kind of universal appeal, that universality comes (perhaps counter-intuitively) from the poet's being as specific as possible; from focusing on the particular image instead of the big idea.

The Poem with Centered Lines or the Seventeen Fonts

How a poem looks on the page matters, and young poets should be encouraged to play with spacing and line breaks and line lengths. However, most contemporary poems do not feature centered lines, and merely clicking "center" on the word processor command bar is a poor substitute for thoughtful consideration of a poem's visual appearance. (Note that greeting cards typically feature centered lines, and we've already warned you about those.) Likewise, switching fonts willy-nilly rarely does much for a poem; rather than spending time debating between Garamond and Arial and Century Gothic, the young poet is well advised to spend time considering a poem's language.

The "Shocking" Poem

It might seem transgressive to write a poem, say, from the point of view of a serial killer. All that blood and gore, right? And yet you're humanizing the killer! Like that television show Dexter, only it's a poem! But anytime you set out to shock your reader, you're limiting the poem before you even start. True shock is harder to achieve than you might expect, and sensationalized images of violence are merely another kind of cliché—just as sentimental in their own way as red roses and fluffy kittens.

The Poem Where the First Word of Each Line Is Capitalized Because Autocorrect Wanted It That Way

Some poets do capitalize the first word of each line, and there's certainly a tradition of it in poetry written in English. However, most contemporary American poets eschew that first-word capitalization in favor of more sentence-driven capital letters. Capitalizing the first word of each line calls attention to these beginning words in ways you might not always want; it emphasizes each line as a new place of beginning. It slows the reader down ever so slightly and can make enjambed lines a little awkward to read. It lends a poem a sort of high formality, an old-fashioned look. None of this is to say don't do it, but if you do, do so because you've considered the effect it has and not because autocorrect did it without your input. (You can turn this particular feature off in your software, and you'll probably want to.)

Note that variations of this kind of poem are "The Poem That Is Double-spaced Because of Default Line Spacing," "The Poem With Indented Lines Because of Paragraph Tabs," "The Poem where the Font Changes in the Middle" and others. The best remedy for this is to learn to use your word-processing program so that decisions about how the poem appears on the page are made by you and not your software.

The Poem That Obscures More than It Reveals

It often happens that when a young poet is introducing their poem before a workshop, they'll tell the story behind the poem—and the event that inspired the poem turns out to be more engaging or moving than the poem itself. The natural question: Why didn't you just tell us that in the poem? The job of the poem is not to pull a mask made of metaphor and flowery language over the powerful moments of our lives. Rather, the poem should seek to explore these events through language; sometimes that means complicating the story, but just as often it means clearly expressing the story so that the poem can build on that foundation (look, for instance at Jamaal May's "The Gun Joke," which makes its narrative backbone perfectly clear, but is no less rich and complex for that).

The Poem That Is Unaware of Its Gaze

Poems are often sparked by the relationship between the writer and the subject, and when there is distance or longing between them, the poem can sometimes get weird by objectifying its subject rather than finding empathy with it. The "male gaze," for example, is that perspective from a masculine point of view that sexually objectifies women by portraying them as creatures that exist for men to look at and use for their own pleasures. A poem grounded in the male gaze actually ends up dehumanizing its subject rather than elevating it or creating empathy like a poem should.

The Poem That Teaches You a Lesson

Sometimes a poem can try too hard to teach its readers a lesson about life. Racism is bad. Economically underprivileged people are people too. Adopting a dog from a shelter is more morally responsible than buying one from the pet store. The problem with the poem isn't the lesson itself—in fact, sometimes the particular lesson is a great topic for a poem. Usually, it's how the poem is prioritizing the need to teach the lesson over the writing of a poem, and the result is that both poem and lesson fail to land for the reader.

The Poem That Wants You to Believe

Sometimes a poem just wants to be about God. Or Allah. Or the Goddess. Faith or spirituality are, obviously, terrific subjects for a poem; there is a tradition of writing about holiness in poems. But sometimes a poem like this can get so caught up in advocating for a particular type of faith that it begins to feel preachy, more like a sidewalk sermon than a poem.

The Poem That Is Too Afraid of Being Any of the above Poems

It's never a good idea to base your art around things not to do, but the above poems are the kinds of poems that often stand in the way of a young poet developing their skill sets. Still, sometimes a great poem is made because the writer had the courage to break some of the rules that were set in front of them and figure out a way to succeed despite the pitfalls. This is what art sometimes does—it pushes at the boundaries of what we think we should and shouldn't do. It takes clichéd or tired tropes and subverts them to create something new. It's not that a young poet should necessarily avoid writing these kinds of poems—we've all written them, and we will write them again. The point here isn't to stifle you or create a new set of rules. Rather, we want you to push past the familiar, push past what's easy. If you know what you're getting yourself into, you can stop treading on hackneyed ground and move toward crafting poems that are daring, original, and yours alone.

11

The Importance and Ethics of Imitation

Why does this book—whose primary purpose is to help you learn and practice writing poems—include an anthology section? How does reading all those poems help someone write their own poems?

Here's a straightforward truth: We learn to make art by copying what previous artists have done. We learn to write poems by reading successful poems and imitating them. Imitation, conscious or not, is a necessary part of our development as an artist, a writer, a poet. We must learn to read before we learn to write; everything we read teaches us what it is possible to write. When you ask published authors about their motivations and inspirations, their answers inevitably come back to reading.

Some beginning writers may defiantly suggest that they don't like to read for fear that reading what others have done will somehow damage their own work, will make their work too derivative, or will push them away from originality.

They're wrong.

Famed horror novelist Stephen King says, "If you don't have time to read, you don't have the time (or the tools) to write. Simple as that."

He's right.

To write poems in the twenty-first century is to join a conversation that has been ongoing for as long as our species has been gathering in groups. How can you join that conversation if you have no idea what has been said before? These beginning writers who avoid reading tend to produce work that is, to the contrary of their intentions, unoriginal and familiar.

An essential part of your growth as a writer and poet is to learn to read as a poet reads. That is, read to learn. Read to borrow. Read to grow. Read with an open mind. Do not be quick to dismiss. Read against your taste; seek out work that makes you uncomfortable; seek out poems you know you could never write. The act of reading, like the act of writing, should be playful, creative, energetic. For a poet, it's important to be expansive in your tastes. To appreciate widely. The easiest thing in the world is to be snobbishly dismissive of things we do not like. But what good does that do us? How does that make us smarter, or better thinkers, or better poets? It does not.

Every poem you read offers its own argument about what a poem is, what it can be. Each poem offers a model for you to use in your own work. That's part of the reason for the poems that appear in this book: to offer you models. When we learn to speak, we learn by imitating the sounds of those speaking to us. Painters learn technique by copying from the work of the masters. So, too, in writing poetry, we learn by imitating the poems we read. Eventually, the goal is for the original source to fall away; what's left is yours and yours alone.

The act of imitation brings with it a certain ethical responsibility. You may have heard a quotation attributed to T. S. Eliot along the lines of "good writers borrow, great writers steal," and yes, part of why we read poems is to find moves we can ourselves use, ways of deploying language that will strengthen our own work. But what Eliot actually said is a bit more nuanced than outright encouraging larceny: "Immature poets imitate; mature poets steal; bad poets deface what they take, and good poets make it into something better, or at least something different."

Something different—that's the key. We've talked about how when you write poems, you're joining a long tradition, a conversation between poets since the beginning of time, and there is very much a tradition of poets writing poems in homage to other poets, inspired by or in response to other poems. A well-known recent example is Roger Reeves borrowing a line from the poet Frank O'Hara, who wrote, "someday I'll love Frank O'Hara" as a line in a poem called "Katy." Reeves in turn wrote a poem titled "Someday I'll Love Roger Reeves," and included a credit line under the poem announcing that the poem was "after Frank O'Hara." (Using "After" is a conventional way for poets to indicate the poem drew inspiration from a previous work; you usually see it italicized and tabbed over, under the title.) It's important to note that Reeves's poem is nothing like O'Hara's, really, other than the direction prompted by the borrowed line-turned-title. Then, after Reeves's poem was published, the poet Ocean Vuong wrote his own version titled "Someday I'll Love Ocean Vuong," noting that it was after both Reeves and O'Hara. Vuong's poem, too, took the idea in a new direction, and after it was published in *The New Yorker*, there was something of a flurry of contemporary poets writing "Someday I'll Love" poems. (You can easily find the poems that started this trend online if you're interested.)

Sometimes, though, the line between homage and plagiarism can seem a little blurry—and, alas, on occasion some poets blow right through that line into outright copying. Don't do this. If you're not sure if you've changed the poem enough to make it fully yours, you probably haven't. It matters, too, whose work you're borrowing from. It's one thing to adapt a line from one of Shakespeare's most famous sonnets or from Edgar Allen Poe's "The

Raven," but quite another to borrow from a classmate's unpublished piece that you read in workshop. The poet Rachel McKibbens, whose own work was plagiarized by another writer, wrote on Twitter that using "after" doesn't mean "I wrote this poem after you already wrote it," but "after reading this poem I was inspired to write this whole other poem."

It's not enough to play mad libs with another writer's poem—"Jeep Commercial Disguised as a Love Poem" that uses "because" as anaphora might remain too close to Matthew Olzmann's original to publish (unless there are other significant changes in tone, theme, language, and even then, it would surely demand an "after"). If the rhetorical move or concept that is most notable about the original is also the most notable thing in your poem, you probably haven't changed it enough to publish. And the "publish" part matters. You can definitely write that Jeep commercial poem if you want to experiment with Olzmann's subject and techniques. You'll surely learn something. But until you make the poem your own, it should remain in your notebook, or as a class assignment—not sent into the world with your name on it to be made public as if it were entirely new.

A big part of the reason for this is not merely the academic faux pas of plagiarism, but something deeper about the reason we make art in the first place. McKibbens again: "Who are we, if not our words? Who are we if we are not allowed to tell our own stories? I survived my own vanishing. I arrive in my art. That is where I map my forgiveness, my sorrow, my joys. Let it be mine. Don't change a single word of it." To publish a poem is to assert that it is a thing you have made.

All of this is not to scare you away from imitating poems, especially as you're learning to write them. Poet and science fiction writer Ursula K. LeGuin said, "You have to learn by reading good stuff and trying to write that way. If a piano player never heard any other piano player, how would he know what to do?" So, yes, imitate. Do so to learn. To attempt to write like another poet will inevitably teach you something about your own voice, your own tendencies, your own aesthetic preferences. It will expand your own capabilities. And when it's done well, and done enough, the source poem will fall away entirely and in its place will be something new— something you have made.

12

Forms (Fixed and Broken, Traditional and Contemporary)

Let's talk about formal poetry. (We were trying to resist making a joke here about getting your poems dressed up in tuxedos and ball gowns, but obviously we could not entirely pass up the opportunity. By this point in the book, we assume you expect nothing less.)

At any rate, formal poetry is a way to describe poems that follow a prescribed pattern, usually based in rhythm and/or a particular rhyme scheme or repetition. The opposite of formal verse is free verse, which generally does not rhyme and likely does not follow a set metrical pattern. Note that free verse does not mean entirely without structure or organization; on the contrary, free verse can be just as intricately assembled as a formal poem, but it generally invents its own structure rather than adhering to a preexisting pattern. These patterns are often known as fixed forms, received forms, or traditional forms: fixed because they are set in advance of the poem's being written; received because they were passed down from literary history and received by the current poet; traditional because they are, well, traditional.

Indeed, you have no doubt encountered fixed forms in previous poetry or literature classes and textbooks. Shakespeare's sonnets are perhaps the most famous poems in the English language, and the sonnet is among the most traditional of traditional forms. For a long time, the teaching of poetry writing has privileged form as the way into writing poems; in this book, clearly, we have taken a different approach. There are a couple of reasons for this. First, most—though by no means all—contemporary poetry is free verse, and that's the current conversation young poets are stepping into. Second, some young poets can mistake the rote following of the mechanics of a form for successfully making a poem; we'd prefer that you focus on expression, invention, imagination, and the rhetorical use of language at the beginning stages of your poetry life rather than counting syllables and bending syntax into a certain rhyme scheme.

However—and this is a big however—there is tremendous benefit to studying and attempting formal verse. Certainly, writing successful poems in fixed forms isn't so easy as merely following a template, filling in the blanks—it requires a nuanced understanding of the elements of poetry. Formal poetry when done well gains great strength from the interplay between the constraint of the formal pattern and the far-reaching exploration of the language. As you might guess, this is quite a feat to pull off as a writer, no matter how experienced you are. But much of the work we do as writers is to rise to just such challenges.

Twentieth-century literary theorist Kenneth Burke describes form in a work of literature as the "arousing and fulfillment of desires. A work has form in so far as one part of it leads a reader to anticipate another part, to be gratified by the sequence." In other words, from a reader's perspective, there's pleasure to be found in pattern establishment and recognition. There's a particular kind of delight, for instance, in knowing that a certain rhyme is on its way but not knowing what the specific word will be until it arrives. For a poet, writing in received or fixed forms offers a path to inciting that pleasure.

Whenever there's a pattern, there also exists the thrilling possibility of breaking that pattern. The poet William Olsen calls the work done in the opening lines of a poem "the lyrical contract" the poet establishes with the reader—immediately, within those first few lines of your poem, you've set us up with certain expectations about rhythm, voice, tone, diction, syntax, point of view. Then it's up to you whether you live up to that contract: fulfill its terms or don't, your call entirely. But if you break it, do so deliberately, with an eye toward the rhetorical impact of doing so. Some contemporary poets have gotten great mileage out of deliberately breaking forms; a poem, for example, that announces itself as a "Broken Sonnet" both benefits from the traditional form and stakes its claim as something new, a rupture from the past. It's also common for poets to choose to echo previous lines instead of repeating them exactly when a form, such as a pantoum, technically calls for a precise repetition. Similarly, many contemporary sestina writers slightly vary the forms of their end words to keep the poem from feeling too stifled by the form.

Nor are all forms traditional. We have not exhausted the possibilities by any means. Terrance Hayes recently invented a form he named a Golden Shovel, named after a phrase from Gwendolyn Brooks's poem "We Real Cool." In a Golden Shovel, the last words of each line are taken, in order, from a line or lines of another poem (often, though not always, from a poem by Brooks herself). Now there's a whole anthology's worth of Golden Shovels. Similarly, Jericho Brown created what he calls the Duplex, a poem written in couplets where the first line of each couplet repeats (more or less) the last line of the couplet above it.

As you can see, there are plenty of current poets working in form, both traditional and contemporary. Diane Seuss's book of sonnets, *frank: sonnets*, won the 2022 Pulitzer Prize; Hayes's own collection *American Sonnets for My Past and Future Assassin* was a finalist for the 2018 National Book Award. Dorothy Chan often works in what she calls triple sonnets; her collection *Babe* includes a number of them. These poets and others bring sonnets (and other forms) to contemporary readers both by working within the received traditions and by making the forms their own.

A Quick Guide to Fixed Forms

An exhaustive inventory and in-depth description of fixed forms is beyond the scope of this particular textbook. But here's a starting place for those interested in trying their hand at fixed forms. If you want more, Appendix B lists a number of great books for further reading. Online, the websites for the Poetry Foundation and the Academy of American Poets offer definitions and examples of a vast range of forms, as well as the history of the forms.

Abecedarian: A 26-line poem in which each poem begins with a successive letter of the alphabet, in order from A to Z.

Acrostic: A poem in which the first letter of each line spells out a word or phrase.

Ballad: A lengthy narrative poem, usually written in quatrains following a rhyme scheme of either ABAB or ABCB within the stanzas.

Bop: A recent form invented by Afaa Michael Weaver that consists of three stanzas (6 lines, 8 lines, 6 lines), each followed by a repeated line or refrain. The first stanza introduces the problem, the second expands it, the third either solves it or reckons with the failure to solve.

Cinquain: A five-line rhymed poem, often ABAAB or ABBAB.

Ghazal: An ancient Arabian form consisting of five to fifteen couplets. Typically each line is fully end-stopped and the couplets are grammatically independent from each other, but the end word of the second line in each couplet is the same. The final couplet often includes the poet's name.

Haibun: A Japanese form consisting of a prose poem followed by a haiku. The haiku should expand upon or evoke some feeling or image from the prose poem without explaining it.

Haiku: A Japanese form consisting of three unrhymed lines. Often rendered in English as five syllables in the first line, seven in the second, five in the third, though many translators or writers of haiku do not follow the precise syllable count. The final line generally offers a kind of turn or resolution—a response to the image or problem of the first two lines.

Limerick: There once was a man from Nantucket, and so on. The form consists of five lines following a strict anapestic rhythm and usually an AABBA rhyme scheme.

Pantoum: A poem written in four-line stanzas in which the second and fourth lines of each stanza are repeated as the first and third lines of the next. Often the last stanza circles back to connect to the first.

Rondeau: A French form, the rondeau is composed of fifteen lines divided into a quintet, a quatrain, and a sestet. The second and third stanzas use the first line of the poems as their last line. Typically follows a rhyme scheme of AABBA, AABr, AABBAr, with "r" representing the repeated refrain line.

Sestina: This is a tough one! A sestina is thirty-nine lines, with six 6-line stanzas followed by a 3-line envoy. The first six stanzas repeat the same six end words in a prescribed order:

1. ABCDEF
2. FAEBDC
3. CFDABE
4. ECBFAD
5. DEACFB
6. BDFECA
7. (envoy) ECA or ACE—and the envoy uses the BDF end words within these final three lines.

Sonnet: Fourteen lines of iambic pentameter following a particular rhyme scheme. The two most common types: Shakespearean sonnets consist of three quatrains and a couplet: ABAB CDED EFEF GG; Petrarchan sonnets consist of an octave and a sestet: ABBA ABBA CDECDE or ABBA ABBA CDCDCD. One of the rhetorical keys to the sonnet is that the opening lines present a problem and then a turn or resolution is offered along with the change in rhyme—so, in the final couplet for a Shakespearean sonnet, or in the sestet for a Petrarchan. There are many, many variations on the sonnet form throughout the history of poetry, including the American sonnet, which typically obeys only the fourteen-line requirement of the traditional form, forgoing any particular meter, syllable count, or rhyme scheme.

Villanelle: This form consists of five tercets followed by a quatrain. The first and third lines of the opening stanza are repeated alternately as the final lines of each subsequent tercet and then as the final two lines of the poem. Line 1, thus, repeats as lines 6, 12, and 18. Line 3 repeats as lines 9, 15, and 17. The first and third line of each tercet rhyme, along with the first line of the final quatrain. The middle line of each tercet rhymes with each of the other middle lines. So, the rhyme scheme looks like ABA ABA ABA ABA ABA ABAA.

13

Prosody

Put simply, prosody is the study of sounds and drumbeat in poetry. At the heart of prosody is a method of studying a poem called scansion. On the one hand, it's helpful for a poet to be able to control a poem's music and rhythm, and scansion gives the poet language to identify and describe what the poem is doing. On the other hand, scansion can be a difficult thing to understand, partly because it's quite technical, and partly because the sounds and rhythm of a poem can be difficult to hear. For most people it takes years of practice listening to language to master scansion, so this chapter is just a starting place for that work. Here, we frame prosody in these terms: scansion as a systematic means by which a poet can describe a poem's rhythm, and how to approach poems using this system.

Scansion: The Basics

Meter is the basic rhythmic structure in a poem. Scansion is the method by which a poem is broken down into its system of rhythmic units. When a poet scans a poem, they listen to the poem's stressed and unstressed syllables and attempt to determine its pattern of sounds, line by line. Many methods of poetry instruction begin with a series of exercises that ask the student to scan a poem for meter, to sharpen their ears for the sounds and rhythms of language. Some people love scanning poems for meter because it can feel like a game or a puzzle. What is the poem doing rhythmically and how does it work? Other people find the game too hard to play or the puzzle too difficult to work with because at times the rhythms feel arbitrary and the rules too arcane. Regardless of how fun or difficult you find scansion to be, what's important is that learning scansion gives poets a way to speak directly and specifically about what they hear in a poem's rhythm.

Metered Feet and Lines

Scansion is most often used when studying metrical verse—that is, poetry that is written with meter as a primary organizing principle. In scanning a poem, the poet can notate the poem's rhythmic structures by listening to it line by line and breaking it down into units of accented and unaccented syllables. These units—called feet—are typically units of two or three syllables that are categorized according to the placement of stresses. Scanning a poem involves identifying the kinds of feet and counting the number of feet per line. Here are some terms used to describe the most common feet and lines in poems. As noted below, we have capitalized and underlined the <u>DUM</u> in order to show where the stressed syllables are.

Common Feet in Poetry		*Metered Lines in Poetry*	
Iamb	da-<u>DUM</u>	Monometer	one foot
Trochee	<u>DUM</u>-da	Dimeter	two feet
Spondee	<u>DUM</u>-<u>DUM</u>	Trimeter	three feet
Pyrrhic	da-da	Tetrameter	four feet
Dactyl	<u>DUM</u>-da-da	Pentameter	five feet
Anapest	da-da-<u>DUM</u>	Hexameter	six feet
Amphibrach	da-<u>DUM</u>-da	Heptameter	seven feet
Amphimacer	<u>DUM</u>-da-<u>DUM</u>	. . . and so on . . .	

—

<u>DUM</u>: stressed syllable

da: unstressed syllable

Breaking things down into feet and lines via scansion is the poet's way of describing what it is that is happening rhythmically in the line. Five dactyls on a line is Dactylic Pentameter. Six amphibrachs on a line is Amphibrachic Hexameter. And no, you don't need to know these terms to hear the rhythms; you have probably listened to a song or sung in the car or in the shower or on the karaoke stage without too much trouble following along with the music. This is because you already know how to listen for rhythm. Singing along with a song is enacting what you already know about how the rhythms of language work (singing on key might be a different story, depending). Scansion gives language to the rhythms we already hear. Identifying how these rhythms work becomes easier when you apply the terminology to actual language, the feet to some words they describe. Try saying these examples aloud to hear them. Note that we've left out the spondee and the pyrrhic below because single words don't regularly scan in those patterns.

Feet	Rhythm	Examples
Iamb	da-<u>DUM</u>	Tonight (to-<u>NITE</u>), Alike (a-<u>LIKE</u>)
Trochee	<u>DUM</u>-da	Welcome (<u>WEL</u>-come), Jungle (<u>JUN</u>-gle)
Dactyl	<u>DUM</u>-da-da	Poetry (<u>PO</u>-e-try), Elephant (<u>EL</u>-e-phant)
Anapest	da-da-<u>DUM</u>	Contradict (con-tra-<u>DICT</u>), Interrupt (in-ter-<u>RUPT</u>)
Amphibrach	da-<u>DUM</u>-da	Appeal (a-<u>PEE</u>-al), Example (ex-<u>AM</u>-ple)
Amphimacer	<u>DUM</u>-da-<u>DUM</u>	Memory (<u>MEM</u>-o-<u>REE</u>), Champion (<u>CHAM</u>-pee-<u>UN</u>)

If this seems like weird, specialized terminology, that's because it is. Specialized studies require a specific vocabulary to convey their subjects, and as students of poetry, we can turn this to our advantage in that this gives us a specific language that allows us to accurately describe the drumbeat in a line of poetry and how the poem uses rhythm.

Scansion: Metrical Verse

If you are using this book in a class, your instructor will likely have their own examples for you to practice your scansion. If you are reading on your own, you can find lots of examples of metrical verse to scan on the internet. Shakespearean sonnets are a perfect place to start training your ear and playing with scansion, because if there is a puzzle to be solved, the Shakespearean sonnet offers up the answer freely: the lines in this kind of sonnet are pretty much always iambic pentameter—five iambs on each line. For example, Shakespeare's Sonnet 18. Here's the first four lines, the first one scanned for you:

shall <u>I</u> / com-<u>PARE</u> / thee <u>TO</u> / a <u>SUM</u>- / mer's <u>DAY</u>?
Thou art more lovely and more temperate:
Rough winds do shake the darling buds of May,
And summer's lease hath all too short a date;

Look at that first line and sound it out for yourself to hear the rhythm and then scan the rest. You'll find one moment in the poem where it gets a little difficult. Is it "thee <u>TO</u> / a" or "<u>THEE</u> to / a"—it makes sense that the speaker of Sonnet 18 might naturally stress "thee," especially given that they are speaking to someone. Or why can't the stress fall on the "a?" How does a poet navigate something like this?

As poet Emilia Phillips says in their essay "Scansion and Contemporary Poetry," sometimes we have to differentiate conversational English from "the poem's English"; that is, figuring out the poem's metrical goal helps us know where the stress belongs even if the meter conflicts with our ear for conversational language. This is important because the way people talk conversationally—the way they pronounce words and accent syllables—is entirely contextual. Accent and pronunciation differs from country to country, from region to region, and even from neighborhood to neighborhood. Even when we do speak the same, an accented syllable is not an absolute value. The accent on a syllable can also vary according the speaker's emphasis, mood, dialect, and emotional state, which can get confusing. Sonnet 18 is pretty easy—while people's conversational English can vary, the poem's English is constant because a metrical poem has a discernible goal. In the case of Sonnet 18, the goal is iambic pentameter. So all we have to do is observe how the rhythm of language fits into the meter of each line.

Additionally, look at our feet/word examples above. Is "contradict" an anapest (con-tra-<u>DICT</u>) or an amphimacer (<u>CON</u>-tra-<u>DICT</u>)? Same goes for interrupt (in-ter-<u>RUPT</u> or <u>IN</u>-ter-<u>RUPT</u>). The answer is that it depends on the line on which they appear because scanning for meter is about working with the poem's English on the line, more than the rhythms of single spoken words.

Scanning Poetry: Substitution

It's nice when a metered poem falls into a metrical pattern easily, but that's not always the case. Look, for example, at Shakespeare's Sonnet 130. It's a Shakespearean sonnet so it's iambic pentameter, right? This should look familiar.

> My <u>MIS</u>- / tress' <u>EYES</u> / are <u>NO</u>- / thing <u>LIKE</u> / the <u>SUN</u>;
> Coral is far more red than her lips' red;
> If snow be white, why then her breasts are dun;
> If hairs be wires, black wires grow on her head.

These lines scan like they should, except for the second one. The first foot of the second line can't be an iamb. <u>CO</u>-ral is a luscious orangey-red and co-<u>RAL</u> is something a rancher might do to care for their cattle. We can't make that foot fit the poem's English. It scans like this, different from the rest of the poem:

> <u>CO</u>-ral / is <u>FAR</u> / more <u>RED</u> / than <u>HER</u> / lips' <u>RED</u>;

So how do poets of yore write verse that adheres strictly to metrical patterns? The answer is that they don't always stick to the meter. Once we know the poem's English is iambic pentameter, we might see moments like this where the poem's pattern breaks. This is called substitution, which means that the poet has substituted one foot for another, in this case a trochee for an iamb, a <u>DUM</u>-da for a da-<u>DUM</u>. So we can call this iambic pentameter with a trochaic substitution in the first foot. If you are scanning and are finding too many substitutions in a metrical poem, you are either scanning an irregular meter or you haven't quite identified the poem's English.

Scanning is mostly used in the study of metered verse, so trying to scan every line of every poem you come across in your life might be maddening—free verse poems elude scanning because they are not structured with meter in mind. One thing to remember is that for most contemporary poets, meter is not the endgame when writing or reading poems. The aim of scansion for free verse poems isn't necessarily to "get the right answer," but to better hear a poem's drumbeat, the rhythms of language as they work in poetry.

Scansion: Non-Metrical Verse

As we've said elsewhere in this book, contemporary poetry has moved away from metrical verse toward free verse, but it's important to note that while free verse poems are not bound to their meter, we can still describe their rhythms using the tools of scansion. Look, for example, at "Introduction to Poetry" by Billy Collins the first stanza is free verse, meaning that it doesn't follow any strict metered system. We can listen to its pattern of stressed and unstressed syllables and see this.

I <u>ASK</u> them / to <u>TAKE</u> a / <u>PO</u>-em	da-<u>DUM</u>-da / da-<u>DUM</u>-da / <u>DUM</u>-da
and <u>HOLD</u> it / <u>UP</u> to / the <u>LIGHT</u>	da-<u>DUM</u>-da / <u>DUM</u>-da / da-<u>DUM</u>
<u>LIKE</u> a / <u>CO</u>-lor <u>SLIDE</u>	<u>DUM</u>-da / <u>DUM</u>-da-<u>DUM</u>

We can argue about how to split those lines into feet, but it's a pointless argument because "Introduction to Poetry" doesn't rely on meter as an overarching rhetorical structure. However, what scanning the poem does reveal is its lack of metrical regularity, which emphasizes what happens in that second stanza: a single line of iambic tetrameter:

Or <u>PUT</u> / an <u>EAR</u> / a-<u>GAINST</u> / its <u>HIVE</u>

The change in rhythmic strategy from unpatterned syllables to strict meter sonically enhances the way the line is highlighted by setting it apart on its own line. Similarly, the first line of the next stanza could also be metrical: it could be trochaic pentameter, but it's only one line, followed by a line of iambic trimeter with an anapestic substitution in the third foot.

<u>I</u> say / <u>DROP</u> a / <u>MOUSE</u> in- / <u>TO</u> a / <u>PO</u>-em
and <u>WATCH</u> / him <u>PROBE</u> / his way <u>OUT</u>

In this sense, a free verse poem doesn't forsake rhythm as much as it simply isn't structured in a regular rhythmic pattern, and we can use the tools of scansion to describe the poem's rhythm in concrete terms. Try reading Collins's poem aloud and see if you can't hear what we have described here. It's okay if it's difficult to get the terminology right away; that's a problem only if accurate terminology is the endgame (like someone is quizzing you). You probably didn't need this chapter to hear this (or any) poem's rhythms, but this way of describing rhythm—prosody—allows us to articulate what we hear in a poem, and how we might create our own rhythms in poetry.

SECTION IV

An Anthology of Contemporary Poetic Modes

Introduction

The following anthology of contemporary poems is arranged by poetic modes. There are twenty modes here, and each suggests a particular approach to the subject. Note that we aren't talking about types of poems, but lenses through which the poet views the world in order to make a poem. It might be tempting to look at the modes as types of poems, and indeed sometimes mode and type overlap: love poems, for example, are specific kinds of poems, but the mode is one that uses desire as its lens on its subject. Or take the environmental mode: we have included a number of different poem types as examples of that mode—nature poems, poems about places, and eco-poems. We aren't suggesting that these things are all the same, just that they all use the poet's sense of place as a means of accessing their subjects through poetry.

This idea of studying writing according to its mode doesn't originate with us. Dating as far back as the nineteenth century, writing students have been asked to operate in four modes: description, exposition, narration, and persuasion. In the past 200 years teachers have innovated ways of thinking about writing beyond modes, but these are still strategies by which a writer approaches the work they do on the page as they try to capture the world and convey it to the reader using language. Which is the work poets do, too.

As you read the poems in this anthology, you'll notice lots of overlap here and lots of gray area. It's unlikely, perhaps even impossible, for a poem to be operating precisely and solely in one particular mode. Thus, Matthew

Olzmann's poem is a love poem, an apostrophe, and a list poem. Layli Long Soldier's "38" is a documentary poem but it also asks the reader to confront some political truths. And as you encounter more poems in the world, you will no doubt discover poems with found bits in them, poems that list things, poems that use apostrophe for just a line or two before dropping the direct address. In this sense, these modes are not a means for reductive categorization, but ways of approaching a poem by way of its interface with the world, by its relationship to other poems in terms of rhetorical lens, poetic tradition, and by its use of the elements of poetry.

We offer these poems not as any kind of comprehensive survey of the state of contemporary poetry, but as a starting place. A poet's reading life must be vast and varied. Not every poem will connect with every reader, but we believe that each poem in this collection teaches something valuable about what a poem can be, what work it can do. So start here. Read and re-read these poems. When you find a poem you especially like, seek out more work by that poet. Seek out similar work by other poets. Find interviews with poets where they mention poets they like or are influenced by, and read the work of those poets. When you discover a mode you like, look up some of the other poets we mention to learn how the mode's history might influence your understanding of contemporary poetry's many possibilities. Read, read, read. In this manner, you will broaden and deepen your understanding of the complex connections between language and experience. Your own poems will be better for it.

Apostrophe

An apostrophe is a poem addressed to "you," a specific entity, as opposed to a generic you or a you who is actually the speaker's self. This specific entity is often a dead or absent person, but might also take the form of a personified object as the speaker turns away from the reader or the poem's topic to the addressee where they discover or reveal inner thoughts or high emotion. (Note that a poem addressed to a person might also be an epistolary poem; that is, a poem in the form of a letter to that person, as the Skeets poem here is.) Apostrophe is a mode seen in many classical poems. For example, John Donne addresses death personified in "Death Be Not Proud," John Keats addresses the bird in "Ode to a Nightingale," and Walt Whitman famously addresses an absent ship's captain in "O Captain! My Captain!"—the captain serving as a stand-in for US president Abraham Lincoln after his assassination in 1865.

Whether it is used as a device for a few lines of a poem or as a mode that drives the entire poem, apostrophe creates a kind of intimacy as the reader has the sensation that they are observing a communication from the poet to the addressee. It's a performed intimacy: it's not a real intercepted communication, after all, but a poem with an implicit audience of readers beyond the ostensible addressee.

To The Mountains
Eileen Myles

when I look out
at you
how absurd to think
of Diet Coke
killing me
I'm flying through
the air
and there you are
white and dangerous
who's kidding who

To Juan Doe #234
Eduardo C. Corral

I only recognized your hair: short,
neatly combed. Our mother

would've been proud.
                 In the Sonoran desert
your body became a slaughter-

house where faith and want were stunned,
hung upside down, gutted. We

                         were taught

to bring roses, to aim for the bush. Remember?
You tried to pork

a girl's armpit. In Border Patrol
                     jargon, the word

for border crossers is the same whether
                they're alive or dead.
When I read his flesh fell

off the bones, my stomach rumbled,
                      my mouth

watered. Yesterday, our mother said,
            "My high heels are killing me.
Let's go back to the funeral."

                   You were always

her favorite. Slow cooking a roast
melts the tough tissue between the muscle fibers;
tender meat remains.

       Remember the time
I caught you pissing
          on a dog? You turned

away from me. In the small of your back
I thought I saw a face.
              Split lip,
broken nose. It was a mask.
          I yanked it from your flesh.
     I wear it often.

Love Letter to a Dead Body
Jake Skeets

on our backs in burr and sage
                                        bottles jangle us awake
                            cirrhosis moon for eye

fists coughed up
                            we set ourselves on fire

copy our cousins
                                        did up in black smoke
                        pillar dark in June

Drunktown rakes up the letters in their names
                        lost to bone
                                        horses graze where their remains are found

and you kiss me to shut me up
                                    my breath bruise dark in the deep

leaves replace themselves with meadowlarks
                                                cockshut in larkspur

ghosts rattle bottle dark and white eyed
                        horses still hungry
                                        there in the weeds

Crow Flying Overhead with a Hole in Its Wing
Kendra DeColo

I looked up and saw you this morning

flying over a Tex-Mex restaurant

the hole in your wing

the size of a bottle cap

I googled what it means

and read about parasites

but nothing about whether it is

a benediction

to see an animal flying

with this perfect portal in its wing

through which I saw the sky

through which its jeweled language

leaked muted and streaky

through which I heard

the first song I ever played my daughter

holding her near the window

that overlooks our street

through which I saw everything

I had been afraid of

which was a kind of death

which was a kind of

abandon

buckling toward joy

as I have fallen to my knees

in grief

but have never known

what it sounds like

to sing without expecting

mercy

through which the wind

might touch us

which is the only

benediction I need

Ars Poetica

An ars poetica is a poem that makes a statement about the nature of poetry. The same surely could be said of all poems: each poem is its own argument for what a poem is. But in the case of an ars poetica, this statement is explicitly part of the project of the piece. Sometimes the statement is clear about the role of poetry in everyday life or how readers should approach poetry. Or sometimes the poet approaches the subject more obliquely or metaphorically with the title declaring the poem's intent.

There is a long tradition of writing in this mode, dating back some 2,000 years to Horace's "Ars Poetica," written around 19 BCE. To contextualize the poems we've collected here, it's perhaps helpful to look at poems like W. B. Yeats' "Adam's Curse," Emily Dickinson's "Tell All the Truth but Tell It Slant," Jane Kenyon's "Briefly It Enters, and Briefly Speaks," or Frank O'Hara's "Why I Am Not a Painter" as traditional examples of how poets explicitly explore the complex nature of the value of poetry and how to write it.

Introduction to Poetry
Billy Collins

I ask them to take a poem
and hold it up to the light
like a color slide

or press an ear against its hive.

I say drop a mouse into a poem
and watch him probe his way out,

or walk inside the poem's room
and feel the walls for a light switch.

I want them to waterski
across the surface of a poem
waving at the author's name on the shore.

But all they want to do
is tie the poem to a chair with rope
and torture a confession out of it.

They begin beating it with a hose
to find out what it really means.

Ars Poetica
Traci Brimhall

It happens as we set down one story
and take up another. We see it—the car,

the skid, the panic, the woman's body, a stain
on snow like blood in a dancer's shoe.

People bend over, afraid to touch her
in case she might rise, a bird startled to find

there wasn't more light on the other side
of the window. The body in so much pain

the soul can no longer keep it. This is how
it happens—something asleep in the earth awakens

and summons us. You feel fingers on your neck
and say, *Take me to the snow*, and it takes you.

[Sometimes I Can't Feel It, What Some Call]
Diane Seuss

Sometimes I can't feel it, what some call

beauty. I can see it, I swear, the conifers

and fat bees, ferns like church fans and then

the sea, its flatness as if pressed by stones

like witches were, the dark sand ridged

by tides, strewn with body parts, claws,

the stranded mesoglea of the moon jellyfish,

transparent blob, brainless, enlightened in its clarity.

I stand there, I walk the shore at low tide, the sky

fearless, not open to me, just open, there it is,

the wind, cold, surf's boom drowning out

thought, I can photograph it, I can name it

beautiful, but feel it, I don't know that I am

feeling it, when I drown in it, maybe then.

No Context in a Duplex
Omar Sakr

"Tensions are escalating." "Mow the grass down."
 Stretch past pain to find poetry, the way home.

 Pen the past to find home. Write even the rain.
Israel, ghost nation, stains the orchards.

 Is rage enough to sustain a whole nation?
I dream of Palestine. Free, alive.

 Pull the line toward life, ask the dreamer:
Who gave the order, who profits from slaughter?

To make a border, make a slaughter.
 O history, O language, burst without love!

With love only, gauge the story—I said with
 Love—listen from the river to the sea.

 People riven from homeland list in grief.
Ten sons ululating. Mothers in the grass.

Aubade & Nocturne

An aubade is a dawn song, a poem of the morning. It traditionally captures the moment when two lovers must part at dawn—which means that the poem might greet the rising of the day mournfully. It's at once a poem of beginnings and of endings, of being together and of impending separation. In John Donne's "The Sun Rising," for example, the speaker dismisses the sun so that he might stay in bed with his love. Other classic aubades include poems by William Shakespeare, Amy Lowell, and Sir William Davenant (all simply titled "Aubade"), and more modern ones include Louise Bogan's "Leave-Taking" and Philip Larkin's "Aubade."

Conversely, the nocturne is a night song, a night scene, a night prayer. It's a poem of sleeplessness, frequently associated with spiritual contemplation. From "A Nocturnal upon St. Lucy's Day" by John Donne to "Sleepless City" by Federico Garcia Lorca to "A Clear Midnight" by Walt Whitman, the nocturne is frequently a poem that positions the speaker alone in the night as they encounter or observe the unknown—the darkness or the dead or something eternal like Heaven or God. Sometimes in the night, the waking world must be abandoned so that the speaker can contemplate their origins or discover the kind of wisdom that is delivered in dreams.

We have grouped these two kinds of poems together because they are counterpoints to one another, ruminations sparked by the hour of the day, by their association with light and darkness. Contemporary poems in the aubade and nocturne modes don't necessarily contain all of their traditional elements—the aubade's parting of lovers and the nocturne's direct address to the spiritual are sometimes absent, but the contemplations and emotions they evoke remain. The aubade is often bittersweet and the nocturne is often mysterious. These kinds of poems are often titled for their mode, reinforcing the poetic traditions they follow and announcing up front the poetic work they are about to do.

Aubade with Bread for the Sparrows
Oliver de la Paz

The snow voids the distance of the road
and the first breath comes from the early morning
ghosts. The sparrows with their hard eyes
glisten in the difficult light. They preen
their feathers and chirp. It's as though they were one
voice talking to God.
                                  Mornings are a sustained hymn
without the precision of faith. You've turned the bag
filled with molding bread inside out and watch
the old crusts fall to the ice. What's left
but to watch the daylight halved by the glistening ground?
What's left but an empty bag and the dust of bread
ravaged by songsters?
                                  There are ruins we witness
within the moment of the world's first awakening
and the birds love you within that moment. They want
to eat the air and the stars they've hungered for, little razors.

Little urgent bells, the birds steal from each other's mouths
which makes you hurt. Don't ask for more bread.
The world is in haste to waken. Don't ask for a name
you can surrender, for there are more ghosts to placate.
Don't hurt for the sparrows, for they love you like a road.

Aubade Ending with the Death of a Mosquito
Tarfia Faizullah

—at Apollo Hospital, Dhaka

Let me break

        free of these lace-frail
        lilac fingers disrobing

the black sky

        from the windows of this
        room, I sit helpless, waiting,

silent—sister,

        because you drew from me
        the coil of red twine: loneliness—

spooled inside—

        once, I wanted to say one
        true thing, as in, I want more

in this life,

        or, the sky is hurt, a blue vessel—
        we pass through each other,

like weary

        sweepers haunting through glass
        doors, arcing across gray floors

faint trails

        of dust we leave behind—he
        touches my hand, waits for me

to clutch back

        while mosquitoes rise like smoke
        from this cold marble floor,

from altars,

        seeking the blood still humming
        in our unsaved bodies—he sighs,

I make a fist,

        I kill this one leaving raw
        kisses raised on our bare necks—

because I woke

        alone in the myth of one life, I will
        myself into another—how strange,

to witness

        nameless, the tangled shape
        our blood makes across us,

my open palm.

Nocturne
Li-Young Lee

That scraping of iron on iron when the wind
rises, what is it? Something the wind won't
quit with, but drags back and forth.
Sometimes faint, far, then suddenly, close, just
beyond the screened door, as if someone there
squats in the dark honing his wares against
my threshold. Half steel wire, half metal wing,
nothing and anything might make this noise
of saws and rasps, a creaking and groaning
of bone-growth, or body-death, marriages of rust,
or ore abraded. Tonight, something bows
that should not bend. Something stiffens that should
slide. Something, loose and not right,
rakes or forges itself all night.

Nocturne
Kiki Petrosino

Last night, the one I loved
before you went before me, walking
with his bride.

I followed with my broken
feet & coat unlatched. He called
her *cake* & *coin* & *wing*

& told her of a place so high
the pines grow small
as thumbs.

They went talking into
the trees the wedding trees
the trees   only I

felt the earth a dark
cut on my gums I held
my teeth in such cloud

of grit. *Hosanna.*
Then came I to the brink
of this tower room

where I have watched
the corsair ships, their iron dazzle
like a field of ghosts.

You must never sail from me
into the blind seep of that
blue mist.

I mean to tell you   *no*
in my language, slow
with blood

no   from my cakewhite
belly I say *The night*
is a knife of salt & every star
sleeps on a bed of smoke

yet still you go from me, more gone
than glass, your skin

an acre of tallgrass speeding
behind the window
& the halves of my head

make a hoofbeat
a thing not born, but flooded
with sound—

It's true, it is true

No music
in the world except
what I jaw

& my jaws are black
and fearsome mine.

Documentary

Some poems take it as their purpose to document events and experiences. Sometimes the poem might examine personal experiences from the speaker's life, sometimes those of other people, and sometimes the poem blends personal experiences with historical events.

Poems in this mode often work to bear witness, sometimes to create a record for posterity, sometimes to provide new perspectives on their subjects. Whatever the mission, poems in this mode try to make sense of the public and personal worlds, although often the beauty of the poem comes through the journey toward meaning rather than the destination. Readers interested in reading more documentary poems might do well to seek out works by Muriel Rukeyser, Patricia Smith, Natasha Trethewey, C. D. Wright, Claudia Rankine, and William Carlos Williams, just to name a few.

Rape Joke
Patricia Lockwood

The rape joke is that you were 19 years old.

The rape joke is that he was your boyfriend.

The rape joke it wore a goatee. A goatee.

Imagine the rape joke looking in the mirror, perfectly reflecting back itself, and grooming itself to look more like a rape joke. "Ahhhh," it thinks. "Yes. A *goatee*."

No offense.

The rape joke is that he was seven years older. The rape joke is that you had known him for years, since you were too young to be interesting to him. You liked that use of the word *interesting*, as if you were a piece of knowledge that someone could be desperate to acquire, to assimilate, and to spit back out in different form through his goateed mouth.

Then suddenly you were older, but not very old at all.

The rape joke is that you had been drinking wine coolers. Wine coolers! Who drinks wine coolers? People who get raped, according to the rape joke.

The rape joke is he was a bouncer, and kept people out for a living.

Not you!

The rape joke is that he carried a knife, and would show it to you, and would turn it over and over in his hands as if it were a book.

He wasn't threatening you, you understood. He just really liked his knife.

The rape joke is he once almost murdered a dude by throwing him through a plate-glass window. The next day he told you and he was trembling, which you took as evidence of his sensitivity.

How can a piece of knowledge be stupid? But of course you were so stupid.

The rape joke is that sometimes he would tell you you were going on a date and then take you over to his best friend Peewee's house and make you watch wrestling while they all got high.

The rape joke is that his best friend was named Peewee.

OK, the rape joke is that he worshiped The Rock.

Like the dude was completely in love with The Rock. He thought it was so great what he could do with his eyebrow.

The rape joke is he called wrestling "a soap opera for men." Men love drama too, he assured you.

The rape joke is that his bookshelf was just a row of paperbacks about serial killers. You mistook

this for an interest in history, and laboring under this misapprehension you once gave him a copy of Günter Grass's *My Century*, which he never even tried to read.

It gets funnier.

The rape joke is that he kept a diary. I wonder if he wrote about the rape in it.

The rape joke is that you read it once, and he talked about another girl. He called her Miss Geography, and said "he didn't have those urges when he looked at her anymore," not since he met you. Close call, Miss Geography!

The rape joke is that he was your father's high-school student—your father taught World Religion. You helped him clean out his classroom at the end of the year, and he let you take home the most beat-up textbooks.

The rape joke is that he knew you when you were 12 years old. He once helped your family move two states over, and you drove from Cincinnati to St. Louis with him, all by yourselves, and he was kind to you, and you talked the whole way. He had chaw in his mouth the entire time, and you told him he was disgusting and he laughed, and spat the juice through his goatee into a Mountain Dew bottle.

The rape joke is that *come on*, you should have seen it coming. This rape joke is practically writing itself.

The rape joke is that you were facedown. The rape joke is you were wearing a pretty green necklace that your sister had made for you. Later you cut that necklace up. The mattress felt a specific way, and your mouth felt a specific way open against it, as if you were speaking, but you know you were not. As if your mouth were open ten years into the future, reciting a poem called Rape Joke.

The rape joke is that time is different, becomes more horrible and more habitable, and accommodates your need to go deeper into it.

Just like the body, which more than a concrete form is a capacity.

You know the body of time is *elastic*, can take almost anything you give it, and heals quickly.

The rape joke is that of course there was blood, which in human beings is so close to the surface.

The rape joke is you went home like nothing happened, and laughed about it the next day and the day after that, and when you told people you laughed, and that was the rape joke.

It was a year before you told your parents, because he was like a son to them. The rape joke is that when you told your father, he made the sign of the cross over you and said, "I absolve you of your sins, in the name of the Father, and of the Son, and of the Holy Spirit," which even in its total wrongheadedness, was so completely sweet.

The rape joke is that you were crazy for the next five years, and had to move cities, and had to move states, and whole days went down into the sinkhole of thinking about why it happened. Like you went to look at your backyard and suddenly it wasn't there, and you were looking down into the center of the earth, which played the same red event perpetually.

The rape joke is that after a while you weren't crazy anymore, but close call, Miss Geography.

The rape joke is that for the next five years all you did was write, and never about yourself, about anything else, about apples on the tree, about islands, dead poets and the worms that aerated them, and there was no warm body in what you wrote, it was elsewhere.

The rape joke is that this is finally artless. The rape joke is that you do not write artlessly.

The rape joke is if you write a poem called Rape Joke, you're asking for it to become the only

thing people remember about you.

The rape joke is that you asked why he did it. The rape joke is he said he didn't know, like what else would a rape joke say? The rape joke said YOU were the one who was drunk, and the rape joke said you remembered it wrong, which made you laugh out loud for one long

split-open second. The wine coolers weren't Bartles & Jaymes, but
it would be funnier for the rape joke if they were. It was some pussy
flavor, like Passionate Mango or Destroyed Strawberry, which you
drank down without question and trustingly in the heart of Cincinnati
Ohio.

Can rape jokes be funny at all, is the question.

Can any part of the rape joke be funny. The part where it ends—haha,
just kidding! Though you did dream of killing the rape joke for years,
spilling all of its blood out, and telling it that way.

The rape joke cries out for the right to be told.

The rape joke is that this is just how it happened.

The rape joke is that the next day he gave you *Pet Sounds*. No really. *Pet
Sounds*. He said he was sorry and then he gave you *Pet Sounds*. Come
on, that's a little bit funny.

Admit it.

Split
Cathy Linh Che

I see my mother, at thirteen,
in a village so small
it's never given a name.

Monsoon season drying up—
steam lifting in full-bodied waves.
She chops bắp chuối for the hogs.

Her hair dips to the small of her back
as if dipped in black
and polished to a shine.

She wears a deep side-part
that splits her hair
into two uneven planes.

They come to watch her,
Americans, Marines, just boys,
eighteen or nineteen.

With scissor-fingers,
they snip the air,
point at their helmets

and then at her hair.
All they want is a small lock—
something for a bit of good luck.

Days later, my mother
is sent to the city
for safekeeping.

She will return home
only once to be given away
to my father.

In the pictures,
the cake is sweet
and round.

My mother's hair
which spans the length
of her áo dài

is long, washed, and uncut.

A Family History Is Sacred
Joshua Jennifer Espinoza

(Place the sky in glass too thick for me to bite through. Give me a void
big enough to contain what I am about to spill.)

On a full moon evening, my grandfather divided the landscape in two.
One side was sunlit, the other bathed in dark purple shadow.
He gripped my shoulder and pointed to the stars. *Those aren't enough*,
    he said.
As we drove down a hillside blooming with faces of women I'd never be
I cried. *I'll give you something to cry about*, he laughed, turning the
    clouds red.
He crested us through blood-rain, still laughing, laughing so hard
his head became a blur of mockery. I am him, somehow.
And yet, not at all. Not at all. I am violet but not violent. I am not
    regarded
as a person, but a threat. (The first time my grandfather walked into
a building where only white people worked, everyone asked him
what he was doing there.) As we pulled to the roadside, drenched
in memory, I wondered what I was doing with him. What
he was doing with me. I couldn't possibly dream in enough color
to ever show myself. So I closed my eyes and let the landscape go fully
dark. I pressed my fingers against my eyelids and made my own stars.
I took a photograph of my father dressed as a woman (that my
mother once showed me) and I memorized it upon the skin of
my bones. Now when my sky turns purple and dark and light and
    blood-red
it is not memory, but song I turn to. I sing the word *woman* over and
    over
until I lose the meaning and slip backwards into my all alone body.

38
Layli Long Soldier

Here, the sentence will be respected.

I will compose each sentence with care by minding what the rules of writing dictate.

For example, all sentences will begin with capital letters.

Likewise, the history of the sentence will be honored by ending each one with appropriate punctuation such as a period or question mark, thus bringing the idea to (momentary) completion.

You may like to know, I do not consider this a "creative piece."

In other words, I do not regard this as a poem of great imagination or a work of fiction.

Also, historical events will not be dramatized for an interesting read.

Therefore, I feel most responsible to the orderly sentence; conveyor of thought.

That said, I will begin:

You may or may not have heard about the *Dakota 38*.

If this is the first time you've heard of it, you might wonder, "What is the Dakota 38?"

The Dakota 38 refers to thirty-eight Dakota men who were executed by hanging, under orders from President Abraham Lincoln.

To date, this is the largest "legal" mass execution in US history.

The hanging took place on December 26th, 1862—the day after Christmas.

This was the *same week* that President Lincoln signed The Emancipation Proclamation.

In the preceding sentence, I italicize "same week" for emphasis.

There was a movie titled *Lincoln* about the presidency of Abraham Lincoln.

The signing of The Emancipation Proclamation was included in the film *Lincoln*; the hanging of the Dakota 38 was not.

In any case, you might be asking, "Why were thirty-eight Dakota men hung?"

As a side note, the past tense of hang is *hung*, but when referring to the capital punishment of hanging, the correct tense is *hanged*.

So it's possible that you're asking, "Why were thirty-eight Dakota men hanged?"

They were hanged for the Sioux Uprising.

I want to tell you about the Sioux Uprising, but I don't know where to begin.

I may jump around and details will not unfold in chronological order.

Keep in mind, I am not a historian.

So I will recount facts as best as I can, given limited resources and understanding.

Before Minnesota was a state, the Minnesota region, generally speaking, was the traditional homeland for Dakota, Anishnaabeg and Ho-Chunk people.

During the 1800s, when the US expanded territory, they "purchased" land from the Dakota people as well as the other tribes.

But another way to understand that sort of "purchase" is: Dakota leaders ceded land to the US Government in exchange for money and goods, but most importantly, the safety of their people.

Some say that Dakota leaders did not understand the terms they were entering, or they never would have agreed.

Even others call the entire negotiation, "trickery."

But to make whatever-it-was official and binding, the US Government drew up an initial treaty.

This treaty was later replaced by another (more convenient) treaty, and then another.

I've had difficulty unraveling the terms of these treaties, given the legal speak and congressional language.

As treaties were abrogated (broken) and new treaties were drafted, one after another, the new treaties often referenced old defunct treaties and it is a muddy, switchback trail to follow.

Although I often feel lost on this trail, I know I am not alone.

However, as best as I can put the facts together, in 1851, Dakota territory was contained to a 12-mile by 150-mile long strip along the Minnesota river.

But just seven years later, in 1858, the northern portion was ceded (taken) and the southern portion was (conveniently) allotted, which reduced Dakota land to a stark 10-mile tract.

These amended and broken treaties are often referred to as The Minnesota Treaties.

The word *Minnesota* comes from *mni* which means water; *sota* which means turbid.

Synonyms for turbid include muddy, unclear, cloudy, confused and smoky.

Everything is in the language we use.

For example, a treaty is, essentially, a contract between two sovereign nations.

The US treaties with the Dakota Nation were legal contracts that promised money.

It could be said, this money was payment for the land the Dakota ceded; for living within assigned boundaries (a reservation); and for relinquishing rights to their vast hunting territory which, in turn, made Dakota people dependent on other means to survive: money.

The previous sentence is circular, which is akin to so many aspects of history.

As you may have guessed by now, the money promised in the turbid treaties did not make it into the hands of Dakota people.

In addition, local government traders would not offer credit to "Indians" to purchase food or goods.

Without money, store credit or rights to hunt beyond their 10-mile tract of land, Dakota people began to starve.

The Dakota people were starving.

The Dakota people starved.

In the preceding sentence, the word "starved" does not need italics for emphasis.

One should read, "The Dakota people starved," as a straightforward and plainly stated fact.

As a result—and without other options but to continue to starve—Dakota people retaliated.

Dakota warriors organized, struck out and killed settlers and traders.

This revolt is called the Sioux Uprising.

Eventually, the US Cavalry came to Mnisota to confront the Uprising.

Over one thousand Dakota people were sent to prison.

As already mentioned, thirty-eight Dakota men were subsequently hanged.

After the hanging, those one thousand Dakota prisoners were released.

However, as further consequence, what remained of Dakota territory in Mnisota was dissolved (stolen).

The Dakota people had no land to return to.

This means they were exiled.

Homeless, the Dakota people of Mnisota were relocated (forced) onto reservations in South Dakota and Nebraska.

Now, every year, a group called the Dakota 38 + 2 Riders conduct a memorial horse ride from Lower Brule, South Dakota to Mankato, Mnisota.

The Memorial Riders travel 325 miles on horseback for eighteen days, sometimes through sub-zero blizzards.

They conclude their journey on December 26th, the day of the hanging.

Memorials help focus our memory on particular people or events.

Often, memorials come in the forms of plaques, statues or gravestones.

The memorial for the Dakota 38 is not an object inscribed with words, but an *act*.

Yet, I started this piece because I was interested in writing about grasses.

So, there is one other event to include, although it's not in chronological order and we must backtrack a little.

When the Dakota people were starving, as you may remember, government traders would not extend store credit to "Indians."

One trader named Andrew Myrick is famous for his refusal to provide credit to Dakota people by saying, "If they are hungry, let them eat grass."

There are variations of Myrick's words, but they are all something to that effect.

When settlers and traders were killed during the Sioux Uprising, one of the first to be executed by the Dakota was Andrew Myrick.

When Myrick's body was found,

                      his mouth was stuffed with grass.

I am inclined to call this act by the Dakota warriors a poem.

There's irony in their poem.

There was no text.

"Real" poems do not "really" require words.

I have italicized the previous sentence to indicate inner dialogue, a revealing moment.

But, on second thought, the words "Let them eat grass" click the gears of the poem into place.

So, we could also say, language and word choice are crucial to the poem's work.

Things are circling back again.
Sometimes, when in a circle, if I wish to exit, I must leap.
And let the body   swing.
From the platform.

                              Out

                                        to the grasses.

Ekphrasis

Ekphrastic poems take as their subject matter another piece of art. But it's not just about picking a topic for the poem; the writer of an ekphrastic poem must evoke and bring its subject to life for a reader who is unfamiliar with the inspiring piece while simultaneously recasting or interpreting the piece. Often an ekphrastic poem works from a painting or photograph, but it's just as reasonable to work from a comic strip, a movie scene, or any other artistic medium in order to make a poem.

And it's generally not enough to simply describe another piece of art; the poet must also in the process of engaging with another work create a poem that stands both on its own and in dialogue with the original. John Keats, for example, in his famous poem "Ode on a Grecian Urn," doesn't just describe the urn, but instead brings to life the figures painted on the urn, and in the process creates meaning in the poem by defamiliarizing and amplifying the artifact's appearance and construction. Similarly, Anne Sexton's "The Starry Night" is written after the famous painting by Vincent Van Gogh by imagining the scene brought to life. William Carlos Williams' poem "Landscape with the Fall of Icarus" uses as its source the painting of the same name by Flemish painter Pieter Bruegel the Elder, capturing both the painting and the Greek mythological event. The possibility for ekphrasis in poems is limited only by a poet's imaginative experiences with art.

History Lesson
Natasha Trethewey

I am four in this photograph, standing
on a wide strip of Mississippi beach,
my hands on the flowered hips

of a bright bikini. My toes dig in,
curl around wet sand. The sun cuts
the rippling Gulf in flashes with each

tidal rush. Minnows dart at my feet
glinting like switchblades. I am alone
except for my grandmother, other side

of the camera, telling me how to pose.
It is 1970, two years after they opened
the rest of this beach to us,

forty years since the photograph
where she stood on a narrow plot
of sand marked *colored*, smiling,

her hands on the flowered hips
of a cotton meal-sack dress.

1935
Naomi Shihab Nye

You're 8 in the photograph,
standing behind a table of men
dipping bread in hummus.
Men on small stools
with variant headdresses,
men so absorbed in their meal
they don't see anything but food,
rough wooden table,
tiny plates,
fresh mound of bread
ripped into soft triangles.

I wish I had found this picture
while you were still alive.
Did they give you the last bite?
You beam as if you owned the whole city,
could go anywhere in Jerusalem,
watch over eating with affection,
waiting your turn.

My new friend had this picture
on her wall. You spoke inside
my head the moment before I saw it.
Now the picture hangs
beside my desk, holding
layered lost worlds where
you are, not only the person I knew
but the person before the person I knew,
in your universe, your life's possible story,
still smiling.

Quinta Del Sordo
Monica Youn

Saturn Devouring His Son (Francisco Goya, 1819-1823)

how can I
ask you to

absolve me
my fingers

still greasy
with envy

gaudy oils
still smearing

the dim walls
the quiet

chamber of
my mouth

Stutter
Evelyn Araluen

Hold the body   the baby   the urge
          to hold that stutters muscle
          that cradles warm air
crush yours into mine to tell me what I'll miss
          the way you move through a room

give me proximity like a threat then give it
again so I'll remember it real good

I like best to find me suggestive
like best the self   to let you move into what's left
like it best when you can't tell me anything
it's best when I want into dark
               what I don't have to say aloud

there's nothing to say but
          to bring to the room a mercy of limbs
I came to give your hands a burden
I came to your hands the cradle of wrist

it'll look good for me to look good doing that
               like it best like that like I let you do like I mean it
it's best if we only remember through the body
to build muscle around it before you go

the urge to reach you stutters   body
it speaks from the choke of my throat
don't let us let the air know   this is our most vulnerable
the crush of things   the proximity that might kill
          don't let the room empty before
               I've built the muscle to remember
don't go until I can like it like that

Elegy

The word "elegy" derives from the Greek *elegos*, meaning "mournful song." Although the mode is associated with the elegiac couplet (alternating lines of dactylic hexameter and pentameter; see Prosody), the elegy as we know it is a lamentation, a meditation on grief, an exploration of mourning for the deceased. Traditionally, the elegy is composed of three parts: an expression of sorrow, a word of praise for the dead, and consolation in the knowledge that the deceased has moved on.

Matthew Olzmann says, "The job of the elegy isn't to simply 'announce' grief, but to make it palpable so that we can comprehend its depth and magnitude," and elegies are often structured to mimic the process of grieving, where the poet moves from a stunned sense of loss to a new way of seeing the world. Contemporary elegies vary widely in form and content as they explore loss or death. A young writer might look at classic elegies like John Milton's "Lycidas," Thomas Gray's "Elegy Written in a Country Churchyard," and Walt Whitman's "When Lilacs Last in the Dooryard Bloom'd" in order to contextualize elegies by contemporary poets such as those collected here.

Elegy with lies
Bob Hicok

This lost person I loved. Loved for a hundred years.
When I find her. Find her in a forest. In a cabin
under smoke and clouds shaped like smoke. When I find her
and call her name (nothing) and knock (nothing)
and build a machine that believes it's God and the machine
calls her name (nothing) and knocks (nothing).
When I tear the machine down and she runs from the cabin
pointing a gun at my memories and telling me
to leave, stranger, leave, man of hammers.
When I can't finish that story. When I get to the gun
pointed at my head. When I want it to go off.
When everything I say to anyone all day long
is bang. That would be today. When I can't use her name.
All day long. Soft as cotton, tender as kiss. Bang.

The Role of Elegy
Mary Jo Bang

The role of elegy is
To put a death mask on tragedy,
A drape on the mirror.
To bow to the cultural

Debate over the aesthetization of sorrow,
Of loss, of the unbearable
Afterimage of the once material.
To look for an imagined

Consolidation of grief
So we can all be finished
Once and for all and genuinely shut up
The cabinet of genuine particulars.

Instead there's the endless refrain
One hears replayed repeatedly
Through the just ajar door:
Some terrible mistake has been made.

What is elegy but the attempt
To rebreathe life
Into what the gone one once was
Before he grew to enormity.

Come on stage and be yourself,
The elegist says to the dead. Show them
Now—after the fact—
What you were meant to be:

The performer of a live song.
A shoe. Now bow.
What is left but this:
The compulsion to tell.

The transient distraction of ink on cloth
One scrubbed and scrubbed
But couldn't make less.
Not then, not soon.

Each day, a new caption on the cartoon
Ending that simply cannot be.
One hears repeatedly, the role of elegy is.

Inside My Mother
Ali Cobby Eckermann

my mother screams as I touch her hair
attempting to brush away the coarseness with my hands
to entwine twigs filled with leaves into her locks
a tiara of green to soften her face
and our tears dry now my mother is frailing
she talks only to those who have gone before
no longer seeing my love, no longer needing

and the wailing bursts from our mouths
as she sinks to the ground, her mother the earth
my mother the dying
throws sand in her face, tasting the grit
in her mouth and wailing louder throws herself
forward, pushing her breasts into the softness
of the earth her mother and
my mother the dying

crawls down into that final embrace
her conversation incoherent now
as if like a child she is practicing words
for the lifetime to come
and the syllables loud and guttural spill
over the sand her mother the earth
and I walk away leaving her there

in the cradle, safely nestled in the roots
of that tree, safe in her country
our solace her grave

The Biting Point
Catherine Smith

Thirty years dead and still curmudgeonly,
my grandfather is driving me through
the fog-numbed streets of Crystal Palace
at five a.m. He's in the plaid dressing gown
he wore to die in, and he's shaved,
badly, flecks of dark blood flecking his chin.
We're the only Austin 1100 on the road;
he crunches through the gears,
blaming the damp, bad oil, the years
it sat cobwebbed in the garage.
He slows for the lights, not best pleased
when the engine stalls—no part of his plan,
I know, to crank the key three times before
the damned thing fires—he's often told me
a good driver knows a car's temperament
like the back of his hand. As a milk float
toots behind us, he mutters, frowns,
eases one foot off the clutch as the other
trembles over the accelerator.
Listen to that! He's triumphant; the engine
warbles its surprise. *Like opera!*
That's known as the biting point, girl,
I'm just telling you so's when you get
A husband, you'll know what's what.
We coast down Fountain Drive, the car
sighs and dreams, a purring baby now.
He sits straight, sliding the wheel for a bend,
as the BBC transmitter sparkles
and winks in the distance—the last thing
he ever mentioned, the last fixed light.

Environmental

From the Ancient Greeks to the Romantics to the Modernists to poets of the present day, poets have always been drawn to place as a source of poetry. Some poems in this mode use nature as a source of inspiration and subject matter. Others ask questions about how individuals fit into their environments. Still others focus on the relationship of a specific place to the people who inhabit it.

The range of poems that work in the environmental mode is wide and extensive. The pastoral, for example, has traditionally been associated with country landscapes and rural life, but in contemporary poetry, it can refer to any poem that has at its heart the landscape, whether rural or urban. Other poems in this mode idealize nature, romanticize an escape to the wilderness, or simply marvel at the beauty of the natural world. More recently, eco-poetics has been on the rise: poems concerned with the Anthropocene and the damage our planet has suffered at the hands of humankind. Poems about historical settings, about landmarks and sites of incarceration, about oilfields and rainforests and oceanscapes—the possibilities seem endless, but a poem written in this mode is generally about more than the poet's environment. It uses the environment to explore the relationship between the physical world and the poem's other concerns, whether love or grief or some other existential question.

Look for example at "Tintern Abbey" by Wordsworth or "The Rhodora" by Ralph Waldo Emerson as classic poems that celebrate nature while Andrew Marvell emotes through his depiction of nature in "The Garden." Emily Dickinson's garden poems are as grand as those poems by Gerard Manley Hopkins that celebrate nature's spirituality. More recently, Gary Snyder and Mary Oliver are known for their use of the natural world in their poems, and poets such as Jorie Graham and Forrest Gander approach the mode with an eye toward environmentalism and the negative impacts of humans on the world.

Landscape with one of the earthworm's ten hearts
Laura Kasischke

and also a small boy with a golden crossbow,
and a white rabbit full of arrows.
Also snow. And the sky, of course, the color
of a gently stirred winter soup.

I am the inert figure behind the barren apple tree.
The one who wonders for what purpose
the real world was created. I ruin everything by being in it, while one
of the earthworm's hearts, deep in the ground, fills up the rest
of the landscape with longing, and fiery collisions, and caves
full of credit cards and catalogues. You can tell

I hear it, too, by the look on my face:

That inaudible thumping insisting without believing
one is enough is enough is enough.

In Chicano Park
David Tomas Martinez

No matter if half the park is concrete
and stanchions supporting a bridge,

near industrial buildings yellow in the sun,
their stalks of smoke soaring awake,

next to empty lots and bus stops
without seats or signs or schedules,

near houses bright with paint
the color of dented cans of Spam,

men walking the streets to work
look longingly towards their doors.

No matter if all the murals decay
and the statue of Zapata falls,

more months pile to be swept, and years
ironed, folded, and put away in drawers,

and if jail bars bite off chunks of your view,
remember a wise gambler's words on craps:

call for the dice back. And between rolls,
wipe the dust off the dice, as bills coil a foot

in the wind because life is a wild emotion
lying in the grass, soon to be green.

Not even bags of chips, cheetahs with wind,
avoid being tackled, gouged, and ripped apart.

We all eventually submit, are arched over
by a hyena grin and growl in the sun.

Soon the spots will show and the world will pull tight with relief
as the jungle rallies around us, as we smile now and cry later.

How to Locate Water on a Desert Island
Karen Skolfield

Darling, these are the palm trees
we've endlessly discussed, their closeness
to dinosaurs and leather. Plants produce
spores and send their children in the air.
It's the wrong time to think
of all the houseplants I've neglected, but still.
That night the praying mantis case
hatched in the kitchen: insects so small
and perfect that for a moment we believed
in their prayer. Of course sticks
can walk and the roots of trees gather
forgotten rains. Even science
can't make up its mind about the divining
rod trembling in the old man's hand:
is it the fork or is it his body
endlessly seeking its source? Here shade
has a brand new meaning. An art form
and our bodies bend to fit in the shapes
laid out for us. Rest for a moment my love,
my comma in the dark. The air around us
explodes in plumage. Watch where the birds go.

Rings of Fire
Craig Santos Perez

    Honolulu, Hawai'i

We host our daughter's first birthday party
during the hottest April in history.

Outside, my dad grills meat over charcoal;
inside, my mom steams rice and roasts

vegetables. They've traveled from California,
where drought carves trees into tinder—"*Paradise*

is burning." When our daughter's first fever spiked,
the doctor said, "It's a sign she's fighting infection."

Bloodshed surges with global temperatures,
which know no borders. "If her fever doesn't break,"

the doctor continued, "take her to the Emergency
Room." Airstrikes detonate hospitals

in Yemen, Iraq, Afghanistan, South Sudan . . .
"When she crowned," my wife said, "it felt like rings

of fire." Volcanoes erupt along Pacific fault lines;
sweltering heatwaves scorch Australia;

forests in Indonesia are razed for palm oil plantations—
their ashes flock, like ghost birds, to our distant

rib cages. Still, I crave an unfiltered cigarette,
even though I quit years ago, and my breath

no longer smells like my grandpa's overflowing ashtray—
his parched cough still punctures the black lungs

of cancer and denial. "If she struggles to breathe,"
the doctor advised, "give her an asthma inhaler."

But tonight we sing, "Happy Birthday," and blow
out the candles together. Smoke trembles

as if we all exhaled
the same flammable wish.

Found Poems

A found poem is a poem in which the words are not written by the poet but, quite literally, found and then arranged into a poem. The poet's task here is to recast the language, to make art from that which originally might not have been intended as artful. It might seem like a cheat, to take a piece of text you discover and claim it as your own poem, but there's more to found poetry than this—it's about discovering meaningful language and repurposing it using the tools of poetry.

In its purest form, a found poem is wholly created with text unaltered from another source, the recasting happening through spacing or lineation. However, found poems can also be created through erasure, blacking out or omitting portions of the original to allow new meaning to arise from the original language. Found text might also be incorporated into the poet's own language, the original text finding new meaning when contextualized in the poem.

This kind of meaning-making from found sources can be seen in a variety of places. Ezra Pound includes historical documents and letters in *The Cantos*. Tristan Tzara explained that a Dadaist poem is made by cutting a text into pieces and drawing them at random from a bag. And the cento is a kind of poem created by collaging together verses or passages from other poems, the tradition of which goes back to the ancient Greeks. Many contemporary poets continue this tradition of playing with found texts to create and uncover poetry on the page.

One-Star Reviews of the Great Wall of China
Aimee Nezhukumatathil

(a found poem)

This is *not* an experience of a lifetime.

It was awful. I couldn't enjoy
the scenery because I was too busy
trying not to trample
or be trampled. Besides that,
it was great. Ha ha, just kidding:

                                        I hated it.

The crowds are crazy!
The pollution is crazy!
No one can speak English!

Back in my day the walls were more beautiful and they didn't have to
be so tall. I didn't feel good with my leg that day, and my wife really
wanted to visit all the Chinese Wall and I said "Ok, let's do it!" but I
soon understood that it was definitely too long for me and I got tired. I
failed in front of my wife because of this wall, so I'm not going back.

It was raining.
It was foggy.
It was raining.

Too much fog.
Too much rain.

It's a wall.

Cascade
Rajiv Mohabir

> *(with words and phrases from the video "How Whales Change*
> *Climate" and "Whale Poop Pumps Up Ocean Health" in Science*
> *Daily)*

But now, a trophic surprise. Looking from above what little
you imagine. Nitrogen and iron in fecal whale pumps nourish
copepods, swarms of krill, and phytoplankton that
photosynthesize, removing carbon from the sea as they fall to
the seabed, changing global climes. Saints or prophets, whale
kind write Genesis with their feces—otherwise what you call
waste. In fact, more plumes mean more silver menhaden skitter
sardines, herring, mackerel, triggerfish, capelin, fusiliers, and
sandeel, flash as nutrients cycle back up to the photic zone
caused by the churning of water, mixed up and down the water
column by cetacean bodies, making more oxygen, keeping
plankton stores respirating, sinking carbon to the depths. More
small schools of fish mean more bottlenose and common
dolphin pods and orcas, more great whale congregations of Sei
Minke, blue and Bryde's. The lunge-feeder feeds its prey who
feeds their predator. Black tip and copper sharks, gannets,
gulls, shearwaters, sea lions, seals, and tuna torpedo through a
din of one billion tightly bound bodies, picked until a shimmer
of scales rains to the floor.

Underwater, sight
curves. Beneath you spirals
a galaxy of fish.

Through a Glass Lightly (Cento for Beginners)
Kate Fagan

The nasturtium is to itself already
a memory. It opens its leaves
its fire
ribbed impression in the grass
that forms like shadow.
I see it plain
as a living fretwork
in the distortion of sound,
press a leaf to a winter dream
of your hand
translated, given.
Our love calls and we lie
in the future of cells dividing,
a water drop
clean in its own shape.
A nasturtium between itself
and us, showing the light.
Time to be born.

Note: The source texts for this poem are Arkadii Dragomoschenko, parts 1, 2, 3, 4, 5, 6, 7, and 9 of "Nasturtium as Reality"; and Seamus Heaney, parts 1, 3, and 4 of "Bone Dreams," parts 6 and 11 of "Station Island," parts 3 and 4 of "Field Work," "Summer Home," and "The Peninsula."

Elegy
Shazea Quraishi

For a boy of eight or ten
the worm can be
a great teacher, especially

a strong, healthy creature
kept in damp moss
to clean and harden his skin.

Such a worm,
hard, bright
and brilliantly red

should be fished
on a No. 10 or 8 offset hook
or even a 6.

Any limber pole
with a length of line from the tip
will do

but an old, soft fly rod
with a simple reel
and 10-pound monofilament is best.

So equipped, a boy can go
to any trout water in spring and early summer
when the water is high

cast his worm in
and let the current carry it to
the likely spots.

Some places are good for big fish
some for small fish
and some are a waste of time.

There is a difference between the feel
of the lake or river bed
and the feel of a fish mouthing the worm.

There is a way of raising the rod tip firmly to strike
the hook into the fish
without breaking the leader.

There is a right moment for this
and a wrong moment.
One must be quicker with a little fish than a big one.

The testing time and the real learning time
is in summer and fall
when the water is low and clear.

Best now to work upstream
approaching the fish from behind
keeping the head low and the rod low

stalking the fish
rather than searching,
sneaking up on the likely places.

The cast is a delicate sidearm swing that slides
the worm forward
through the air (drawing coils of loose line

from the left hand)
and plops it in at the head of the run.
It comes drifting back.

The line is slowly and carefully recovered
through the rings of the rod
keeping pace but never pulling on the worm.

Suddenly the line stops
holds against the current
and the fish is there.

The time will come
when the boy is ready to fish a fly
and the worm has little more to teach him.

Mountain lakes or lowland lakes,
rushing streams
or quiet meadow streams,

tidal estuaries
or saltwater shallows,
all have their charms and moods.

Spring, summer, and fall,
the fly-fisherman moves quietly through them,
disturbing little, seeing much.

Note: This poem employs text from A Primer of Fly-Fishing *by Roderick Haig-Brown (William Morrow and Company, New York, 1964).*

List Poems

A list poem is just what it sounds like: a list. The poet working in list mode is often focused on the poem's inventory, on presenting information or images or metaphors without need for connecting language: conjunctions, sentence structure, or even verbs. The logic of a list poem is often implicit rather than explicit, juxtapositional rather than sequential, meaning and subtext and commentary arising from the raw inventory as the reader imagines or discovers the value of the items by focusing on the items themselves. And because a poem written in this mode doesn't explain or comment on its items, it often relies heavily on its title to establish a key frame for understanding the list that follows.

Sometimes, the list poem is viewed as territory for children—poets like Jack Prelutzky, Shel Silverstein, and others use lists to play with a poem's inventory in silly ways that are fun for kids to read and speak aloud. However, like all the modes, the rhetorical power of a list is in its flexibility of use for a variety of responses. Many poems contain lists in them, moments where the poet rattles off items one after the other in the midst of whatever else is happening in the poem. Meanwhile, poems like Allen Ginsberg's "Howl" and Walt Whitman's "I Hear America Singing" and "Spoon Ode" by Sharon Olds use lists as their primary rhetorical strategy, allowing the poem's meaning to arise from the act of cataloging.

Things That Didn't Work
Catie Rosemurgy

Touching, seriousness, snow.
The short list of lovers anyone has ever had, both of whom
have turned into long, quiet rivers.

Geraniums and their bruises that ruin
the clean edges of summer. The mother wiping
her son's cheek with spit.

Picture frames. Targets. The psychological
boundaries described in books.
Any shape or line whatsoever.

Split It Open Just to Count the Pieces
Oliver Baez Bendorf

> *One might consider that identification is always an ambivalent process.*
> — *Judith Butler*

Call me tumblefish, rip-roar, pocket of light,
haberdash and milkman, velveteen and silverbreath,
your bitch, your little brother, Ponderosa pine,
almanac and crabshack and dandelion weed. Call me
babyface, kidege—little bird or little plane—thorn of rose
and loaded gun, a pile of walnut shells. Egg whites
and sandpaper, crown of Gabriel, hand-rolled sea,
call me cobblestone and half-pint, your Spanish
red-brick empire. Call me panic and Orion. Pinocchio
and buttercream. Saltlick, shooting star, August peach
and hurricane. Call me giddyup and Tarzan, riot boy
and monk, flavor-trip and soldier and departure.
Call me Eiffel Tower, arrondissement, le garçon,
call me the cigarette tossed near the leak
of gasoline. Call me and tell me that Paris is on fire at last,
that the queens of Harlem can have their operations
and their washing machines. Call me seamless,
call me sir. Call me tomorrow's inevitable sunrise.

Glass Jaw Sonnet
Gabrielle Calvocoressi

Glass jaw, chicken neck, bag of bones, heart sick.
Knuckle head, bug eyes, lily-livered chump.
Sweet feet. Heavy handed, gutless, headstrong,
Weak-kneed, barrel-chested, hairless, loose-lipped,
Lion hearted redneck. Hair of the dog.
Brainiac, bow-legged, slack-jawed punk. Head
Strong. Sweet spot. Gut Shot. Back away. Meat hooks.
Lazy eye, on the chin, stink eye, reed thin.
Face only a mother could love. Back down.
Nerves of steel, limp wrist, square jaw. Thin skinned, Soft-
Skull, small of the back, heart strings, limp wrist, green
Eyed monster, cauliflower ear. Knock-kneed,
Slim waisted, eye of the tiger. In God's
Arms. Thick neck. Ass backward. Harden my heart.

Love Poems

On the one hand, a love poem is a classification of a type of poem written by one person for another. Many such poems are one-dimensional because they are steeped more in sentiment than in poetry, more in declarations of love than conveying an emotional experience to the reader. Love poems of this kind are often the stuff of greeting cards and missives that are best kept private because their goal is simple communication: the professing of love.

There are lots of famous love poems you might already know, Shakespeare's "Sonnet 18," Lord Byron's "She Walks in Beauty," and Elizabeth Barrett Browning's "How Do I Love Thee," to name just a few. These poems are foundational to how we understand the relationship between expressing high emotion and poetry. And because the tradition of the love poem goes so far back, combined with the fact that so many love poems are written in the name of affirming love, it's easy for contemporary love poems to end up sentimental and cliché. Not that those classic poems are cliché, but more that the ground they cover has at this point been trampled by generations of subsequent writers.

When a writer sits down to write in the mode of the love poem, however, something different is at work. Sure, it can still be about the speaker's feelings for their loved one, but as a mode, the love poem makes desire physical for the reader. A poem in this mode views its subject using desire or affection as its lens. Love is an emotion worth writing about, worth shouting about over rooftop and mountain, but a poem written in this mode doesn't simply profess love; it also evokes the feeling of love, the particular sensation of love as it's felt by the poem's speaker. Or it might take as its mission the complication of love, challenging personal or societal assumptions about intimacy and relationships, bringing a fresh perspective to a potentially hackneyed subject.

The Bus Ride
Jenny Johnson

When she turns from the window and sees me
she is as lovely as a thrush seeing for the first time all sides of the sky.

Let this be a ballet without intermission: the grace of this ride beside her
on the green vinyl, soft thunderclaps in the quarry.

Let me be her afternoon jay,
hot silo, red shale crumbling—

Mountain Dew Commercial Disguised as a Love Poem
Matthew Olzmann

Here's what I've got, the reasons why our marriage
might work: Because you wear pink but write poems
about bullets and gravestones. Because you yell
at your keys when you lose them, and laugh,
loudly, at your own jokes. Because you can hold a pistol,
gut a pig. Because you memorize songs, even commercials
from thirty years back and sing them when vacuuming.
You have soft hands. Because when we moved, the contents
of what you packed were written *inside* the boxes.
Because you think swans are overrated and kind of stupid.
Because you drove me to the train station. You drove me
to Minneapolis. You drove me to Providence.
Because you underline everything you read, and circle
the things you think are important, and put stars next
to the things you think I should think are important,
and write notes in the margins about all the people
you're mad at and my name almost never appears there.
Because you make that pork recipe you found
in the Frida Kahlo Cookbook. Because when you read
that essay about Rilke, you underlined the whole thing
except the part where Rilke says love means to deny the self
and to be consumed in flames. Because when the lights
are off, the curtains drawn, and an additional sheet is nailed
over the windows, you still believe someone outside
can see you. And one day five summers ago,
when you couldn't put gas in your car, when your fridge
was so empty—not even leftovers or condiments—
there was a single twenty-ounce bottle of Mountain Dew,
which you paid for with your last damn dime
because you once overheard me say that I liked it.

You Don't Know What Love Is
Kim Addonizio

You don't know what love is
but you know how to raise it in me
like a dead girl winched up from a river. How to
wash off the sludge, the stench of our past.
How to start clean. This love even sits up
and blinks; amazed, she takes a few shaky steps.
Any day now she'll try to eat solid food. She'll want
to get into a fast car, one low to the ground, and drive
to some cinderblock shithole in the desert
where she can drink and get sick and then
dance in nothing but her underwear. You know
where she's headed, you know she'll wake up
with an ache she can't locate and no money
and a terrible thirst. So to hell
with your warm hands sliding inside my shirt
and your tongue down my throat
like an oxygen tube. Cover me
in black plastic. Let the mourners through.

When I Tell My Beloved I Miss the Sun,
Paige Lewis

he knows what I really mean. He paints my name

across the floral bed sheet and ties the bottom corners
to my ankles. Then he paints another

for himself. We walk into town and play the shadow game,
saying *Oh! I'm sorry for stepping on your*

shadow! and *Please be careful! My shadow is caught in the wheels
of your shopping cart.* It's all very polite.

Our shadows get dirty just like anyone's, so we take
them to the Laundromat—the one with

the 1996 Olympics-themed pinball machine—
and watch our shadows warm

against each other. We bring the shadow game home
and (this is my favorite part) when we

stretch our shadows across the bed, we get so tangled
my beloved grips his own wrist,

certain it's mine, and kisses it.

Lyric

We're not referring here to words meant to be set to music, as in song lyrics, although that is the original sense of the phrase lyric poems. Traditionally, the lyric poem is a short, intense, composition that expresses deep personal feelings. The term comes from the ancient Greeks, meaning verse accompanied by a lyre, although many cultures claim their own kinds of lyric poetry. Classically, in English, readers can look to poems by John Donne, Percy Bysshe Shelley, and William Wordsworth, among the many poets writing in this mode.

For contemporary poets, working in the lyric mode means writing a poem that is driven not necessarily by narrative or storytelling, but by some other impulse: intensity of emotion or image or sound. Associations may be more idiosyncratic or personal; the story being told may be more obscured by the language or imagery. These are the aspects of vertical movement that create depth for a poem, but also that result in poems that might evoke an initial "Huh? I don't get it" upon first read. And while the lyric mode is often described in opposition to the narrative mode, the two often work in tandem in some way or another. Even more than any other mode, lyric poems ask the reader to sit and reflect, to read slowly, to let go of expected associations or narrative linearity, which can be a challenge for readers, but one that can be well worth the effort.

I Have to Go Back to 1994 and Kill a Girl
Karyna McGlynn

It's no wonder   I'm always tired   with all these tract houses—
    It's night & cold
on my belly in   the undeveloped field now
    I have to bury her
clothing inside   a black garbage bag in plot D
police cars roll   past but continue   down the treeless parkway
    even after shining
their lights on   me in my freshman sundress
    I can only assume
they don't see   the significance of my presence
but I must say   1994 is a simpler   time—not everyone is suspect
    I crawl up next to
my old house   & look through a lit window
    my mother reads
a book in bed   I want to knock   on the glass, there's something
    I need to tell her

Tell Me Again about the Last Time You Saw Her
Gary L. McDowell

The telephone on the moon has been ringing
continuously

since 1969   The footprints
ache to answer it

See red Mars
rise

Driving becomes difficult with only the road
in your way   What shatters on it

but light, each moon claiming the other false

The best kind of torture
is the voluntary kind

Ghosts revered for their sense of smell:

fingerling potatoes roasted in olive oil
and sea salt

And on the couch   Paranoia
curled-up in the shape

of a child's skeleton

Downhearted
Ada Limón

Six horses died in a tractor-trailer fire.
There. That's the hard part. I wanted
to tell you straight away so we could
grieve together. So many sad things,
that's just one on a long recent list
that loops and elongates in the chest,
in the diaphragm, in the alveoli. What
is it they say, *heart-sick* or *downhearted*?
I picture a heart lying down on the floor
of the torso, pulling up the blankets
over its head, thinking this pain will
go on forever (even though it won't).
The heart is watching Lifetime movies
and wishing, and missing all the good
parts of her that she has forgotten.
The heart is so tired of beating
herself up, she wants to stop it still,
but also she wants the blood to return,
wants to bring in the thrill and wind of the ride,
the fast pull of life driving underneath her.
What the heart wants? The heart wants
her horses back.

The Return of Music
Kazim Ali

The bridge of birches stretches down to the horizon.
A ridge of wings descending into the leaves.

Turn now in a note sent thither.
Thither around and the wind strikes.

Orange, the trees are aflame.
Scarlet. Called here, you came.

Light carving shadows into tree bark.
You translate this into other languages, all antiquated and still.

An anthem of ether. Shorn, you always wondered:
what willful course have you carved through your history?

In the tree-capped valley, the lustrous wind chafes through.
Leaf fence uncurl. The valley wends the way the music went.

The sapphire sky, unbelievable, but there.
These moments against the years you cannot believe.

This hover of music winging down from the mountains
you cannot believe.

But here in the trees, here above the river, here as the season
stitches itself into fog then frost, you will.

Here as you unfold, unsummon, uncry, you will.

Unopened, you will. Unhappen, you will.

These moments against the years, you will.

Unmoment you will.

Unyear you will. Unyou you will.

Unwill you will—

Meditation

If writing is a form of thinking—and we believe that it is—then it's natural that sometimes a poet is interested in thinking about something in a poem. The meditative mode begins in contemplation, in deep rumination about an idea, an experience, an event—about anything. The speaker thinks and reflects and moves the reader through a poem driven by the process of thought, moving toward a heightened level of thinking or awareness about its subject. This doesn't necessarily mean the speaker discovers a higher truth or an emotionally calm state—as in much of poetry, beauty, and meaning arise on the journey rather than at the destination.

Some examples of the meditative mode from history might include poems like "Tintern Abbey" by Wordsworth and "What Is Our Life" by Sir Walter Raleigh, and more recently, poems like "Let America Be America Again" by Langston Hughes, "The Road Not Taken" by Robert Frost, "The Room of My Life" by Anne Sexton, and "Dirge without Music" by Edna St. Vincent Millay. It's true that rumination and reflection are common features throughout poetry, but poems in the meditative mode tend to be explicit about the process of contemplation.

Good Bones
Maggie Smith

Life is short, though I keep this from my children.
Life is short, and I've shortened mine
in a thousand delicious, ill-advised ways,
a thousand deliciously ill-advised ways
I'll keep from my children. The world is at least
fifty percent terrible, and that's a conservative
estimate, though I keep this from my children.
For every bird there is a stone thrown at a bird.
For every loved child, a child broken, bagged,
sunk in a lake. Life is short and the world
is at least half terrible, and for every kind
stranger, there is one who would break you,
though I keep this from my children. I am trying
to sell them the world. Any decent realtor,
walking you through a real shithole, chirps on
about good bones: This place could be beautiful,
right? You could make this place beautiful.

Song
Tracy K. Smith

I think of your hands all those years ago
Learning to maneuver a pencil, or struggling
To fasten a coat. The hands you'd sit on in class,
The nails you chewed absently. The clumsy authority
With which they'd sail to the air when they knew
You knew the answer. I think of them lying empty
At night, of the fingers wrangling something
From your nose, or buried in the cave of your ear.
All the things they did cautiously, pointedly,
Obedient to the suddenest whim. Their shames.
How they failed. What they won't forget year after year.
Or now. Resting on the wheel or the edge of your knee.
I am trying to decide what they feel when they wake up
And discover my body is near. Before touch.
Pushing off the ledge of the easy quiet dancing between us.

Jet
Tony Hoagland

Sometimes I wish I were still out
on the back porch, drinking jet fuel
with the boys, getting louder and louder
as the empty cans drop out of our paws
like booster rockets falling back to Earth

and we soar up into the summer stars.
Summer. The big sky river rushes overhead,
bearing asteroids and mist, blind fish
and old space suits with skeletons inside.
On Earth, men celebrate their hairiness,

and it is good, a way of letting life
out of the box, uncapping the bottle
to let the effervescence gush
through the narrow, usually constricted neck.

And now the crickets plug in their appliances
in unison, and then the fireflies flash
dots and dashes in the grass, like punctuation
for the labyrinthine, untrue tales of sex
someone is telling in the dark, though

no one really hears. We gaze into the night
as if remembering the bright unbroken planet
we once came from,
to which we will never
be permitted to return.
We are amazed how hurt we are.
We would give anything for what we have.

Redneck Refutation
John Kinsella

I didn't connect regardless
how much I participated, it's a vocab thing
though not to do with skills of expression;
                              ejecting bullets
from the breech, freezing whole carcasses
of home-slaughtered sheep, the contradictions
roll the same roads, and families
still come to visit:
                    crops in the bush, sullen days
coming down off bad speed, scoring from the old bloke
shacked up with teenage girls,
                      his bull terrier
crunching chickens;
              a flat in the city is a deal
that can go either way, and the economics
of the paddock are the call-girl's profit;
                          the ford fairmont
runs against the speed camera, and blind grass
poisons sheep—sightless like the minister
amongst his flock,
              the school teacher,
                        the father
who won't let his son play netball because it will turn him,
like an innocent bitten by a vampire, into a pervert—or worse—
a poofter. Outside, you can't know that those
who speak in short, inverted sentences
always have fences in a state of disrepair,
                        line length
and wire length are directly proportional,
eloquent subdivider of land, intensive pig farmer,
will let nothing in or out, though the space around the pig-shed
is large and open, mainly used for hay cutting
while all sons play Guns 'n' Roses' *Appetite for Destruction*,
timeless classic . . . apotheosis, serrated road edge
where a termite mound astoundingly remains intact: there
are no generics, no models of behaviour.
                        It's not that my
name is a misnomer: it's who owns
a particular conversation.

Narrative

While narrative is an element of many poems, this mode refers to poems driven primarily by the storytelling impulse and relying largely on the narrative arc to provide the poem with a structure. They start with a problem or catalyst and proceed from there, though they are still poems after all, and how the story proceeds might not always be a straight line toward a particular climax.

The narrative mode seems like it's everywhere in poetry because this is primarily the poem's horizontal movement—wherever a poem tells a story or recounts something that has happened or is happening, the poet is working with the narrative mode. Some well-known poems driven by their narratives might include the epic poems by Homer, "The Rime of the Ancient Mariner" by Samuel Taylor Coleridge, and "Hero and Leander" by Christopher Marlowe, just to name a few. And sometimes, the narrative poem is extended as it is in works like *The Canterbury Tales* by Geoffrey Chaucer, *Don Juan* by Lord Byron, and *Aurora Leigh* by Elizabeth Barrett Browning.

It's important to note that while the narrative is often presented in opposition to the lyric, these modes present the poet with more of a continuum than a binary.

Teacher of the Year
David Kirby

This year last year's Teacher of the Year
    broke an office window having sex with a student
at Laurie's university, Laurie tells me,
    and I say, "Ummmm . . . broke it with what?"
and she says that's what everybody wants to know,
    like, the head? The booty? The consensus is

it was a foot bobbing UP and down and UP
    and down and then lashing out in a final ecstatic
spasm, crash! Then comes surprise, giggles,
    shushing noises. Somebody finds out,
though. Somebody always finds out:
    my first Mardi Gras, when I was ten,

I remember passing a man saying,
    "Oh, come on, baby, why can't we let BY-gones
be BY-gones?" and shaking his cupped hands
    as though he is comparison-shopping

for coconuts while peering pleadingly
        into the pinched face of his female companion,

whose own arms are folded tightly across her chest,
        and even then I thought, Hmmm! Bet I know
what those bygones are! I.e., that they have
        nothing to do with who ate that last piece of cake
or brought the car home with the gas tank empty
        and everything to do with sex stuff.

Laurie is in town with Jack, who is a therapy dog,
        and she tells me she takes Jack to homes
and nursing centers to cheer up old-timers,
        and after their first visit, she asked
the activities coordinator if she should do
        anything differently, and the woman says,

"Could you dress him up?" And Laurie says,
        "Excuse me?" and the woman says,
"They really like it when the dogs wear clothes."
        My analysis: having seen people act like dogs
all their lives, toward the end, elderly people
        find it amusing when dogs act like people.

A German shepherd could be Zorro, for example,
        and a chow Elivus as a matador. A poodle could be
St. Teresa of Avila, a border collie Sinatra.
        A yorkie could be a morris dancer
and a sheltie a gandy dancer or vice versa.
        A schnauzer could be Jayne Mansfield.

Dogs could pair up: imagine a boxer
        as Inspector Javert chasing a bassett hound
as Jean Valjean under the beds, around
        the potted plants, in and out of the cafeteria.
Or a bichon frise as Alexander Hamilton fighting
        a duel with a Boston terrier as Aaron Burr.

On the romantic side, there could be
        a golden lab and a chocolate lab
as Romeo and Juliet or a Samoyed and a husky
        as Tristan and Isolde, though it wouldn't been good
to let their love end the way doggie love does:
        the posture isn't nice, and the facial expressions

are not the kind of think you want to think about
      when you're thinking about this kind of thing.
Up to a point, you want to know it all,
      then the more you know, the less you want to know.
Though you can't help wondering:
      a shoulder? An elbow? A knee?

Lighter
Dorianne Laux

> *"Aim above morality."*
> *—Ruth Gordon, Harold and Maude*

Steal something worthless, something small,
every once in awhile. A lighter from the counter
at the 7-Eleven. Hold that darkness in your hand.
Look straight into the eyes of the clerk
as you slip it in your pocket, her blue
bruised eyes. Don't justify it. Just take
your change, your cigarettes, and walk
out the door into the snow or hard rain,
sunlight bearing down, like a truck, on your back.
Call it luck when you don't get caught.
Breathe easy as you stand on the corner,
waiting, like everyone else, for the light to change,
following the cop car with your eyes
as it slowly rolls by, ignoring the baby
in its shaded stroller. Don't you want
something for nothing? Haven't you suffered?
Haven't you been beaten down, condemned
like a tenement, gone to bed hungry, alone?
Sit on a stone bench and dig deep for it,
touch your thumb to the greased metal wheel.
Call it a gift from the gods of fire.
Call it your due.

Dynamite
Anders Carlson-Wee

My brother hits me hard with a stick
so I whip a choke-chain

across his face. We're playing
a game called *Dynamite*

where everything you throw
is a stick of dynamite,

unless it's pine. Pine sticks
are rifles and pinecones are grenades,

but everything else is dynamite.
I run down the driveway

and back behind the garage
where we keep the leopard frogs

in buckets of water
with logs and rock islands.

When he comes around the corner
the blood is pouring

out of his nose and down his neck
and he has a hammer in his hand.

I pick up his favorite frog
and say If you come any closer

I'll squeeze. He tells me I won't.
He starts coming closer.

I say a hammer isn't dynamite.
He reminds me that everything is dynamite.

In Which Christina Imagines That Different Types of Alcohol Are Men and She Is Seeing Them All
Christina Olson

Gin was nice enough but had tiny teeth: little ships
of white. Whiskey showed up an hour late,
took me and my one good dress

to a crab shack. We cracked boiled crawfish, swept
our fingers over the tablecloth, left butter behind.

I hid in the back of the coffee shop—crouched
behind whole beans—and scoped out Rum, then left
without introducing myself. Maybe it's cruel of me

but I just wasn't feeling exotic. Bourbon
and I had fun, but it was all cigarettes

and ex-wives. Tequila was ever the gentleman, blond
and smooth as caramel. Bought all my rounds
and when I came back from the bathroom he,

my wallet, my car: all gone. The bartender didn't look
sorry. My mother set me up with Brandy

and I should have known that he'd be the type
to own small dogs. I don't like poodles.
I saw Gin again last night; both of us out

with other people. His: a redhead. I waved anyway,
and when he smiled, all sharp points

and bloodied gums, well, *that* was when I fell in love.

Triple Sonnet for Being a Queer in a Family of Straights
Dorothy Chan

If my family had a reality television show,
      I'd jet off the minute my scene was over,
ready for fried chicken and milkshakes
      on a plane with a secret lover, both of us
in short skirts, our tops wrapped in pink furs,
      because why do more than what's contractually
obligated on a show that glorifies straight people
      and their straight drama: how many proposals
and weddings and kitchen talks and breakdowns
      in the middle of Kowloon, Hong Kong can one
season even handle? Or what about the finale
      of the summer when I arrive at the eight-course
family dinner and a young man's waiting for me,
      and I came hungry—not just for him, and this is

      a scam. This is a setup. This a get-me-out-
of-here-ASAP-because-I-clearly-don't-fit.
      This is straight people who just happen to be
my family mocking me by inviting a complete
      stranger to dinner. And how boring is he with
his startup and finance degree, as he blabs on
      and on while I'm trying to eat my garlic lobster.
Dear Producers: stop scamming me for ratings.
      I know you want me pregnant with this man's baby
by the middle of next season, so you can plan
      the Primetime wedding special, and how scandalous:
A child out of wedlock! The perfect straight family
      drama that'll be solved with his proposal, filled
with red and pink roses and a jazz band playing

in the park, but I'll say no. And network, I've just
      wasted your money, or did I? I'm worth every
penny, baby, and I'm a spoiled brat—a secret
      camera whore, because do you know what it feels like
to be the hottest one who's labeled "single"
      out of family spite and sibling rivalries,
and I've got no time for that, ready to jet off
      with a secret lover to Singapore for a waterfall
photoshoot, and don't you go chasing us there,
      our tight bikinis and one-piece cutouts, and none

of this is for ratings—we're just trying to live
       our lives, and Hello, Primetime, your formula's
so straight, it's stale, but what would you know?
       Basic cable, you've got no idea what you're missing.

Occasional

An occasional poem is one written to recount or commemorate a particular event, whether it be a birthday, a graduation, a first date, a divorce—no event is too small to be recognized with a poem. This mode is traditionally associated with public events and poems delivered orally. Poets working in the occasional mode face the challenge of delivering a specific message to a general audience about the occasion while retaining the sense of mystery and ambiguity that is inherent to poems. This isn't to say that accessibility and mystery are mutually exclusive, just that the poet has to negotiate the differences between these things as they write.

There are many different kinds of poems that might be included in a study of this mode. An epithalamium is a poem delivered in honor of a bride and groom at their wedding. A dirge is a poem that expresses grief at a funeral. Pindar's victory odes marked the accomplishments of athletes in the Olympic Games, and inaugural poems are read at the inauguration ceremonies for heads of state. There are lots of classic examples of poems in the occasional mode, too. Alfred, Lord Tennyson's famous poem "The Charge of the Light Brigade" remembers the Battle of Balaclava during the Crimean War. Elizabeth Bishop's "Cape Breton" marks a personal occasion, the poet's visit to Cape Breton, Massachusetts. In "The Day Lady Died," Frank O'Hara mourns the death of jazz singer Billie Holiday.

Move-in
Janine Joseph

California, 1991

Aba had never seen a crane   but called the white bird branching
from the street-front pepper tree   a crane
and though we knew her eyes   were whiting with cataracts
we hipped our boxes   and stood nodding on the walk

Without miracle its wings untucked   and our beagles split
airstrips of hackles up their coats   Fact and in full-color
there it was   The tallest bird in North America!
J. whooped   And so it was

Hey welcome   the neighbors said and said
it's earthquake season   You all ought to strap down
the wall-to-wall-ware   the china and mom's
Madonna & Child carved   into a wheel of holywood

The waves'll start in the living   room they said and shake out
like rattlesnakes   from there   the epicenter   and head
to where the children'll sleep   Things could get bad?   I asked *Fast*

After Our Daughter's Autism Diagnosis
Kamilah Aisha Moon

I watched the backs
of college girlfriends
trailing off to mobile lives.
I watched them
until they were blips.

Ours was a sacred exile
then. Waterfalls
of words between us;
silhouettes in love,
tending our own.
The hours, clouds
floating past —
beds in the sky
where rain slept.

—

I often wake up dizzy,
the sun mocking us
as it douses her face.

My husband
says nothing,
his kisses
shallow.

What we don't say
we eat.

Halloween
Sandra Beasley

Somewhere in town tonight,
a woman is discovering
her inner Sexy Pirate.

This is not to be confused
with one's inner Sexy Witch,
Sexy Kitten, Sexy Librarian,
Sexy Bo Peep, Sexy Vampire,
Sexy Race Car Driver, or
inner Sexy Ophthalmologist.

She forgot to buy ribbon,
so she threads the corset's eyelets
with gym shoes laces.
She re-poofs the sleeves
of her buccaneer blouse.

Arrrr, she says to the mirror.
Argh, the mirror sighs in return.

Once I asked my mother why
anyone would wear tights like that
to net a fish.
Wouldn't your legs get cold?
Wouldn't your heels slip
on the wet deck of a ship? *Shush,*

my mother said, adjusting the wig
on her Sexy Cleopatra.

Somewhere in town tonight,
a sitter sets out the pumpkin.
A girl studies its fat head.
They punch its eyes in, so
it can see. They cut its mouth out,
so it can smile. *Now you bring it*

to life, the sitter will say.
And where its seeds had been,
the girl will place a flame.

Yolanda: A Typhoon
Sarah Gambito

How much our hands are God's
to be running fingers over braille cities.
We are this hand pushed through our womb.
Weeping with each other's blood in our eyes.
I dreamed that I slept with the light on.
I was asleep in my mother's bed because my father was out to sea
and my claim on him was to feel the frets of my death sure to come.
Sweet, small fishing rod. Ears of wind rushing through many jellied trees.
We were on this cardboard earth with its puffing volcanoes,
miniature baseball players and horrible winds
scored by musician's hands.
Stand in the strong ear of this love.

Ode

An ode is similar to an apostrophe in that it's typically addressed to a particular person or object, but the ode specifically praises and celebrates its subject. Traditionally, there are three main types of odes. The Pindaric Ode takes its name from the ancient poet Pindar, who set his poems to music; also known as the Greek Ode, this form consisted of three parts: a beginning (strophe), a middle that responded to the beginning (antistrophe), and a summary of the first two parts (epode) that was written in a different meter than the rest of the poem. The Horatian Ode, named for the Roman poet Horace, is set in quatrains or couplets using strict meter throughout. The Irregular Ode observes meter and rhyme but in no regular pattern like either the Pindaric or the Horatian. Some classic odes you might look up include "The Progress of Poesy" by Thomas Gray, "Ode to a Nightingale" by John Keats, and "Ode to the West Wind" by Percy Bysshe Shelley.

Poets have continued writing poems of appreciation and approval beyond these three forms. We recognize poems like "Sea-Heroes" by H.D., "In Celebration of my Uterus" by Anne Sexton, "Homage to my Hips" by Lucille Clifton, and many other poems of praise as being odes as poets, including those writing in the present day, continue to adapt the traditional concept of the ode to a variety of subject matters and rhetorical stances.

Ode to Jay-Z, Ending in the Rattle of a Fiend's Teeth
Hanif Willis-Abdurraqib

teach us how to hustle so / hard that they / never come for our daughters
and / feast upon their dancing limbs or / the thick tangles of hair swarming
/ over their dark eyes / have we prayed at your feet / long enough for them
to keep / what they came here with / after they are entombed in / the dirt /
this is what is happening / in our America right now / another black girl was
emptied / in Brooklyn last night and / I watch this on the news in Ohio and
weep / even though I know that it is not / my mother / because the girl on TV
has no name other than *gone* / and my mother held on / to her name until
her body / became ash / until she was a mountain of white / powder / that's
that shit / we take razor blades to / and drown / the whole hood in / that shit
that got us out / the projects / and left whole families / of men / starved and
longing / is this what becomes / of the women we love / consumed even in
death by / a flock of men / who have mistaken their grief / for a persistent
hunger / that comes again each / sweat-soaked morning with / a new set of
freshly forgotten corpses / overflowing in its arms / after coming down from
/ the cross / how did you fix your hands / to hold a child without / covering
her in decades / of blood / and have you taught her / to run yet / not the
way we run / into the arms of a lover / but the way you ran / before the first
gold record hung / in a home far enough away / from the block / you finally
stopped / hearing the clatter of ravening jaws / clashing together at sunset /
we still hear it out here / it gets louder with each / black girl hollowed out
/ and erased / if you can't feed them into silence / again / can you at least
rap for us / over all this noise / everyone I love has had / the hardest time /
sleeping

Ode to Buttoning and Unbuttoning My Shirt
Ross Gay

No one knew or at least
I didn't know
they knew
what the thin disks
threaded here
on my shirt
might give me
in terms of joy
this is not something to be taken lightly
the gift
of buttoning one's shirt
slowly
top to bottom
or bottom
to top or sometimes
the buttons
will be on the other
side and
I am a woman
that morning
slipping the glass
through its slot
I tread
differently that day
or some of it
anyway
my conversations
are different
and the car bomb slicing the air
and the people in it
for a quarter mile
and the honeybee's
legs furred with pollen
mean another
thing to me
than on the other days
which too have
been drizzled in this
simplest of joys
in this world
of spaceships and subatomic
this and that

two maybe three
times a day
some days
I have the distinct pleasure
of slowly untethering
the one side
from the other
which is like unbuckling
a stack of vertebrae
with delicacy
for I must only use
the tips
of my fingers
with which I will
one day close
my mother's eyes
this is as delicate
as we can be
in this life
practicing
like this
giving the raft of our hands
to the clumsy spider
and blowing soft until she
lifts her damp heft and
crawls off
we practice like this
pushing the seed into the earth
like this first
in the morning
then at night
we practice
sliding the bones home.

Bipolar II Disorder: Third Evaluation (Ode to the Brain)
Eugenia Leigh

I am trying to cherish
this terrible city, this glittering city.

Oh, how its residents dance!
The basal ganglia

whiskey-whooping its luminous messages.
The tilted cerebellum

kicking offbeat. And the lobes—
all my disorder-

ly lobes—lush
and tuxxed, bopping in a line

not quite a line,
shaking their sparklers to receive me.

My Magic 8-Ball brain
spins with twenty answers for everything—all twenty,

yes. Yes, god-orb. Yes, sunstone.
Yes, synth-pop skull

fritzing with pop rocks. Yes, clock
miswound, clock on coals, clock

shotput to Elysium
and speeding with light. Tonight, I will not curse

the jagged slivers
you, crushed ornament, have

scattered everywhere.
I've neglected you for far too long,

you too-sweet fruit bruising in one blue spot, but—yes—
still good.

Ode to the First Time I Wore a Dress & My Mother Did Not Flinch
torrin a. greathouse

My palm still recalls the shape, crushed
velvet's soft-jagged pull that makes
my thin jaw ring, my teeth a row
of tiny bells. How it stained my skin's
silhouette the color of a newborn
bruise, before first-puberty made
mayhem of my skin, unbraided
genes to watch their blueprint spill,
moth's unfinished body from split
cocoon. In my mouth boyhood was a fawn,
stomach lined with nettle blooms, a dog
retching grass, bright red of a silver neck
-lace torn from my throat by a boy who bit
small moons from his fingernails
& told me all the ways he could break
my body & no one would even
notice. He left my mouth dry as velvet,
scrubbed from a buck's bone crown, rouge
across a tree's pale face & I loved him
for it. Wanted him to love me back like any
-thing other than a boy. Window. Perfect
pebble. Shooting star. Pen knife. Painted
pair of lips. My mother helped me tighten
the straps, lent me her smallest heels,
& watched me dance with a violent boy's
gentle name on my tongue. I can't
imagine how both of them will see this
velvet slip as nothing more than tender
skin to be shed bloody from a *boy*
to make from him a man.

Persona

A persona poem is one ostensibly written from the point of view of a speaker other than the poet. Persona comes from the Latin for *mask*, and these poems typically tend to make that mask obvious, finding a way to signal to the reader who's speaking. Often poets write from the point of view of historical or fictional figures; this allows the reader the dual pleasure of seeing the world or an event in a particular way, but also drawing on the reader's preexisting knowledge of the speaker or situation. The persona itself becomes at once an illusion and an allusion.

The persona poem is done in the first person, which is how the poet dons the mask, and it often uses apostrophe as the speaker monologues to the reader. Arguably, the most well-known persona poem is a dramatic monologue by Robert Browning—in "My Last Duchess," Browning adopts the character of the Duke of Ferrara, who talks to the reader about a painting of his late wife. A similar technique is used by Sylvia Plath in "Lady Lazarus," Margaret Atwood in "Siren Song," and John Ashbery in "Daffy Duck in Hollywood" as the poets play with the voice of their characters to discover new perspectives on the world. The persona need not always be that of a well-known figure; Ai wrote many persona poems, "Cuba, 1962" for example, giving voice to characters who were marginalized or abused. Robert Hayden's "[American Journal]" is in the voice of an alien visiting the United States. Persona poems are a way of having serious fun writing about serious topics.

Trumpet Player, 1963
Mark Halliday

> *And when I get to Surf City I'll be shootin' the curls,*
> *And checkin' out the parties for surfer girls.*

When Jan and Dean recorded "Surf City"
there must have been one guy—

I see this trumpet player (was there even a horn section in that song?
Say there was)—

I see this trumpet player with his tie askew
or maybe he's wearing a loose tropical-foliage shirt
sitting on a metal chair waiting
for the session to reach the big chorus
where Jane and Dean exult
Two girls for every boy
                       and he's thinking
of his hundred nights on his buddy Marvin's hairy stainy sofa
and the way one girl is far too much and besides
he hasn't had the one in fourteen months, wait,
it's fifteen now.
Surfing—what life actually lets guys ride boards
on waves? Is it all fiction? Is it a joke?
Jan and Dean and their pal Brian act like it's a fine, good joke
whereas this trumpet player thinks it's actually shit,
if anybody asked him, a tidal wave of shit.
Nobody's asking.
The producer jiggles in his headphones. He wants more drums
right after *all you gotta do is just wink your eye!*
This producer is chubby and there is no chance,
my trumpet player thinks, that this chubhead gets
two swingin' honeys at any party ever and besides
on a given night a man only has one cock, or
am I wrong? And besides, you wake up wanting five aspirin
in an air lousy with lies, or half-lifes.
And that's with only one girl.

But why am I so pissed here, he thinks,
when all these guys are hot for a hit?
Because I'm deep like Coltrane and they're all shallow,
right? Or because
I'm this smelly sour session man with a bent nose
and they're all hip to this fine joke?

The song is cooking, it's nearly in the can,
everybody has that hot-hit look
and my trumpet man has a thought: Sex
is not really it—what they're singing about—
they're singing about being here.
This dumb song is *it*:
this studio, this is the only Surf City,
here. And that's the great joke.

Okay, surf dicks, I am hip. But
there's gonna be pain in Kansas, he thinks,
lifting his horn and watching for the cue,
when they hear about Surf City and believe it.

Wonder Woman Dreams of the Amazon
Jeannine Hall Gailey

I miss the tropes of Paradise—green vines
roped around wrists, jasmine coronets,
the improbable misty clothing of my tribe.

I dream of the land of my birth. They named
me after their patron Goddess.
I was to be a warrior for their kind.

I miss my mother, Hippolyta.
In my dreams she wraps me tightly
again in the American flag,

warning me, "Cling to your bracelets,
your magic lasso. Don't be a fool for men."
She's always lecturing me, telling me

not to leave her. Sometimes she changes
into a doe, and I see my father
shooting her, her blood. Sometimes,

in these dreams, it is me who shoots her.
My daily transformation
from prim kitten-bowed suit to bustier

with red-white-and-blue stars
is less complicated. The invisible jet
makes for clean escapes.

The animals are my spies and allies;
inexplicably, snow-feathered doves
appear in my hands. I capture Nazis

and Martians with boomerang grace.
When I turn and turn, the music plays louder,
the glow around me burns white-hot,

I become everything I was born to be,
the dreams of the mother,
the threat of the father.

The Lammergeier Daughter
Pascale Petit

That night, I opened your wardrobe and found
a trophy of vultures, their necks pierced

by hanger hooks. I saw at once
that you hunted everything I loved—

the griffon, the Himalayan, the lammergeier,
who haunted our home with wheeling cries.

I peeled off my skin then, and robed myself
as a bird bride. Veiled in morning mist

I married the sky. Of course, you aimed
at my heart, but as the bullet tore through me

I wrapped my talons around your skull,
lifted you high, and dropped you as a lamb

drops newborn from his mother
onto the snow-fleeced earth.

I landed beside you on the quilt.
And when the flesh-eaters had done their work,

it was I, your lammergeier daughter,
who devoured your bones—look, Father,

how they slide down my throat like rifles.

Anna May Wong Blows Out Sixteen Candles
Sally Wen Mao

When I was sixteen, I modeled fur coats for a furrier.
White men gazed down my neck like wolves

but my mink collar protected me. When I was sixteen,
I was an extra in *A Tale of Two Worlds*. If I didn't pour

someone's tea, then I was someone's wife. Every brother,
father, or husband of mine was nefarious. They held me

at knifepoint, my neck in a chokehold. If they didn't murder
me, I died of an opium overdose. Now it's 1984

and another white girl awaits her sweet sixteen. It's 1984
and another white girl angsts about a jock who kisses

her at the end of the film. Now it's 1984 and Long
Duk Dong is the white girl's houseguest. He dances,

drunk, agog with gong sounds . All around the nation,
teens still taunt us. Hallways bloat with sweaters, slurs.

When I was eight, the boy who sat behind me brought pins
to class. "Do Asians feel pain the way we do?" he'd ask.

He'd stick the needles to the back of my neck until I winced.
I wore six wool coats so I wouldn't feel the sting. It's 1984

so cast me in a new role already. Cast me as a pothead,
an heiress, a gymnast, a queen. Cast me as a castaway in a city

without shores. Cast me as that girl who rivets center stage
or cast me away, into the blue where my lips don't touch

or say. If I take my time machine back to sixteen, or twenty,
or eight, I'd blow out all my candles. Sixteen wishes

extinguish and burn. The boy will never kiss me at the end
of the movie. The boy will only touch me with his needles.

Portrait

One of the things you'll often hear about the work poems do is that they paint a picture and poems in the portrait mode do so rather explicitly. Whereas the persona poem allows the poet to adopt a mask, the portrait poem creates meaning through the description of a person or entity as its focus. Often, the subject of the portrait can be another personality, as in Wordsworth's Lucy poems, or, more recently, the poems of Jake Adam York, in which the poet writes about people who were killed in the name of civil rights in America. Or the poem might try to portray the self, as in "Self-Portrait" by Rainer Maria Rilke, "Phenomenal Woman" by Maya Angelou, "I, Too" by Langston Hughes, and "Self Portrait in a Convex Mirror" by John Ashbery. We might note how a portrait might extend to the animal world too, but whatever the case, the portrait works by what the poet uncovers through the act of portrayal.

On the other hand, contemporary poets often complicate their self-portraits by portraying the self as something else. In this way, the poet creates a complex or unusual juxtaposition between the idea of the self and another thing that the self tries to inhabit. It's a way of challenging our concept of who we are, of recreating the self in a different context.

Lone Star
Nick Makoha

for George Weah

Lone Star, you were a man on the run
when you picked the ball up on the edge
of your penalty box. A planet at your feet,
San Siro stadium sealed tight so nothing
escapes. The crowd a pair of eyes as you
moved toward the light. One man in costume
dancing across the pitch as if he were liquid
weight, a flicker, black Orpheus with five minutes
to go. The opposition's error believing that you
were on your own. Past the halfway line
was the future, wide open like the shores of Liberia.
You ran like a man with a ship to catch. Like smoke
you had a story to tell. The boy from a village
without a well, who never spoke of money or the war.
At their forty yard line you struck the ball like a match.
Released from your spell it curled into their goal.

My Mother Talks in Numbers
Eileen Chong

What is home?
Forty years of morning, noon, and night.

Tell me about your childhood.
Thirty-seven mouths open under a tin roof.

What is happiness?
Eighteen in my sailor suit, spray from the waterfall—

Why did you marry?
Five years of coins.

How many tears?
One thousand, eight hundred, and ninety-eight pearls.

Do you love your mother?
Two hands, ten fingers, six children.

How many miles have you come?
Sixty-four thousand and twenty-five gull-wings.

Do you love me?
The rain falling, falling, over thirteen thousand dawns.

Pol Pot in Paris
Adam Aitken

Oh happy child, kindly teacher—were you a fake?
Like you I'm taciturn
but when I give an order who's to hear?
Paris, I found it cold but didn't read very much.
No one knows what you thought of its weather,
the river, the churches or the metro.
You preferred a book on the Soviets to girls in Montmartre.
I too would rather recite Verlaine
than take notes on electronics.
If I had a history and traditions, I don't remember.
Would you understand me?
I too lived on an allowance
of uncomfortable epithets
cobbled from Buddha and Marx:
"Physical beauty is an obstacle to the will to struggle."

Late nights drinking weren't your thing.
Sweet words of girls "mask evil hearts".
A fun holiday on a tractor in Belgrade.
"The wheels of revolution never stop, roll on
to crush all who dare to walk in its path."
We could have been lifetime friends, together
rooting out evil, picking mushrooms,
sipping coffee in the Latin Quarter,
mediocre, polite, soft spoken
migrants meandering in overcoats.

The others marry French girls, you join a work brigade
digging ditches in Zagreb.
In the 15th arrondissement, Rue Latellier
mid-winter, dog shit everywhere.
On the river it's 20 francs
for *La Grande Revolution Française*.
We could've talked, taken notes for a memoir:
did you join the party before or after the festival
in East Berlin? Did you buy that shirt
before or after the coup d'état?

In Marseille you boarded the *Jamaique*.
Your tiny shadow cast a conspiracy
of epic dimensions, and there, in the oily backwash
and the silver wake, a complete solution.
I too went home, dreaming of a family
I would never have, and the one I would.

Self-Portrait as Mae West One-Liner
Paisley Rekdal

I'm no moaning bluet, mountable
linnet, mumbling nun. I'm
tangible, I'm gin. Able to molt
in toto, to limn. I'm blame and angle, I'm
lumbago, an oblate mug gone notable,
not glum. I'm a tabu tuba mogul, I'm motile,
I'm nimble. No gab ennui, no bagel bun-boat: I'm one
big megaton bolt able to bail
men out. Gluten iamb. Male bong unit.
I'm a genial bum, mental obi, genital
montage. I'm Agent Limbo, my blunt bio
an amulet, an enigma. Omit élan. Omit bingo.
Alien mangle, I'm glib lingo. Untangle me,
tangelo. But I'm no angel.

Protest

The very act of writing a poem is itself a political act; to write a poem is to resist the dominant culture, which tends to devalue poetry (alas!). A poem that is overtly political in its content is almost by its nature a poem that protests something, a poem that stands up for something the poet believes in even as it stands against those forces that might threaten that thing. These are poems of social justice, poems of outrage, poems of citizenry that empower and embolden people as much as they resist the forces that would oppress and suppress.

This kind of poetry is vital to poetry's history and tradition. Poems like "What Kind of Times Are These" by Adrienne Rich, "America" by Allen Ginsberg, "Still I Rise" by Maya Angelou, and "I Want the Wide American Earth" by Carlos Bulosan stand against oppressive nations and ideologies similar to the way that many contemporary poems call our attentions to individuals and populations who are unfairly persecuted by governments, to the ways that political topics are inseparable from people's everyday lives. It would be a mistake to think of protest poems as being purely a product of twentieth- and twenty-first-century America—John Dryden, Alexander Pope, William Blake, and Elizabeth Barrett Browning are just a few of the English poets who wrote poems steeped in the politics of their day. Wherever and whenever there is social unrest, you'll find poetry being written in response.

Poems of protest explicitly grapple with the kinds of contemporary political issues we might see on CNN. However, unlike an overpaid television pundit, the job of the poet is not merely to argue for a given point of view or deliver a quick sound bite. The job of the poet is to explore, to expose, to complicate, to question. A poem that has its mind made up from the start is not a poem; it's propaganda. There's a time and place for propaganda, to be sure, but not in your poems. Protest poems are important, even essential, in a civil society. (And even more so in an uncivil society.)

from **Reaching Guantánamo**
Solmaz Sharif

Dear Salim,

Love, are you well? Do they   you?
I worry so much. Lately, my hair   , even
my skin   . The doctors tell me it's.
I believe them. It shouldn't
     . Please don't worry.
                         in the year, and moths
have gotten to your mother's
                         , remember?
I have enclosed some   —made this
batch just for you. Please eat well. Why
did you   me to remarry? I told
          and he couldn't   it.
I would never   .
Love, I'm singing that   you loved,
remember, the line that went
"   "? I'm holding
the   just for you.

Yours,

The Gun Joke
Jamaal May

It's funny, she says, how many people are shocked
by this shooting and the next and next and the next.
She doesn't mean funny as in funny, but funny
as in blood soup tastes funny when you stir in soil.
Stop me if you haven't heard this one:
A young man/old man/teenage boy walks into
an office/theater/daycare/club and empties
a magazine into a crowd of strangers/family/students.

Ever hear the one about the shotgun? What do you call it
when a shotgun tests a liquor store's bulletproof glass?
What's the difference between a teenager
with hands in the air and a paper target charging at a cop?
What do you call it when a man sets his own house on fire,
takes up a sniper position, and waits for firefighters?

Stop me if you haven't heard this one:
The first man to pull a gun on me said it was only a joke,
but never so much as smiled. The second said
this is definitely not a joke, and then his laughter crackled
through me like electrostatic—funny how that works.
When she says it's funny she means funny
as in crazy and crazy as in this shouldn't happen.
This shouldn't happen as in something is off. Funny as in
off—as in, ever since a small caliber bullet chipped his spine,
your small friend walks kinda' funny and his smile is off.

Two Guns in the Sky for Daniel Harris
Raymond Antrobus

When Daniel Harris stepped out of his car
the policeman was waiting. Gun raised.

I use the past tense though this is irrelevant
in Daniel's language, which is sign.

Sign has no future or past; it is a present language.
You are never more present than when a gun

is pointed at you. What language says this
if not sign? But the police officer saw hands

waving in the air, fired and Daniel dropped
his hands, his chest bleeding out onto concrete

metres from his home. I am in Breukelen Coffee House
in New York, reading this news on my phone,

when a black policewoman walks in, two guns
on her hips, my friend next to me reading

the comments section: *Black Lives Matter*.
Now what could we sign or say out loud

when the last word I learned in ASL was *alive*?
Alive—both thumbs pointing at your lower abdominal,

index fingers pointing up like two guns in the sky.

Animals
Hayan Charara

The phone call, from my wife.
She's hungry, *she's pregnant,*
someone kicked her

in the stomach—we have to.
I say yes, but the reply
I keep to myself is,

We don't have to do a goddamn thing.
A dog. I'm talking about a dog
I would have otherwise left to starve.

Now though, five years since,
I love this animal, Lucy,
more than I can most people.

                    *

A boy names his dog and five cats
after our Lucy. The boy, my brother,
born in Henry Ford's hometown,

lives now in Lebanon,
which the Greeks called Phoenicia,
and they tried but failed

to subdue it, same as the Egyptians,
Hittites, Assyrians, Babylonians,
Alexander the Great, Romans, Arabs,

Crusaders, Turks, the British,
the French, the Israelis.
There, my father built a house

with money earned in Detroit—
as a grocer, with social security.
Also there, the first alphabet

was created, the first law school built,
the first miracle of Jesus—
water, wine.
                    *

On the first day
the bombs fall they flee
and the boy asks

to go back for Lucy,
the dog. As for the cats,
No. They take care of themselves.

One week into it
he wonders who feeds them,
who fills the water bowls.

Maybe the neighbors,
the mother thinks out loud.
The father is indignant: *Neighbors—*

what neighbors? They're gone.
The mother is stunned:
What do you mean, gone?

After a month, everyone forgets
or just stops talking about
the animals. During the ceasefire

my father drives south,
a thirty-minute trip that lasts
six hours—wreckage upon wreckage

piled on the roads, on what is left
of the roads. The landscape
entirely gray, so catastrophic

he asks a passerby how far
to his town and is told,
You're in it.

                        *

My father finds three of the cats,
all perforated, one headless.
The dog is near the carport,

where it hid during lightning storms,
its torso splayed in half
like meat on a slab, its entrails

eaten by other dogs
scavenging on the streets.
Look. They're animals.

Which is to say, there are also people.
And I haven't even begun telling you
what was done to them.

APPENDIX A

100 Poetry Experiments

Here's a word in favor of writing from prompts, or exercises, or assignments. It might feel a little artificial, right? Like cheating somehow, to have written a poem about your mother and the sunset over Lake Michigan not merely because you were moved to do so, but because you were given an assignment to write a poem about your mother and the sunset over Lake Michigan. Here's a secret: we poets all give ourselves assignments all of the time.

There are a couple of reasons for this. One, it works. It certainly works a good deal better than never writing a poem until we are specifically moved to do so. That works sometimes, but it means an awful lot of time spent in between poems, more waiting than writing. Two, it can sometimes get boring, writing only the poems you have in your head already. An assignment is a way of getting outside of yourself. If you say, "Okay, I'm going to write a poem where every line starts with either the letter A or a color, and I have to include a watermelon and a sidewalk and a piece of dialogue I overhear at the coffee shop while I'm writing," you have no idea where that poem is going to end up. It's a great way to surprise yourself.

Chances are, if you're using this textbook in a class, your teacher is going to offer you prompts for at least some of your poems. Don't resist the prompts; embrace them. To go back to that initial spark we're always looking for to get us started, to turn the kindling of our daily lives into the fire of a poem, think of the prompt as the flint to the steel of your own ideas. Striking them together is the quickest way to start the fire you're after. There's a reason we're calling them experiments here—the point is to try things and see what happens. To, you know, experiment.

Another thing about writing prompts is that they offer constraints. Complete freedom to let the poem go wherever it ends up wanting to go is at once both the greatest and most frustrating thing about writing poems. In offering the poet some restrictions, the prompt also provides the writer with some guidance. Write a poem that seems like it's about to make rhymes, but never actually does. Write a poem that talks back to the next song you hear on the radio. Write a poem that contains a horse, a body part, and something on your television. Sure, a prompt can take options away from a writer, but it also offers a writer the challenge to make art out of the ingredients that have been offered—not unlike one of those cooking shows where the contestants are asked to make a meal from a predetermined list of ingredients. And as in those shows, one of the beautiful things about this is that no two poets will write the same poem from a given prompt. Just as one chef makes gazpacho and another makes salsa out of those heirloom tomatoes, you will write the poem that only you can write and the person next to you will write the poem only they can write.

Obviously the prompts in this appendix offer a starting place, but they're just that: a start. If you're not presently enrolled in a poetry class, find another poet and make up assignments for each other. There are also lots of places to find writing prompts online, and there are books and books devoted to writing prompts. You can always make them up for yourself, too—coming up with challenges for your poet-self can get the creative mind working.

As you're using the experiments below or seeking out other prompts to get you started on a poem, bear in mind that the best prompts often push more on form than on content. That is, they offer some kind of structure around which you drape whatever ideas or subject matter you like. This makes sense, because often when we're struggling with getting started, it's not a matter of not knowing what to write about, but not knowing how to write it.

Of all the infinite shapes of all the poems in the world, how do you even begin? It can be exceedingly helpful, then, when a prompt offers you scaffolding.

T. S. Eliot wrote, "When forced to work within a strict framework the imagination is taxed to its utmost—and will produce its richest ideas. Given total freedom the work is likely to sprawl." The kind of constraint provided by a meaningful prompt or poetry assignment offers just this framework. We often do our best work when we're pushing against something, fighting with the difficult or uncomfortable part of a writing challenge. (The chapter on Forms in this book delves more deeply into this concept.)

It has been said that the best way to kill a poem is to begin it knowing exactly what you want it to say—and sometimes when we begin with the subject matter, that's what happens. So instead, begin with shape. Forcing the words into a particular shape means you will have to adjust the words, and that allows for the possibility of discovery in the process. When this is working at its best, you discover something both about what you want to say and the best shape in which to say it.

Given all that, here's a series of writing prompts—experiments—to help get you started writing poems. When one of the experiments references one of the elements of poetry, a particular rhetorical device, or one of the modes described in the anthology, look it up. We have already discussed the value of constraints on the creative process, so challenge yourself to make art out of the ways that the prompts put constraints on your writing process. Do them one at a time. Or mix and match them. Whatever you want—just try to have fun writing poems.

Play.

Experiment.

1. Write an aubade that is also an elegy.

2. Write a poem that uses a line from a song as its title. The poem should be about anything but that one song. Credit the song in an epigraph.

3. Write a poem that paraphrases a song. Avoid using the actual song lyrics in the poem.

4. Write a poem that begins but does not end.

5. Write a poem you would not show your mother.

6. Write a poem you would not show your teacher.

7. Write a poem that is something else in disguise (along the lines of Matthew Olzmann's "Mountain Dew Commercial Disguised as a Love Poem").

8. Write a poem that tells the origin story of someone in your family (the way superheroes have origin stories, usually involving lab accidents or destroyed home planets).

9. Write a poem that is a sequel (or a prequel) to one of the poems in this anthology. Credit the initial poem.

10. Write a nocturne that is also a protest poem.

11. Write a poem for your future self to find.

12. Write a poem about a well-known historical event from the point of view of a witness to that event. You can make up the witness or assume the point of view or someone who was present or even involved in the event. "My Aunt Gertrude Watches from a Dallas Sidewalk as JFK Is Shot" or "Mary Todd Lincoln Watches Her Husband Deliver the Gettysburg Address" or "Simon Cowell Watches Confetti Fall on Kelly Clarkson's Head."

13. Write a poem that argues with one of the poems in this anthology. (Call it "Kim Addonizio Is Wrong About Love," or "Billy Collins Is Wrong About Poetry Students," or something along those lines.)

14. Write a poem that makes your readers hungry. Maybe even for food.

15. Write a found poem that is also a self-portrait.

16. Write a sad poem with a funny title.

17. Write a funny poem with a sad title.

18. Write a poem that values image over narrative.

19. Write a poem that starts with the line "You're not going to believe this, but . . ." then take out that line before you show the poem to anyone.

20. Write a poem that uses an actual headline from a newspaper (or a news website) as its title.

21. Write an elegy for someone who isn't dead yet.

22. Write a poem from the point of view of an animated character.

23. Write a poem that is a letter to your fourteen-year-old self.

24. Write a poem that begins with "My name is____" and explores what it's like to be you.

25. Write an ars poetica that is also an ode to a very specific object from your childhood.

26. Write a list poem in which the listed items seem to have no obvious, logical connection to each other. Then use the title to suggest a connection.

27. Write a poem that goes through every doorway it creates.

28. Write a poem that observes without interpretation.

29. Write a poem that interprets without observation.

30. Write a meditative poem that muses on the flawed nature of memory.

31. Write a poem that reboots one of your earlier poems.

32. Write a poem inspired by a recent dream but don't acknowledge that it's a dream. Bring it to life instead.

33. Write a poem that privileges music over meaning.

34. Sit quietly in a public space for twenty minutes and make a list of everything you can hear. Use that list as the starting place for a poem.

35. Write a poem that looks like a sonnet but isn't.

36. Write a poem that is a sonnet but doesn't look like it.

37. Write a poem about the current season that reverses the usual associations we have about that season. Pay special attention to image and mood.

38. Write a protest poem that contradicts itself.

39. Write an aubade that uses an extended metaphor.

40. Write a poem that makes use of colloquial language or slang.

41. Write a poem that is built from contemporary slang combined with archaisms.

42. Invent a poet. (A good poet.) Write that poet's most famous poem.

43. Go to a gallery or an art museum and spend an hour looking at a work of art and thinking about it. Yes, an hour. Then write an ekphrastic poem about the art.

44. Go to a gallery or an art museum and instead of looking at the titles of the artwork, name them yourself. Write those names down so you

can remember them—you now have a list of poem titles. Choose one and write the poem that goes with the title.

45. Write a poem that calls attention to a little-known but important historical event. Privilege the sentence over the line, but make sure it's a poem and not an essay.

46. Write a poem that does not know where to begin.

47. Write a poem that scares you.

48. Write a poem about yourself from the point of view of someone who knows you only in a specific context (such as your Sunday School teacher, your guidance counselor, the person who sells you the same latte every morning).

49. Write a poem in three parts in which each part explores the same event from a different point of view: one first person, one second person, one third person.

50. Write a poem about what you want most in the world. What would happen if you got it?

51. Write a poem that defines the value of something at the beginning. At the end, use the turn to redefine that value.

52. Write a poem in six sections. Use a single sextet in the first section, a quintet in the second, a quatrain in the third and so on, all the way to a single line in the sixth and final line of the poem.

53. Go outside and write a poem that you couldn't have written if you'd stayed inside.

54. Write a poem that is between thirteen and twenty sections long, but keep each section five lines or less. Use at least one weird or impossible image in each section.

55. Write a poem driven by anaphora.

56. Write a portrait of someone or something no one else pays any attention to.

57. Write an ode to an abstract concept. Provide at least one concrete, specific image in every line.

58. Write a poem about how to do something. Do not mention that something.

59. Write a poem about an embarrassing moment from your life.

60. Write a poem about what you would do if you had super powers.

61. Take the previous two poems and braid them together to create one poem.

62. Write a poem that tells a family secret. The secret doesn't have to be true.

63. Write a beautiful poem that threatens to beat someone up.

64. Write a poem that breaks some rule you used to think applied to poetry.

65. Find a poem written in a language you don't understand, Translate that poem based not on what a translating dictionary tells you, but according to what English words the foreign words look like.

66. Write a science fiction poem.

67. Write a poem with a mystery in it.

68. Write a rom-com poem.

69. Write an inaugural poem for any historical US President.

70. Write a contrapuntal elegy.

71. Pick a letter and write a poem where as many words as possible begin with that letter.

72. Write an ode to something you do every day.

73. Rewrite a fairy tale or fable as a lyric poem.

74. Write a poem about math, built with a mathematical structure.

75. Write a poem that uses caesura in lieu of punctuation.

76. Write a poem about the things you will tell your children one day.

77. Write a poem that superimposes one image over another.

78. Write a poem that offers a series of unrelated images, juxtaposed for meaning.

79. Write a poem that opens with a big claim about how the world works. Contradict the claim within a few lines.

80. Write a poem where every line ends with a verb.

81. Write a poem about something you've forgotten.

82. Write a haibun where the prose poem is one mode (say, a love poem) and the haiku is another (say, a protest poem).

83. Write a poem consisting entirely of sentence fragments.

84. Write a poem consisting entirely of questions.

85. Write an abecedarian that is also a narrative.

86. Write a persona poem in the voice of a famous historical or fictional figure. In the poem, reveal something important about yourself (though it appears to be about your persona). Use the title to tell us who the speaker is.

87. Write a poem that uses syllogisms.

88. Write a fixed-form poem that gives up on the form halfway through—but then returns to it at the very end.

89. Write a poem that goes backwards—start at the end and go back to the beginning.

90. Write a poem that makes nonsensical claims and then draws logical conclusions from those claims.

91. Write a poem that bears witness to an injustice you see in the world.

92. Write an ode that relies heavily on music and rhythm.

93. Write a poem that sincerely apologizes for something you have done, but do not literally apologize for anything.

94. Write a poem you wish you'd read.

95. Write an occasional poem about an extremely personal event.

96. Write an apostrophe to someone who probably doesn't remember you, though you have a very specific recollection of them.

97. Write a poem about where your name came from and what it means.

98. Write a poem about the moon that is unlike any of the 10,000,000 poems that have already been written about the moon.

99. Revise one of your poems into another artform: collage, pencil sketch, crayon drawing, popsicle-stick sculpture.

100. Invent your own fixed form. Write the very first poem to ever exist in that form.

APPENDIX B

Additional Reading

Addonizio, Kim and Dorianne Laux. *The Poet's Companion*. Norton, 1997. A book about poetry technique and the writing life.

Agodon, Kelli Russell and Martha Silano. *The Daily Poet: Day-By-Day Prompts for Your Writing Practice*. Two Sylvias Press, 2013. Just what the title promises.

Behn, Robyn and Chase Twichell, eds. *The Practice of Poetry*. Harper Perennial, 1992. A fine collection of poetry exercises created by poets who teach.

Burt, Stephanie. *Close Calls with Nonsense: Reading New Poetry*. Graywolf, 2009. A call to action in favor of reading more poetry, even when it's challenging.

Chavez, Felicia Rose. *The Anti-Racist Writing Workshop: How to Decolonize the Creative Classroom*. Haymarket Books. 2021. A necessary challenge to traditional ways of teaching creative writing.

Corn, Alfred. *The Poem's Heartbeat: A Manual of Prosody*. Copper Canyon, 2008 (originally published in 1997). A study of rhyme, rhythm, and meter.

Doty, Mark. *The Art of Description: World into Word*. Graywolf, 2010. A fairly short book crammed with wisdom about how description works.

Goldberg, Natalie. *Writing Down the Bones: Freeing the Writer Within*. Shambhala, 2005. Suggests a Zen approach to writing, offering a number of prompts and exercises to tap into your creative impulses.

Gonzalez, Rigoberto. *Pivotal Voices, Era of Transition: Toward a 21st Century Poetics*. University of Michigan Press, 2017. Part of the press's "Poets on Poetry" series, with essays and reviews focused on writers of color, especially Latino poets.

Hass, Robert. *Twentieth-Century Pleasures: Prose on Poetry*. Ecco, 1984. Essays on verse by a former United States Poet Laureate.

Hirshfield, Jane. *Ten Windows: How Great Poems Transform the World*. Knopf, 2017.

Hoagland, Tony. *Real Sofistikashun: Essays on Poetry and Craft*. Graywolf, 2006.

Hugo, Richard. *The Triggering Town*. W.W. Norton, 1979. Wisdom on the nature of poetry from a former United States poet laureate.

Hunley, Tom C. *The Poetry Gymnasium: 94 Proven Exercises to Shape Your Best Verse*. McFarland, 2011. A large book of poetry exercises.

Kingston, Maxine Hong. *To Be the Poet*. Harvard University Press. 2002. A witty manifesto on inspiration and memory.

Kooser, Ted. *The Poetry Home Repair Manual*. Bison Books, 2005. A book of advice about how to write poems and live with poetry for young poets by the former US Poet Laureate.

Lerner, Ben. *The Hatred of Poetry*. FSG, 2016. The author explores why so many people say they don't care for poetry and, in the end, offers a defense of the art.

Lockward, Diane, ed. *The Crafty Poet II: A Portable Workshop*. Terrapin Books, 2016. Writing prompts, interviews with poets, and poems aimed at helping you overcome writer's block.

Lockward, Diane. *The Practicing Poet: Writing Beyond the Basics*. Terrapin Books, 2018. Craft tips and sample poems organized in sections devoted to poetic concepts.

Longenbach, James. *The Art of the Poetic Line*. Graywolf, 2007. A brief book that takes a deep dive into how the line functions in poetry.

Lorde, Audre. *Sister Outsider: Essays and Speeches*. Crossing Press, 2007. Classic collection of important essays from an important American thinker.

McDowell, Gary L. and F. Daniel Rzicznek, eds. *The Rose Metal Press Field Guide to Prose Poetry*. Rose Metal Press, 2010. Lots of prose poems and essays by poets on the nature of the prose poem.

Orr, David. *Beautiful and Pointless: A Guide to Modern Poetry*. Harper Perennial, 2012. Opinions about the state of poetry in the twenty-tens.

Paz, Octavio. *The Bow and The Lyre: The Poem, The Poetic Revelation, Poetry and History*. University of Texas Press, 2009. Reflections on the role of poetry in history and in our lives.

Phillips, Carl. *Coin of the Realm: Essays on the Life and Art of Poetry*. Graywolf, 2004. Essays on identity, beauty, and meaning.

Phillips, Carl. *My Trade Is Mystery: Seven Meditations from a Life in Writing*. Yale, 2022. Thoughts on poetry from one of the leading contemporary voices.

Pinsky, Robert. *The Sounds of Poetry: A Brief Guide*. Farrar, Straus, and Giroux, 1999. A useful examination of how sound and syntax work together in poems.

Rilke, Rainer Maria. *Letters to a Young Poet*. Penguin, 2014.

Ruefle, Mary. *Madness, Rack, and Honey: Collected Lectures*. Wave Books, 2012. A compilation of thoughtful lectures on poetics.

Rukeyser, Muriel. *The Life of Poetry*. Paris Press, 1996. A book about the importance of poetry to democracy and life in the United States.

Saje, Natasha. *Windows and Doors: A Poet Reads Literary Theory*. University of Michigan Press, 2014. This one's not for the faint of heart. It's dense and theoretical, but chock full of insight.

Strand, Mark and Eavan Boland. *The Making of a Poem: A Norton Anthology of Poetic Forms*. Norton, 2000. A hefty volume of poetic forms with examples.

Theune, Michael, ed. *Structure & Surprise: Engaging Poetic Turns*. Teachers & Writers Collaborative, 2007. A book about poetic structure featuring essays about model structures by a variety of poets.

Turco, Lewis Putnam. *The Book of Forms*. University Press of New England, 2012. A handbook of poetics with a significant focus on form and fixed forms in poetry.

Voigt, Ellen Bryant. *The Art of Syntax: Rhythm of Thought, Rhythm of Song*. Graywolf, 2009. This book explores the nuances and complexities of the relationship between syntax, sentence, and meaning.

Acknowledgments

Kim Addonizio, "You Don't Know What Love Is" from *What Is This Thing Called Love: Poems*. Copyright © 2004 by Kim Addonizio. Used by permission of W. W. Norton & Company, Inc.

Adam Aitken, "Pol Pot in Paris" from *Eighth Habitation*. Copyright © 2009 by Adam Aitken. Reprinted by permission of Giramondo Publishing.

Kazim Ali, "The Return of Music" from *Far Mosque*. Copyright © 2005 by Kazim Ali. Reprinted with the permission of The Permissions Company, LLC, on behalf of Alice James Books, www.alicejamesbooks.org.

Raymond Antrobus, "Two Guns in the Sky for Daniel Harris" from *The Perseverance*. Copyright © 2021 by Raymond Antrobus, published by Tin House Books, reproduced by kind permission by David Higham Associates.

Evelyn Araluen, "Stutter," from *Dropbear*. Copyright © 2021. Reprinted with permission from the University of Queensland Press.

Mary Jo Bang, "The Role of Elegy" from *Elegy*. Copyright © 2007 by Mary Jo Bang. Reprinted with the permission of The Permissions Company, LLC, on behalf of Graywolf Press, Minneapolis, Minnesota, www.graywolfpress.org.

Sandra Beasley, "Halloween" from *Count the Waves: Poems*. Copyright © 2015 by Sandra Beasley. Used by permission of W. W. Norton & Company, Inc.

Oliver Baez Bendorf, "Split It Open Just to Count the Pieces" from *The Spectral Wilderness*. Copyright © 2015 by Oliver Baez Bendorf. Reprinted with permission from The Kent State University Press.

Traci Brimhall, "Ars Poetica" from *Rookery*. Copyright © 2008 by Traci Brimhall. Reprinted by permission of the author and Southern Illinois University Press.

Gabrielle Calvocoressi, "Glass Jaw Sonnet" from *Apocalyptic Swing*. Copyright © 2009 by Gabrielle Calvocoressi. Reprinted with the permission of The Permissions Company, LLC, on behalf of Persea Books, New York, www.perseabooks.org.

Anders Carlson-Wee, "Dynamite" from *The Low Passions: Poems*. Copyright © 2019 by Anders Carlson-Wee. Used by permission of W. W. Norton & Company, Inc.

Dorothy Chan, "Triple Sonnet for Being a Queer in a Family of Straights" from *Babe* by Diode Editions. Copyright © 2021 by Dorothy Chan. Reprinted by permission of the author.

Hayan Charara, "Animals" from *Something Sinister*. Copyright © 2016 by Hayan Charara. Reprinted with the permission of The Permissions Company, LLC, on behalf of Carnegie Mellon University Press, www.cmu.edu/universitypress.

Cathy Linh Che, "Split" from *Split*. Copyright © 2014 by Cathy Linh Che. Reprinted with the permission of The Permissions Company, LLC, on behalf of Alice James Books, www.alicejamesbooks.org.

Eileen Chong. "My Mother Talks in Numbers" from *A Thousand Crimson Blooms*. Copyright © 2021. Reprinted with permission from the University of Queensland Press.

Billy Collins, "Introduction to Poetry" from *The Apple That Astonished Paris*. Copyright © 1988, 1996 by Billy Collins. Reprinted with the permission of The Permissions Company, LLC on behalf of the University of Arkansas Press, www.uapress.com.

Eduardo C. Corral, "To Juan Doe #234." Copyright © 2017 by Eduardo C. Corral. Reprinted by permission of the author.

Kendra DeColo, "Crow Flying Overhead with a Hole in its Wing" from *I Am Not Trying to Hide My Hungers from the World*. Copyright © 2021 by Kendra DeColo. Reprinted with the permission of The Permissions Company, LLC, on behalf of BOA Editions, Ltd., Rochester, New York, www.boaeditions.org.

Oliver de la Paz, "Aubade with Bread for the Sparrows" from *Furious Lullaby*. Copyright © 2007 by Oliver de la Paz. Reprinted by permission of the author and Southern Illinois University Press.

Jenny Johnson, "The Bus Ride" from *Full Velvet*. Copyright © 2017 by Jenny Johnson. Reprinted by permission of Sarabande Books.

Janine Joseph, "Move-In" from *Driving Without a License*. Copyright © 2016 by Janine Joseph. Reprinted with the permission of The Permissions Company, LLC, on behalf of Alice James Books, www.alicejamesbooks.org.

Laura Kasischke, "Landscape, with one of the earthworm's ten hearts" from *Space, in Chains*. Copyright © 2011 by Laura Kasischke. Reprinted with the permission of The Permissions Company, LLC, on behalf of Copper Canyon Press, www.coppercanyonpress.org.

John Kinsella, "Redneck Refutation" from *The New Arcadia: Poems*. Copyright © 2005 by John Kinsella. Used by permission of W. W. Norton & Company, Inc.

David Kirby, "Teacher of the Year" from *The House of Blue Light: Poems*, LSU Press. Copyright © 2000 by David Kirby. Reprinted by permission of the author.

Dorianne Laux, "Lighter" from *The Book of Men*. Copyright © 2011 by Dorianne Laux. Used by permission of W. W. Norton & Company, Inc.

Li-Young Lee, "Nocturne" from *Rose*. Copyright © 1986 by Li-Young Lee. Reprinted with the permission of The Permissions Company, LLC, on behalf of BOA Editions, Ltd., www.boaeditions.org.

Eugenia Leigh, "Bipolar II Disorder: Third Evaluation (Ode to the Brain)" from *Bianca*. Copyright © 2024 by Eugenia Leigh. Reprinted with the permission of The Permissions Company, LLC, on behalf of Four Way Books, www.fourwaybooks.com.

Paige Lewis, "When I Tell My Beloved I Miss the Sun," from *Space Struck*. Copyright © 2019 by Paige Lewis. Reprinted with the permission of The Permissions Company, LLC, on behalf of Sarabande Books, www.sarabandebooks.com.

Ada Limón, "Downhearted" from *Bright Dead Things*. Copyright © 2015 by Ada Limón. Reprinted with the permission of The Permissions Company, LLC on behalf of Milkweed Editions, www.milkweed.org.

Patricia Lockwood, "Rape Joke" from *Motherland Fatherland Homelandsexuals*. Copyright © 2014 by Patricia Lockwood. Used by

Aimee Nezhukumatathil, "One-Star Reviews of the Great Wall of China" from *Oceanic*. Copyright © 2018 by Aimee Nezhukumatathil. Reprinted with the permission of The Permissions Company, LLC, on behalf of Copper Canyon Press, www.coppercanyonpress.org.

Naomi Shihab Nye, "1935" from *Transfer*. Copyright © 2011 by Naomi Shihab Nye. Reprinted with the permission of The Permissions Company, LLC, on behalf of BOA Editions, Ltd., www.boaeditions.org.

Christina Olson, "In Which Christina Imagines That Different Types of Alcohol Are Men and She Is Seeing Them All" from *Before I Came Home Naked*, Spire Press. Copyright © 2010 Christina Olson. Reprinted by permission of the author.

Matthew Olzmann, "Mountain Dew Commercial Disguised as a Love Poem" from *Mezzanines*. Copyright © 2013 by Matthew Olzmann. Reprinted with the permission of The Permissions Company, LLC, on behalf of Alice James Books, www.alicejamesbooks.org.

Craig Santos Perez, "Rings of Fire" from *Habitat Threshold*. Copyright © 2020 by Craig Santos Perez. Reprinted by permission of Omnidawn Publishing.

Pascale Petit, "The Lammergeier Daughter." Copyright © 2023 by Pascale Petit. First published by the Poetry Foundation in *Poetry* magazine, February 2023. Reprinted by permission of the author.

Kiki Petrosino, "Nocturne" from *Hymn for the Black Terrific*. Copyright © 2013 by Kiki Petrosino. Reprinted by permission of Sarabande Books.

Shazea Quraishi, "Elegy" from *The Glimmer*. Copyright © 2022 by Shazea Quraishi. Reprinted by permission of Bloodaxe Books, Ltd.

Paisley Rekdal, "Self Portrait as Mae West One Liner" from *Imaginary Vessels*. Copyright © 2016 by Paisley Rekdal. Reprinted with the permission of The Permissions Company, LLC, on behalf of Copper Canyon Press, Port Townsend, Washington, www.coppercanyonpress.org.

Catie Rosemurgy, "Things That Didn't Work" from *The Stranger Manual*. Copyright © 2010 by Catie Rosemurgy. Reprinted with the permission of The Permissions Company, LLC, on behalf of Graywolf Press, Minneapolis, Minnesota, www.graywolfpress.org.

Omar Sakr, "No Context in a Duplex." Copyright © 2021 by Omar Sakr. Reprinted by permission of the author.

Diane Seuss, "[Sometimes I can't feel it]" from *frank: sonnets*. Copyright © 2015 by Diane Seuss. Reprinted with the permission of The Permissions Company, LLC, on behalf of Graywolf Press, Minneapolis, Minnesota, www.graywolfpress.org.

Solmaz Sharif, "Reaching Guantanamo" (first section) from *Look*. Copyright © 2016 by Solmaz Sharif. Reprinted with the permission of The Permissions Company, LLC, on behalf of Graywolf Press, www.graywolfpress.org.

Jake Skeets, "38" from *Eyes Bottle Dark with a Mouthful of Flowers*. Copyright © 2019 by Jake Skeets. Reprinted with the permission of The Permissions Company, LLC, on behalf of Milkweed Editions, Minneapolis, Minnesota, www.milkweed.org.

Karen Skolfield, "How to Locate Water on a Desert Island" from *Frost in the Low Areas*, Zone 3 Press. Copyright © 2013 by Karen Skolfield. Reprinted by permission of Zone 3 Press.

Catherine Smith. "The Biting Point" from *Lip*. Copyright © 2012. Reprinted with permission from the Poetry Business.

Maggie Smith, "Good Bones" from *Good Bones: Poems*. Copyright © 2017 by Maggie Smith. Reprinted with the permission of The Permissions Company, LLC, on behalf of Tupelo Press, www.tupelopress.org.

Tracy K. Smith, "Song" from *Life on Mars*. Copyright © 2011 by Tracy K. Smith. Reprinted with the permission of The Permissions Company, LLC, on behalf of Graywolf Press, Minneapolis, Minnesota, www.graywolfpress.org.

Natasha Trethewey, "History Lesson" from *Domestic Work*. Copyright © 1998, 2000 by Natasha Trethewey. Reprinted with the permission of The Permissions Company, LLC, on behalf of Graywolf Press, Minneapolis, Minnesota, www.graywolfpress.org.

Hanif Willis-Abdurraqib, "Ode to Jay Z Ending with the Rattle of a Fiend's Teeth" from *The Crown Ain't Worth Much*, Button Poetry. Copyright © 2016 by Hanif Willis-Abdurraqib. Reprinted by permission of the author.

Monica Youn, "Quinta del Sordo" from *Blackacre*. Copyright © 2016 by Monica Youn. Reprinted with the permission of The Permissions Company, LLC, on behalf of Graywolf Press, Minneapolis, Minnesota, www.graywolfpress.org.

INDEX